PANIC NOW

PANIC NOW?

Tools for Humanizing

IRA J. ALLEN

THE UNIVERSITY OF TENNESSEE PRESS / KNOXVILLE

Library of Congress Cataloging-in-Publication Data

NAMES: Allen, Ira J., author.

TITLE: Panic now? : tools for humanizing / Ira J. Allen.

DESCRIPTION: First edition. | Knoxville : The University of Tennessee Press, [2024] |
Includes bibliographical references. | Summary: "Calling on several discourses
related to the Anthropocene, Ira J. Allen defines the 'polycrisis' now facing humanity
in his search for a means of empowerment amidst unavoidable feelings of dread. The
interrelated threats of climate collapse, an artificial intelligence revolution, a sixth
mass extinction, a novel chemical crisis, and more are all brought to us by what Allen
describes as "CaCaCo," the carbon-capitalism-colonialism assemblage. Underscoring
the legitimacy of panic, this book asks what it means to panic productively. The
author admits no one script will suffice for everyone, but he outlines several attitudes
and practices that have proven to move us through fear to collective action"
—Provided by publisher.

IDENTIFIERS: LCCN 2024017555 (print) | LCCN 2024017556 (ebook) | ISBN 9781621909057
(paperback) | ISBN 9781621909064 (kindle edition) | ISBN 9781621909071 (pdf)

SUBJECTS: LCSH: Panic. | Crises. | Social problems. | Civilization, Modern—21st century.

CLASSIFICATION: LCC HN18.3 .A616 2024 (print) | LCC HN18.3 (ebook) |
DDC 361.1—dc23/eng20240514

LC record available at https://lccn.loc.gov/2024017555

LC ebook record available at https://lccn.loc.gov/2024017556

CONTENTS

PREFACE

It's a question, but let me not be coy. It's also a period, even an exclamation point. When should you panic? Now. In just the six months since I completed this manuscript, the panic-inducing polycrisis it responds to has accelerated. This will continue.

It's not immediately clear that panic is a good or useful way to feel (though I hope to persuade you in this book that it is). But the causes of that feeling present themselves with ever-increasing force.

It's most obvious with regard to the climate emergency. Throughout a 2023 fire season that began early and ended late, more than 45 million acres of Canadian rainforest and boreal forest burned. That's an area larger than the U.S. state of North Dakota razed by fire, nearly nine times Canada's yearly average of 6.2 million acres blanketing vast swathes of North America in thick, choking smoke. That's also just one year, and a comparatively minor moment of climate catastrophe.

Meanwhile, the increasingly rapid disappearance of Antarctic sea ice has begun prompting headlines of the "too late to fix" variety. As sea ice at both poles and—after it—glaciers in Antarctica and Greenland melt, multiple (or dozens, or a couple hundred) feet of sea level rise get locked in, starting in just the next couple decades. And that's to say nothing of methane emissions from melting Arctic permafrost and failing subtropical wetlands. As these carbon sinks become, like burning forests, net carbon emitters, climate change feedback loops speed up. For a couple days in November 2023, global average temperatures topped the worst-case increase over pre-industrial temps imagined by the Paris climate agreement

(+2°C). And yet, these all barely factor into our leaders' calculations of how much suffering the market can bear.

A wounded Gaia begins to refuse ecosystem services to a human population that continues, for now, still to swell.

Carbon-driven global weirding bleeds into, and bleeds out in, a sixth mass extinction that hits new benchmarks for sorrow, loss, and existential threat every month. In late September 2023, more than 100 dolphins were found dead of heat exhaustion when temps topped 102°F / 39°C in the water of the Amazon basin's Lake Tefé. The Amazon, a drought-stricken tropical forest ecosystem for now still dubbed the lungs of the world, is one of the most floridly biodiverse places Earth has ever known. And yet, even as the (wildly catastrophic) rate of Amazon deforestation diminished in September 2023 (to merely extremely catastrophic: a lower *rate* of deforestation is still deforestation), more than 10,000 species, i.e., nonhuman peoples, in this land continued processes of dying out forever.

It was a big month for Amazon disasters of another sort as well. Global e-sales and web hosting behemoth Amazon invested 4 billion dollars in AI startup Anthropic, the supposedly human-friendly alternative to OpenAI (whose primary investors are Microsoft and Facebook/Meta). Google followed with 2 billion dollars of its own. Now, four of the largest tech companies in the world—one of which has the self-declared goal of *becoming the marketplace* and explicit intention of replacing as many human workers as possible with robots, two others of which have been implicated in information-manipulation scandals rising all the way to genocide, and the last of which is merely universally loathed for its monopolistic provision of enterprise software—collectively maintain controlling interests in the automation of intellection, once thought a prototypical human activity. Ed tech companies, meanwhile, exult in the "cognitive offloading" AI will allow students and teachers alike. As though cognitive *loading* were not the central point of education!

Not to be outdone, microplastics and nanoplastics allow themselves each week to be discovered in new "pristine" sites—the deepest ocean, walled off cave systems, the highest peaks. Together with a range of other novel chemicals, many introduced as wonder solutions to still-other crises, they reshape the plasticity of biological being a little more every day. All this amounts, alongside the live threat of nuclear war as an outcome of Russia's invasion of Ukraine and other geopolitical disasters; a gathering global economic depression linked to everything from famine to neofeudalism; and mounting centripetal tensions within long-established political entities (like the United States), to a polycrisis.

Polycrisis is a name for the heap of crises that will be the end of one world, an accumulating and mutually amplifying collection of deferred costs that cannot be paid. This world that is ending cost the crises now ending it to produce. Carbon, capitalism, and colonialism (or CaCaCo, as I detail throughout this book) have together purchased a world—our world—whose deferred costs are falling due with more interest than anyone can afford. So, why panic now? Because our world is ending.

But the end of a world is not the end of everything. Not a sudden event, like a colossal earthquake or asteroid impact. Rather, we are entering (or have been in for some time) a period of staggered collapse.

The CaCaCo world is falling apart. As popular writer and whimsically self-described "doomist" Jessica Wildfire suggests, like anything else, that's a process. In an essay titled "We're Living through the End of Civilization and We Should Be Acting Like It," Wildfire writes, "Humans don't have to go extinct, but the way we're living has to change. There's no hope for this way of life, full of reckless consumption and convenience well beyond the planet's means. The harder we fight, the more denial and delusional thinking we engage in, the worse we're going to make it." When you say things like this, people often jump in to archly observe that *not all humans*. But the people saying that are typically themselves pretty reckless consumers. And a great deal of global humanity, for reasons elaborated in this book, is both stuck in and aspires to the most damaging lifeways of CaCaCo beneficiaries.

Worse yet, an awful lot of people are trying to persuade you that nothing fundamentally needs to change, that innovations in everything from finance to material science will save civilization (such as it is). They are wrong.

Panic gives everyday people a way of confronting the polycrisis that opens onto new possibilities: not for "saving the world," but for preparing next worlds.

As CaCaCo staggers through the next few years or decades of collapse, there will be no shortage of innovations both better and worse. For instance, solar panel efficiency is improving almost, though not quite, as fast as the climate emergency's feedback loops stack catastrophes. Cold fusion pops onto the horizon again and again, a will-o-the-wisp beckoning to a future of energy abundance. Microplastic-eating bacteria are refined. Solar geoengineering strategies (damn the torpedoes! full speed ahead!) are marketed, I mean reported on, with ever-increasing fervor. AI regulation summits are held, declarations made, and policy produced (as with U.S. President Biden's Executive Order of October 2023): all promising to mitigate coming impacts of a technology that can already now replace most labor tasks accomplished by human intellection.

Some of these strategies for navigating catastrophe will pay off. Versions of "normal" will, obscenely, persist. As Wildfire notes, "This is what the end of civilization looks like. Work and school go on. Celebrities throw parties during megafloods. Teenagers freak out because they can't find their favorite makeup at Sephora, because the factories that make it are shut down by a disabling virus. The urgency of normal will persist." But, even as it does, the simple fact of the matter (discussed in the first chapter of this book) is that the CaCaCo world *cannot* produce the technologies— political economic and governance technologies especially—to make good on the balloon payments "normal" now demands.

Not for nothing have the United States and other CaCaCo beneficiary countries refused climate justice pleas from the global south. They prepare for rapidly worsening times ahead as the powerful often have: battening hatches, building walls, describing those at the gates as barbarians who brought suffering on themselves. In Congressional testimony of July 2023, U.S. special envoy on climate change John Kerry reassured legislators that "under no circumstances" would wealthy global north countries make direct payment, offer "climate reparations," to the more immediately devastated poor countries of the global south. As resource availability dwindles further, fortresses will get concomitantly smaller.

Ever more of us, even those currently enjoying comfortable lives in the wealthy countries, will find ourselves outside the gates.

In this context, already the present and intensifying in the near future, concepts like "climate genocide," the "reorganization of violence," and "collapse" feel increasingly salient. This book discusses all three, but stay a moment with the first.

The characteristic lifeways of wealthy CaCaCo people ensure suffering, death, and physical dislocation for billions of (primarily darker-skinned) poor people in decades to come. In global perspective, "wealthy" means the lifeways not just of people buying big yachts with littler yachts inside of them, but also of most working people in the old colonial core and even a large urbanized middle class in former colonies. (Rising seas will displace plenty of rich people, too, but *they* will have somewhere else to go. Crop failures drive famine for the poor, supply chain problems for the rich. This is what wealth means.)

To think of climate genocide, to confront the reality that this future is the logical and unavoidable extension of *who we are deciding in practice to be now*, is to begin to feel how exceptionally badly things are going. A process of staggered collapse is radical, and it is violent, and it is how we live now. People will not bear this forever. As incentive structures fail and apparatuses for repression get overwhelmed, many will try to reorganize the systems of violence that maintain a present "normal." Who, in painful times ahead, will we be?

The billionaires have already been privately panicking. They secure their interests not merely with bunkers and armed drones but equally with ubiquitous surveillance, acceleration of universal indebtedness, and media plumping for "normalcy" itself. For the rest of us, whose interests are far more divided and ambivalent, the time to panic is now.

The aim of this book is to make a case for panicking wisely, both the why of it and the how of it. If enough of us can manage to panic in time, we might yet avoid the worst. We might even humanize, pluralize new visions of a global humanity in deep relation with the more-than-human world. *Panic Now?* is devoted to that possibility, to our collective capacity for making new worlds and new versions of ourselves.

The future is broken, the present irredeemable. But that's not to say "smoke 'em if you got 'em." To the contrary, panicking now lays the only groundwork there could be for genuinely better next worlds. May we build wisely among the ruins of this one.

Introduction

This book isn't for everybody. No book is. But maybe it is for you.

WHERE *PANIC NOW?* STARTS

We're stuck in a doom loop, a downward spiral. Hopelessly so, it can seem. Maybe. Certainly, a mounting collection of increasingly massive and accelerating crises is midstream in the process of finding no resolution.

But that's a historical condition, not some kind of transcendental reality. We're not stuck consuming ourselves and nearly all kin on this planet to death because "that's just how humans are." Tempting as the intellectual cop-out is, there's more to the story than that.

Trying to account for the horror and enormity of climate collapse, an AI revolution spinning out of control, Earth's sixth mass extinction, a novel chemical crisis we still barely understand, and so much more, I've myself fallen at times into thinking of these as products of universal human failings.

Maybe people really are no damn good.

But the reality is trickier. We're stuck today in a weird historical condition: stuck mentally, stuck emotionally, stuck imaginatively, and stuck practically.

This book is my effort to write, feel, and think my own way through and out of that condition. I hope it can help you to do the same.

I'll write in the chapters to follow about something I call CaCaCo, the carbon-capitalism-colonialism assemblage. I'll also write about what we've come to call the Anthropocene—the era, our own, in which CaCaCo humans have reshaped geologic time itself. We CaCaCo humans are stuck in a very specific sort of way. The hopelessness and inability to change or accomplish anything radically different that many people feel are products of a particular moment in world history. And that's all true.

But maybe it's a bit abstract, almost too big to grasp. So, let me start off with a different story of our historical condition, something to bring it all down to earth a little, a way of accounting for how I myself come at all this.

Here's where I'm writing from.

In the beginning was Reagan. And Reagan was with Thatcher. And Reagan was Thatcher. And that was the beginning of the end of the world.

This is a kind of punk rock story, one I'll come back to challenge in a little bit. It's the story I learned coming up, listening to The Dead Kennedys, Propagandhi, and Bad Religion. We could call it the Jello Biafra Theory of Modern History.

On this theory, a lot of new things happened in the Anglophone world in the 1970s, most of them bad for collective global imagining of different futures. Presidents Nixon and Carter, respectively, took the U.S. Dollar off the gold standard and began a rapid-fire process of deregulating businesses and banks. British armed forces massacred Northern Irish protesters without consequence. There was a lot of disco music. Then, in the '80s, the wheels really fell off the bus. In 1979, Maggie Thatcher gained the U.K. prime ministership and began her reign of terror, eviscerating the notion of government as something that provides public goods. Across the pond, after his allies had sabotaged Carter's efforts to get American hostages in Iran freed before election day in 1980, Ronald Reagan (the actor???) acceded to the U.S. presidency.

Together, Thatcher and Reagan crushed unions, sold off public assets, and boosted military dictators around the world. Between automation and offshoring of jobs, labor was weak—through its political avatars, big business struck first. No longer was zealous anticommunism practiced mostly abroad or against select domestic enemies. Now, it was time to dismantle the welfare state writ large, time to change the very notion of governance itself. It was time, Reagan famously urged, to "starve the beast" of government.

One result was that it started seeming impossible for regular people to change the shape of history by seizing control of powerful governments.

Each of these two villains left in their wake a tattered public sphere and diminished democracy. Thatcher's own ill-tempered *bon mot*— "there's no such thing as society"—would organize historical imaginaries for decades to come. The two had triumphed, well before the fall of the Berlin Wall or privatization of Soviet industry in the hands of oligarchs and their Anglo-American partners, in more than just killing off the idea of a global communist experiment. They'd poisoned the well for democratic governance in general.

In their fervor to root out anything smacking of collective popular control, Reagan and Thatcher rendered us all incapable of addressing a whole panoply of looming global catastrophes.

It's a great story.

It's not entirely true, though.

Not that Reagan and Thatcher weren't monsters. They were, and they shaped their decade and beyond (8 years in office for Reagan, 11 for Thatcher). But through the 1980s, new visions of alternative worldmaking continued gaining traction throughout the Anglosphere. Militant radicals continued acting on the world in service of some other world entirely.

In the U.K. and Northern Ireland, the Provisional Irish Republican Army pursued a "Long War" of attrition—over nearly two decades popularly known as the Troubles, they fought the British state for an all-Ireland socialist republic. In the United States, anti-capitalist "globalism from below" radicals found expression in militant ecology and international feminist socialism. Changing the structure of the world had lost much of its labor underpinnings, but the vision was hardly dead. Further south, the EZLN or Zapatistas formed their decentralized ultraleft indigenous organization in 1983, eventually wresting a large chunk of the Mexican state of Chiapas away from federal control. Similar moments of radical possibility continued unfolding throughout much of the world.

So, here we are now. Reagan and Thatcher did plenty of damage, but they couldn't destroy the possibility of changing the world for the better. And yet, CaCaCo and much of the world we know really is falling apart today. We're in the early stages of a staggered collapse, throughout global north and south alike. Matters will get much worse. And we seem frozen, helpless to do much of anything.

This book starts by surrendering the Jello Biafra Theory of Modern History I cut my teeth on. Perhaps another explanation of how we have become so badly stuck can help us to get unstuck. Perhaps a different story about where things went wrong can help us get purchase on our intractable problems in some new ways.

Instead of Reagan and Thatcher, it's helpful to turn to a nearer moment in time: the interval from 1989 through 1992. Between 1989's color revolutions leading to the fall of the Soviet Union and 1992's Rio de Janeiro Earth Summit, something happened to our collective ability to think, feel, and imagine different worlds.

It is almost trite to say that the end of Soviet communism, frighteningly bad as it was in much of its execution, was also the death of a certain kind of global imaginary. Almost trite, but true.

Capitalism imagines a world of competitors. In this war of each against all, the market is a kind of sovereign force. The price-setting magic of "what the market will bear" determines the value of everything—humans, commodities, even political institutions. The world is a marketplace, and though competition need not be cutthroat (and indeed is often collaborative), in this marketplace there are "natural" winners and losers. Each best serves all by serving herself, securing market share. The wisdom of the crowd, which acts as if moved by an invisible hand to converge on prices, will secure the best possible outcomes for all.

Is it the best imaginable world? Perhaps not, but there is no other. It is, at least, the best possible world imaginable.

This is the way of seeing, thinking, and feeling we are stuck in. Scholar Mark Fisher famously, in a book of that title, called it *capitalist realism*.

That might not be so bad if capitalist realism set us up well to solve diffuse planetary crises, such as climate breakdown and global biodiversity loss. But it does not. As I detail in this book, it cannot. We need different imaginaries.

Different imaginaries start with different ways of feeling.

As we lurch ever deeper into predictable disasters, many on the left today feel despair. Or anger, resentment, glumness, or (notoriously) melancholy. We've never finished mourning the loss of a communist vision of the world. Maybe that's indeed our problem. After all, what I've said so far isn't some radical new idea. Lots of people have said much the same.

The end of Soviet communism in 1989 (coupled with China's prior transition to state capitalism) was, for much of the world, the end of any vision of global solidarity.

How can we get started on revolutionary worldmaking if it is, indeed, easier to imagine the end of the world than the end of capitalism? What "next" even *is* there beyond entry into the marketplace, efforts to secure competitive market position, maybe at best something like "effective altruism," where supposedly you're pursuing market success so you can fund noble causes down the line while also seeking to ensure that "ideas that do good" will win out in the market more directly? How can you work for global radical action if the marketplace and its fracturing of non-market solidarities conquers all? Wasn't capitalism's defeat of communism inevitable? Isn't it, after all, in the nature of humans to be competitive?

Such questions look at only the "death of utopianism" end of the 1989–1992 interval.

From 1989 alone, the fall of communism does seem like an "end of history." Certainly, it was the disintegration of a key tension within liberal democracies. Liberalism's focus on individual (property) rights and democracy's on collective public goods and decision-making are at odds. With the Soviet Union and the idea of communism as their external competition, liberal democracies had to maintain some attunement to the democracy bit—even through and after Reagan and Thatcher.

But when communism fell, capitalism was free to jettison the democratic side of the equation. Market liberalism turned out to be, at least within the Anglosphere, an end of history of sorts. We live in the shadows of this end of history. We really cannot imagine the end of capitalism. In many ways, no longer horizon has arisen to replace what communism once offered.

Still, this is just part of the picture. In 1989, after all, there remained in play a globalizing *understanding* of climate change.

Gathering force through the 1980s had been an awareness that beat against the insular imaginary of ultracompetitive, privatizing, liberal capitalism like a hurricane. Globally and within the United States, through the tireless efforts of advocates like NASA scientist James E. Hansen, broad publics had begun to understand that greenhouse gases (GHGs, especially carbon dioxide) were driving global heating and climate change. It was early days of climate change yet, but the science was clear to most people. By 1988, the role of carbon emissions in warming the planet was undeniable.

The rushing-in of public understanding of greenhouse gas climate forcing got so intense that, in 1988, both Democrat Michael Dukakis and Republican George H. W. Bush ran on climate platforms. Everyone knew global climate action was necessary.

Coming in green against his environmentally smudgy Democrat opponent on the campaign trail, Bush promised such climate action. He would convene an international summit to address the issue, inviting the Soviet Union and China alike. "Those who think we are powerless to do anything about the greenhouse effect," Bush thundered in one stump speech, "are forgetting about the White House effect!"

But something different happened after Bush was elected. Almost immediately, as journalist Nathaniel Rich details in *Losing Earth*, a widely anticipated 1989 summit in the Netherlands ended without new agreements.

Around the world, people had been expecting a binding treaty on carbon emissions—something on the model of the 1987 Montreal Protocol that regulated chlorofluorocarbons (CFCs) to protect the ozone layer. Instead, Bush's chief of staff, John Sununu, scurried around Noordwijk (alongside counterparts from the Soviet Union, Japan, and the U.K.), working to scupper any possible deal. Sununu made it clear that he, an engineer, doubted very much the reality of climate change at all. No treaty, binding or otherwise, would proceed from this first big climate conference.

On the one hand it was known, beyond all partisanship or posturing, that human carbon emissions were warming the Earth. The first-ever report from the Intergovernmental Panel on Climate Change (IPCC), in 1990, described this fact as "certain."

On the other hand Sununu, alongside others from Bush's administration, actively worked to obfuscate this reality. Hansen's official government testimony was censored. Exxon and other oil giants began reversing investments in solar and alternative energies and dumping money into obfuscating the science instead.

And yet, movement toward another big climate summit—like greenhouse gas forcing itself—was unstoppable.

So, just prior to the 1992 Rio de Janeiro "Earth" Summit, Bush made his new position forcefully clear: "The American way of life is not up for negotiations. Period." There would be no binding global treaty on emissions. Not in 1992, perhaps not ever.

And yet again: The facts of the situation remained well-understood. For a diffuse, slowly gathering crisis like global warming, markets could not provide solutions in time. There were just too many perverse incentives driving increases in GHGs. Binding global treaties, just like for CFCs and the ozone layer, were necessary. In this regard, 1992 registered a second end of history, maybe a worse one than 1989.

In 1989, the imaginative goal of global solidarity beyond and against capitalism died, or at least took one hell of a beating. In 1992, the understanding that solidarity was needed to address the quintessentially *global* problem of carbon emissions was split into two. This story helps us better understand where we're stuck. Maybe it can even help us to do a few things differently.

It's important to start by seeing that, in the story of the climate crisis (which sets the tone for all of our other crises), there is no "right side of history."

From 1992 forward, half of Americans (and—such is the force of hegemony—citizens throughout much of the rest of the world) would have one truth and the other half another. Each would understand one certain truth and believe one obvious falsehood.

Those looking at the nothingburger of the "Earth" Summit understandably concluded that perhaps climate change was not real after all. Sununu (and untold millions or billions in reality-falsification by fossil fuel giants) must be right. If climate change were such a big deal, Bush would have done something, but he did not! A lie and a truth.

Meanwhile, those taking the science seriously reached an opposite conclusion. Climate change was obviously real, certainly caused by human carbon emissions. Thank goodness such a significant start had been made on addressing it at the Earth Summit! A truth and a lie.

Since 1992, the possibility of planetary solidarities has sunk ever further beneath the weight of this bifurcated picture of the world. Climate change, of course and as every reasonable person knows today, is all too real and all too human-caused. *And*, as has become increasingly (though still not entirely) clear to hopeful fabulists on the other side of the aisle, we've been doing nothing of substance to address it for decades. Relative to the actual scale of the crisis, even the "largest climate bill ever" is fundamentally unserious.

The IPCC itself carries forward this bifurcation. Leaving aside the way its executive summaries get captured by fossil fuel interests and national politics, the underlying science may be the most extraordinary knowledge-building project in human history. Never before have so many nations, interests, and individuals come together to construct such an enormous, rigorous apparatus for understanding the world. The human-hours and collaborative spirit of knowledge-making that underwrite the IPCC constitute a magnificent achievement in themselves, its periodic syntheses and working group reports still more. And yet, nothing much has been done with all this knowledge.

For three decades of Conference of the Parties (COP) summits and IPCC reports, global leaders have met and decided not to engage in binding climate action. This is not only a problem of energy-generation technologies and associated money-power, but is far more a problem of our technologies for living together in societies, a problem of governments and political economies writ large. We lack both imagination and understanding. We don't have the social or political economic technologies necessary to avert catastrophe.

The world is stuck. We are stuck. The epistemic pall of the 1989–1992 interval hangs over us all. And the consequences are beginning to mount. They will grow worse and worse.

Capitalist market forces will surely deliver exciting new innovations. IPCC reports will develop ever-greater nuance and multidimensionality. And climate genocide will steal over whole swathes of the globe. Not only climate genocide, either, but the horrific consequences of various other costs a CaCaCo world has been deferring, and that now are falling due. The climate emergency, though itself barely graspable in its ever-swifter unfolding, is only one dimension of an enormous collective crisis.

The climate crisis twins with a biodiversity crisis or sixth extinction, and these run alongside a novel chemical crisis that has been unfolding for more than half a century. All three are today joined by an AI revolution that threatens, like each of the others, to upend human life as we know it.

Together, these constitute a polycrisis that demands both global imaginaries and locally solidaristic ways of thinking, feeling, and acting toward planetary politics beyond markets and the politics of individual nation-states.

We look to the market to save us, but it cannot. Our political leaders seem powerless to act seriously. When we start to understand how profoundly stuck we are, stymied not only by epistemic polarization but by a debility of the imagination itself, trapped in competing lie-truth combinations about how the world is—well, what is there left to do?

When we really grok the weakness of the stories we've been working with, our embroilment in historical conditions that tend only to the worst— what are we to feel and think?

What else, but panic?

WHERE *PANIC NOW?* GOES

This is just a punk rock song
written for the people who can see something's wrong.
Like ants in a colony, we do our share
But there's so many other fucking insects out there.

—Bad Religion, "Punk Rock Song"

Before it goes anywhere else, this book is headed for panic. We all need to start panicking, and quick.

Things are going badly for humanity, on the whole. This fact got a lot clearer to many otherwise fairly comfortable people after covid-19 began raging through "developed" and "less developed" worlds alike. Here was a kind of best-case-scenario for our current world system (a new disease that wasn't *too* deadly, a rapidly developed vaccine based on prior technology and the disease's proximity to others we know well, a widely respected international health surveillance and emergency response system, high levels of intergovernmental cooperation in managing individual travel and commercial logistics, etc.), and yet it kept killing millions in wave after deadly wave.

Between the disease's emergence in Wuhan, China in late 2019 and the World Health Organization's May 2023 declaration that it was no longer a health emergency, nearly seven million people died worldwide.[1] Thousands around the globe continue, as I write shortly after the WHO's declaration, to die of covid every week. Untold millions more suffer long-term health consequences. The United States, whose citizens had for many years assured one another it was the greatest country on earth, saw over a million covid deaths—the highest mortality rate in the world.

Still, things are not going nearly as badly yet as in years to come. That was just one pandemic. On paper, it was a crisis we had all the tools to address.

Our other budding catastrophes have more complicated and uncertain solutions, or no solutions at all. From the depredations of a pay-as-you-go subscription-model life into which corporate economics force ever more markets to the thundering failures of buildings, glacial walls, and social institutions undercut by the deluges of climate crisis, any realistic appraisal of the coming decades is pretty bleak for most of humanity. Despite many efforts to reassure us, the writing is on the wall. Throughout global north and south alike, millions already recognize that the current world is staggering into collapse and experience a creeping malaise.[2]

Whether quiet despair or useless rage, the malaise comes from not knowing how to name and live collectively with the accumulating crises that drive a staggered collapse. Outside pockets of very or aspirationally wealthy people clinging to the rose-tinted statistics of a Steven Pinker or pivoting to the longtermism of a William MacAskill,[3] we can see well enough: Things are not going great.

But who are "we"? To a large extent, most books' "we"s are implied. Since this book invites readers to feel difficult feelings in solidarity with other people around the world, people whose lives are exceedingly different in most particulars, it's worth spelling out who I'm talking to a little more than is usual.

If you feel stressed by how badly things are going, but don't want to panic: this book is for you. If you suspect world history is proceeding *more* badly than the going stories would have it: this book is for you. If you've been tracking the climate crisis, or the AI revolution, or the novel chemical crisis, or the sixth mass extinction with growing concern, perhaps with a gnawing sense that these are all connected: this book is for you. If you've heard the refrain "don't panic" plenty, and you know they're right to say it, but you also know in a way that's hard to explain that they're wrong, desperately, horribly wrong? This book is for you.

The tools for humanizing offered here are, as suggested by Bad Religion's "Punk Rock Song," for people who can see something's wrong. At the same time, they're necessarily also for a "we" that finds itself in a position to pick up this book at all—not, as I'll return to note from time to time, most of the globe's population. This book's "we" are, as badly as we're doing, doing pretty well in comparison to those most immediately harmed by the polycrisis described here and its many precursors.[4] Not to worry, though: we'll do worse soon.

Panic Now? suggests not just ways of thinking about panic but also ways of thinking and feeling and acting both with panic and after panic for people in comparatively advantaged positions. The book sketches a map for feeling and living through our age of catastrophes that might make sense, might even make our catastrophes less catastrophic, but most of all might make differently organized futures possible a little further down the line, after we've staggered a bit deeper into collapse and societal crumbling. Transformative possibility starts, though it does not end, with the experience of panic.

But don't let me get carried away. This is just a book. It's not going to make anything happen. And, as will become clear through its pages, a good deal of social and ecosystem collapse is already baked into the global organization of life. As Bad Religion had it, "There's so many other fucking insects out there."

The political economic, physical, and infrastructural organization of the world that drives our crises prevents, in the short term, most (though not all) amelioration of them.

There's nothing any collective audience for this book can do to immediately transform our worsening world (which is not the same as saying there's nothing we can do at all). Moreover, even when we read aloud, we read alone. We live our lives at once as isolated dots and helpless clusters within some larger pattern that takes increasingly disastrous form. Each reader of this or any book is less than an iota, not even a mote in the vast cataclysmic swarming of our species in its overtopping of all planetary boundaries. A reader is not a crowd, not a mass, not a movement.

And yet, new crowds and masses and movements will indeed form.[5] They will form to deal with damage already done, as escalating interest comes due on the deferred debts of a global organization of life around carbon, capitalism, and colonialism. Crowds and masses and movements will form as the world we live in disintegrates. But *when* will they form, and *how* will they act when they do? This book offers considerations for answering those questions thoughtfully, with an eye to making—somehow—a better, more humane world of the tumult to come.

Starting with the emotional difficulty necessitated by realism about the state of our world, my aim has been to offer a conceptual framework and practical tools for negotiating crises that appropriately spur panic. In the following chapters, I lay out in some detail our general stuckness in a carbon-capitalism-colonialism assemblage (ch. 1) and panic-inducing polycrisis (ch. 2). We need to know where we are and where we're heading, if we're to have any hope of changing course. Accordingly, these first two chapters are massively endnoted. I want you to be able to go down the rabbit hole for yourself if you'd like (but you don't have to).

Causes for panic established, I move to answer questions about whether panic is useful in the first place and what sorts of possibilities it might awaken (ch. 3). Panic doesn't just strike us and need to be pushed away; it's *for* something. Our task is to understand what. Readers skeptical that panic is ever a reasonable response might find it useful to begin in chapter three before picking back up with chapters one and two. After chapter two, too, the endnotes ease up a bit. This isn't an academic tome, but more a guidebook for panicking wisely.

Returning to our age of catastrophe, the final two chapters lay out some possible directions for panicking judiciously (ch. 4) and conclude with reflections on who the "we" of a truly global humanity might yet be (ch. 5). There are better and worse ways of panicking, and the best bid fair to enable truly different futures than our present darkly promises. This book is as much about what, and *who*, can come of panic as about panic itself.

On that note, I should say that I've myself had to turn back and forth between chapters in the writing of this book. The reality is that, at present, we are far more stuck churning along on desperately bad trajectories than a lot of well-meaning people would like to believe. A sense of possibility can sometimes come from different stories, and the stories I've offered in chapters three through five are efforts to find something that makes sense of our times for myself as much as anyone else. But any sense of possibility that isn't rooted in panic first will fail to grasp the depth of our crises.

And yet, the causes for panic are themselves too great to sit with, unaided and uninterrupted, for long. The visions of possibility in chapters three, four, and five have helped me personally to sustain the difficult feelings of chapters one and two. More, though, it takes *being with* a whole world. Maybe the best sorts of possibility emerge from feeling the prickle of sweat under an afternoon sun's beating intensity, watching wind whip the strong, wide branches of ponderosas on a far hillside, listening for what the dogs hear when they start at deer or skunks alongside the house, tasting the air's heavy wetness just before it turns to rain, and smelling neighbors' woodsmoke as it sneaks in a cracked-open window.

We have to become peoples of this world, people able to stop long enough to breathe in this world deeply, people who align differently with it than we ever have before.

The trouble is that this world we need to align with is dying. So, while it's true that there's no way out but through, it's worth remembering that "through" isn't always linear. Sometimes, to live through panic honestly it's necessary to just go hug a tree or sit in a union meeting for a while. What matters is that we return, in a spirit of honesty and open-hearted love, again and again, to the still-thrumming panic at an ending that undergirds any serious look at the present world.

Because that ending's where all the new beginnings are.

Our crises are massively overdetermined, to a good extent unavoidable. They will proceed in the intensification of today's unevenly distributed suffering: houses swamped and burned, the eerie silence of dead forests, mass involuntary infertility, machinic words that have lost all human meaning. People will flee coastlines and starve as food production gets battered by heat and war. Algorithms will determine who may live and who die as autonomous killing machines are unleashed on the other side of militarized border walls. People will become increasingly unsure of what is real and what not, will harden their internal borders to perceived epistemic foes. And all that precisely at a time when only mass collective action could hope to mitigate the violences of unguided assault vehicles, heat death at the sweltering midlatitudes or in suddenly arising domes elsewhere, suffocation from the smoke of unchecked megafires, endocrine and gene-expression disruptions that reshape the very biological basis of humanity. That's the next couple decades.[6] As time goes by, all this will get more evenly distributed.

The tools of the world that produced today's crises are insufficient for resolving them, since after all these crises are its own deferred costs. In an entropic universe, it took a lot of energy to build and maintain the CaCaCo world, to carve out even its dubious stability. That energy was borrowed at interest, and the world it made can pay neither interest nor principal. The next two chapters don't sugarcoat the organizing logic of it all: things *will* get much worse for most of us, not later on but in our own lifetimes, relatively soon.

And yet, the meaning of the crises currently unfolding remains still unwritten. So, too, the way our responses to them will shape who we ourselves do and can become. The conceptual toolkit *Panic Now?* shares is something ordinary people can use to become differently, both alone and together, to "humanize" in present and coming times of devastation. It's a toolkit for developing practical wisdom in a time of rapidly unfolding crises.

The nature of practical wisdom is that its results aren't guaranteed. It's more an approach or way of thinking and feeling, imagining and understanding, than it is a formula—a way that can sustain uncertainty, even panic. Practical wisdom is a betting style that heavily weights honesty about constraints and, on that basis, looks for unseen possibilities. The bet of this book is that we can learn to panic wisely, in time to avoid the worst and maybe even lay foundations for building new worlds in the ruins ahead.

Wouldn't we be fools to bet against ourselves?

~~Chapter One~~

YOU CAN'T UNWIND A TENSIONED SPRING

To bet wisely, a person needs to understand the odds. For our current organization of world, they aren't great.

This world is a coiled spring. Most springs are stiffened metal that can be compressed or elongated to store energy. A metal's tensile strength allows for that compression or expansion. But no spring has infinite tensile strength. And an overloaded spring's coming loose can be quite explosive! A tensioned spring *wants* to become explosive force.

The potential energy a taut spring stores will have a vector, some direction in which it waits to proceed as work on the world, based on the orientation of the spring. But you can only load a spring so much. A tensioned spring will, well, spring loose when too much force is applied, uncoupling from whatever housing holds it in place.

Our world, a world screwed tight by the machinery of carbon, capitalism, and colonialism, is such a spring. The nature of our disasters has an "explosive dispersal" direction to it. And the complicated legacy of our carbon-capitalism-colonialism assemblage cannot simply be unwound. "The past is never dead," William Faulkner famously observed, "It's not even past."[1] Our badly formed world, which is headed in some horrifically bad directions, coils tight around a past that is not past. There are no external machines with which we might unwind it. The force that screws it ever tighter is the ever greater collection of deferred costs that make this world possible in the first place. All our acting, thinking, and feeling transpires within the dimensions of this coiled spring.

Panicking wisely begins with understanding just how tightly we are wound, how long are our odds of making any better world.

WHERE ARE WE NOW?

There's no way to grasp how reasonable panic is without having a sense of the carbon-capitalism-colonialism assemblage that's where we're stuck now. I've been abbreviating this assemblage CaCaCo; it is (both thankfully and frighteningly) in the early stages of breaking down.

For now, we really are stuck in this bad world, which benefits a few in the short term by imposing devastating costs on the many—and, over the long haul, even on the short-sighted few. The goal here, though, isn't to emphasize villains or encourage crowds to form with an eye to constructing guillotines.

There are a lot books out there that castigate CaCaCo's desperately rich slate of villains, but these preach mainly to the converted or occupy rarefied spaces of scholarly discourse. To their credit, many manage to castigate while also offering nuanced, thoughtful breakdowns of CaCaCo in its forward-lurching systematicity.[2] This book, though, is more a guide for betting wisely on how the spring might break loose.

How are we to make sense, in feeling, reflection, and action, of disastrous storms into which we are collectively thrust? How might the right sorts of panic today help us make it through them and on to fairer seas tomorrow? To ask these questions isn't to downplay the real villainy driving our collective crises, both in the past and in the present,[3] or even to say that redistributions of world-making violence can or should remain unthinkable.[4] To the contrary, the many violences compressing the whole globe to fit into a carbon-capitalism-colonialism assemblage simply *will* be redistributed. The question is: How?

As the CaCaCo world staggers into collapse, its violences will be reorganized in new ways. Pretty as it is to suppose they might simply disappear, there's no grounded rationale for such a belief. Reorganizations of violence may here or there serve just causes. On the whole, though, they're likely to be distressing, traumatizing, and damaging to anything like a social fabric.[5] CaCaCo's mounting troubles cannot reasonably be supposed solvable—either for maintenance of the existing world or replacement by some other—with nonviolent demonstrations, market innovations, and the like. There's just too much force compressed in there, with more added every minute.

Panicking wisely on behalf of a humanizing future means staying a while with troubles that have no ready solutions.

As a phrase, "carbon-capitalism-colonialism assemblage" is pretty alienating. And yet, we can readily discover its operation in our lives.

CaCaCo refers to the organizing conditions for nearly every human person on earth's lived reality. There is almost no corner of the globe where carbon-burning is not the primary source of energy, capitalism does not organize economic production and consumption, and colonialism's legacy and persistent present does not define the social and property relations—oriented by entwined racial and national hierarchies—into which each of us is thrown upon birth.

It's CaCaCo's world. We're all just living in it. But that's a contingent fact of political economic history, not a general human destiny.

CARBON

Carbon is merely an element on the periodic table (the C of CO_2). Building block of life, sure, but like any building block largely inert on its own. As most people have become aware, burning carbon is a primary driver of the climate crisis, and thus is intimately entwined with other large-scale crises. The AI revolution, for instance, requires staggering new carbon emissions; the novel chemical crisis flows from oil through plastics; and the biodiversity crisis is forced by the massive scale of human activity enabled by rearranging carbon. Carbon is at the heart of all our difficulties, but only because these difficulties are the deferred costs of our "normal" version of a world.

As a kind of battery for energy from the sun, various arrangements of carbon can be incinerated to release that stored energy (the battery ranges from trees to coal to compressed gases and other fossil fuels).

When we burn carbon, the resulting greenhouse gases end up trapping ever more of the sun's energy within earth's atmosphere. The devastating consequences in heat and extreme weather from that excess trapped energy are obviously not wonderful, but there's no denying the capacity for metabolizing resources that carbon-burning of the fossil fuel variety opened up. The carbon part of CaCaCo refers to the fact that we heat (and deforest and strip mine and so on) our planet in order to be able to produce and consume more, as a species overall and with far greater intensity since fossilized carbon resources came into the picture. We burn carbon along lines pretty rigidly ordered by capitalism's demand for infinite economic growth and colonialism's distribution of the benefits and immediate consequences of that.

So, it's important to recognize up-front that the climate crisis and all our others are fundamentally about deferred costs coming due. The climate crisis, for example, is a species-wide delayed payment for the *extraordinary* amounts of energy expended via CaCaCo. (Our other crises intersect with this at every level, too.) Rearranging carbon is something humans have always done, but over the last couple hundred years some of us really went wild with it.[6] Now and increasingly unaffordably in the very near future, everyone is paying for that.

Like all living things, humans consume resources to be able to expend energy to metabolize still further resources to sustain various of our populations' particular ways of life. We are one of many biota, busily constructing out our ecological niche to the fullest. The trouble is that through fossil carbon, colonial legal arrangements of the globe, and capitalist systems of production and consumption we've become so good at building out our ecological niche to maximize resource metabolization that we're overshooting, destroying our own niche and everybody else's as well.[7] Today's crises are yesterday's deferred costs.

Producing labor-power to make and do things is energetically costly, more so for humans than for other primates.[8] Throughout most of our species history, we did work on the world with our own bodies or with the coerced cooperation of other humans and of nonhuman animals, drawing along the way on resource offerings of the more-than-human world generally.[9] For many thousands of years, when we burned carbon, it was mostly trees or dung—energetically demanding to collect. Social and engineering technologies, from levers to animal husbandry to slavery, allowed small groups of humans to draw on much more energy than they could themselves produce, but for most of human history the cost of work-energy still involved a lot of direct resource metabolization by living beings.[10] If something was to be done, *some body* had to do it, and every living body requires ongoing sustenance.

It wasn't until the widespread adoption of carbon-burning as an energy source for steam engines that humans began regularly drawing on work-energy many orders of magnitude greater than any living being could produce and expend.[11] Rather suddenly, and ever increasingly, immensely *more* could be done for and by anyone with access to the right arrangements of carbon. Global capitalist growth has meant that, in some ways for better and in many for worse,[12] nearly all humans now live to some extent in the world of that "more"— in deeply structuralized unequal fashion from one place to another.[13]

From coal through methane (what we call "natural" gas), carbon-burning has enabled the redirection of vast quantities of stored energy from the sun. For a while, the cost of that wasn't entirely clear. It seemed like something that could be taken care of later, at least to the people controlling most of the burning. Now, it's later. The deferred costs are falling due, not only as greenhouse gases heat our climate intolerably (in effect, carbon and methane and other emissions make our entire atmosphere into a storage unit for the sun's energy, with cataclysmic results for life), but also as the entire CaCaCo way of life renders ever more other forms of life impossible, reshaping the entire planetary system.

Accordingly, some scholars argue our current geologic era would better be termed the Carbonocene or Capitalocene. Anthropocene is where most people seem to have settled, so I use that, but anyone interested in the stakes of what we call our epoch should check out the various arguments offered in Jason Moore's *Anthropocene or Capitalocene?*.[14]

The swirling weather extremes and changing animal behavior of global weirding, as the twinned climate and biodiversity crises are sometimes together called,[15] can be thought of as long-term prices for several hundred years in which human resource-metabolization was organized with increasing ubiquity around the inhuman energy released by burning carbon fossil fuels: coal, oil, and gas. That carbon-burning became so ubiquitous in the first place happened, at least in part, because of capitalism.[16]

CAPITALISM

Very simply put, capitalism names relations of production and consumption structured by the accumulation of capital.

Capital's definition is endlessly debated (and rightly so), but a lot of it boils down to stored value over and above the cost of providing goods and services in a system that allows for virtually infinite such value storage.[17] The catch is that this stored "surplus value" can only be realized, literally *made real as capital*, in new investments.

In economies that grow overall (and capitalism requires such economies), any given capitalist's capital can be "stored" only via its circulation. Capital can only circulate, *as capital*, through investment in economic institutions that seek to produce market value for capital owners that exceeds the value garnered by workers for their work within the scope of those investments. And here we're back where we started. In effect, capital (by contrast with money, such as the wages you or I earn by working a job) can only be accumulated by those who own as property and can profit from certain kinds of growth-enabling economic institutions. Capital accumulation is capital circulation in new investments. Correspondingly, capitalism as a form of political economy entails ongoing, "infinite" growth.[18]

Capital institutions or assets vary greatly. They include everything from marketplaces themselves (like the NASDAQ or the Bombay Stock Exchange), to limited liability corporations (whether Fortune 500 firm or family farm), to individual factories and other sites of manufacturing or extraction (from the garment manufactories of Dhaka to the coal mines of the Cumberland Gap), to platform capitalism's hybrid edifices of binary code and patterned human behavior (the web interface, cloud servers, and vast surveillance databases of Amazon's global empire, for instance)—and more.

What's crucial is that even as anyone can theoretically own pieces of some of these institutions (shares and other economic derivatives), a very small number of people in actual practice own nearly all of them. Capital institutions or capital assets, in addition to being owned in their majority around the world by a shockingly small percentage of the global population, are distributed along lines defined by colonialism.[19]

Does it have to be that way? Maybe, maybe not. But it *is* that way. Despite any number of well-meaning people's fond wishes and sincere efforts, colonial property structures and national/international hierarchies continue to shape who gets to accumulate capital and how. This does not happen by accident, and nor does it require secret cabals. All it takes is the consistent application of violence, both within countries and between them, to maintain a global legal order organized at its base by colonialism.[20]

Through its historical entwining with colonialism, capitalism accumulates the most resources not only for relatively few members of any given society, but for few societies relative to the diversity of peoples and places in the world.[21] As a system of extraction, production, and consumption, capitalism rewards those who own capital institutions or assets for keeping their costs as low as possible and securing as great a market value as possible for their goods and services. (This, of course, comes largely at the expense of other people, but as long as the whole pie kept growing many of those who owned little or no capital were either willing or violently forced to countenance immediate costs of the system.) The reward for doing capitalism well is more stored value, capital. But again, this capital only becomes real when it is put to some use, invested in new economic institutions. And so the cycle goes.

As a system organized around the "productive accumulation" of capital, which must always be circulating, capitalism entails infinite overall growth. Endless growth of value requires, in turn, infinitely growing consumption of energy and/or other resources. *Rate* of metabolization may vary, but for as long as the universe remains entropic and perpetual motion machines impossible, capitalism's entailment of value growth via circulation in new economic institutions will continue to require increasing resource metabolization.[22]

The costs of growth, as these fall due, are the costs of capitalism as a political economic technology.

Within this framework, burning fossil carbon to release energy, when paired with technologies for converting energy into specific forms of useful work and with state or para-state violence that lowers labor and material costs, proved to be a tremendous amplifier of work-power. Capitalism could long promise virtually infinite value growth in part because, compared to the rest of human history, the immediate unit-cost of energy involved in fossil carbon-burning production was miniscule. This unit-cost of production was reduced further still through colonialism's land- and people-grabs. Under colonialism, capitalists drew on state capacities for violence to maximize the amount of value they could store by reducing labor costs; to secure new markets for capital investment; and to assure themselves of the ability to extract untold resources from what had previously been other peoples' lands.[23]

COLONIALISM

Colonialism is an ordering of the world where dispossession takes on the color of law, and keeps it. That takes a lot of force, but it also takes some very particular ideas about who is and is not a person.

Violent, military dispossession runs alongside complicated legal structures and forms of life, and all have in common that some people lose habitual forms of personhood, including relations to the land itself, while others get something out of that. Ordering of the CaCaCo world was thus deeply entwined with religion, one of humanity's most powerful technologies. The ideas that would in practice become colonialism show up early on in documents like Pope Nicholas V's 1452 papal bull *Dum Diversas*. Here, the Pope authorized Portugal's king Alfonso V to seek out "all Saracens and pagans whatsoever, and other enemies of Christ wheresoever placed," to appropriate all their moveable properties and real estate, "and to reduce their persons to perpetual slavery."[24] This effectively granted papal authority for not only the West African slave trade, but also the expropriation and enslavement of nearly any other person living anywhere on the globe.

Drawing on Glen Coulthard's *Red Skin, White Masks*, Max Liboiron sums it all up powerfully in *Pollution is Colonialism*:

"Colonialism is a way to describe relationships characterized by conquest and genocide that grant colonialists and settlers 'ongoing state access to land and resources that contradictorily provide the material and spiritual sustenance of Indigenous societies on the one hand, and the foundation of colonial state-formation, settlement, and capitalist development on the other.' Colonialism is more than the intent, identities, heritages, and values of settlers and their ancestors. It's about genocide and access."[25]

Colonialism isn't only histories of profitable dispossession and genocide, but just as much the legal structures and material relations those histories put in place. Colonial social structures and physical habits and forms of life remain very much in place today.

The most obvious and gruesome legacies of colonialism are slavery and genocide. The Trans-Atlantic slave trade relied on internationally codified property relations that sought to strip enslaved humans of their humanity entirely, remaking them as legal things rather than persons in perpetuity.[26] And the incursion of Europeans throughout the Americas and Australasia drove genocide of unprecedented scale.[27]

In both instances, what resulted—colonialism's durable product—was an entwined racial and international hierarchy. That product cost the lives and lands of the dispossessed. Colonialism's legal order codified some persons as human and others as less-than-human while also determining that some regions of the world would be able to consume more resources and others would be disposed of without regard for relations to the land.[28]

Though colonialism's particulars have changed many times in the intervening years, each of us today, the world over, is born into roughly this general order.[29]

Colonialism's ongoing racial and national hierarchization is part and parcel of the complex flows of people, products, and profits we later came to call globalization.[30] Globalization tends to be a term for describing post-World War II worldwide economic interconnectedness in general. So, it matters that globalization's winners and losers track fairly closely the history of colonialism—even many decades after most official colonies had won their independence.[31]

To take one smallish (and yet still giant) instance of the way colonialism organizes conditions for "globalized" life, consider the role played by the Group of 7 or G7 in orienting world politics. (Beginning in 1998, by including post-Soviet Russia the G7 for a time became the G8, but it reverted back to G7 after Russia's 2014 invasion of Ukrainian Crimea.[32]) The group includes finance ministers (and presidents or prime ministers) from the United States, Canada, the United Kingdom, Japan, France, Germany, and

Italy. In other words, it's a small club of seven colonial powers, which for a while included another premier colonial power (Russia), and now doesn't.

To a shockingly large extent, the agenda for global policy discussions is hashed out by the G7, covering everything from public health to agricultural finance, climate change mitigation to the strategic outcomes of war.[33] Again, that's just finance ministers and heads of state, plus their invitees, at those meetings. In this non-treaty-established and yet very real intergovernmental coordinating body, seven "former" colonial powers and the European Union hash out an international policy agenda entirely separate from the global governance mechanisms of the United Nations. Together, these G7 members hold less than 12% of the world's adult population and more than half of its wealth.[34] None of these countries is dominated by Black, Brown, or Indigenous people—the historical and ongoing primary victims of a colonial ordering of the world.

In paragovernmental coordinating institutions like the G7, we find a practical codification of colonial hierarchies. A spectrum of humanity is presumed as the basis for who can participate in global agenda-setting, and organizes life even for and through people who might personally object to the notion that there *should* be any such spectrum. This same macro dynamic gets replicated, to greater and lesser extents, within every sovereign territory of any real size. The rigidity of national and racial hierarchies, the way they undergird even aspirationally egalitarian decision-making, is one of colonialism's hard constraints.

You can change who's in and who's out, of course. (Though as the case of post-Soviet Russia's joining and then being suspended from and then permanently leaving the G7 suggests, even that can be tricky.) You can make the core group bigger, call it a G20. But you can't scrap the basic logic.

Colonialism *entails* genocidal organization of access to land on a spectrum of "least" to "most" qualified humanity, with abiding and compounding consequences for decision-making and even survivability.[35] The colonially ordered world is a place where equitable decision-making on and implementation of policies to distribute the costs and benefits of carbon-burning and capitalist accumulation is, strictly speaking, impossible.

Colonialism broadly, then, names a centuries-long process whose legacy has been a very particular organization of the world. It is the political and bureaucratic-judicial technology undergirding our globalized world. This latter perpetuates the general hierarchy, both internationally and within sovereign states, put in place by the old land grabs we more frequently think of when somebody says *colonialism*.

Colonialism entails practices whereby some nation-states get to manage faraway lands—directly or indirectly—on behalf of commerce that provides both raw materials and new markets for capitalism's carbon-driven production of commodities.

The genocide of existing populations and the importation of slave labor-power to colonies were two infrastructural moves that made this arrangement work early on.[36] Others included radical destruction and reordering of social bonds—including with land itself—throughout the Black and Brown world we today call the global south,[37] or mapping practices that designated some territories as sites of extraction and others as recipients of radically increased capacities for resource consumption.[38]

It wasn't until the spread of carbon-burning as a partial replacement for machine-amplified human labor-power, however, that everyone really became *stuck* with colonialism as a global logic.[39] Today, we can see this logic at work in the way even very good initiatives, like efforts to regulate AI or carbon emissions, are organized first and foremost still by the old colonial core: the G7 and European Union, plus whomever else they decide is for now qualified to participate in agenda-setting.

CACACO

So, it's CaCaCo: the shit company. The way carbon, capitalism, and colonialism intertwine through social organization at all levels bodes ill for any habitable future for most of global humanity. It stinks all to hell.

Each of the terms of CaCaCo has imposed unbearable costs not only on the past and present but also on the future. On us. They enabled a form of life with real benefits for some (I can fly across the United States to visit my mother and my brother's family, can bring as gifts consumer goods that, though they'll degrade into microplastics within a few short years, may bring joy in the interim; more broadly, lowering infant mortality and improving access to literacy around the entire world have been CaCaCo achievements for portions of humanity).[40] That form of life, along the way, cost many everything: from Land relations and lives to personhood in perpetuity. For the more comfortable among us (the Steven Pinkers of the world), this has seemed like a pretty good, or at least an okay, trade-off.

Today, what's changing is that CaCaCo's *deferred* costs are falling due. We're in the early moments of a staggered collapse. For a longish time, the CaCaCo political economic system and physical and social technologies were able to shove many of its costs into the future. Now, the future is here. CaCaCo cannot reintegrate all the costs that purchased it.

For a too-reductive, but still useful simplification, think of it through the analogy of student loan debt. Millions of the best-educated people in the United States today will never earn sufficient money to pay back the loans that made their education, and with it their earning power, possible in the first place. Unlike student loan debt, though, there's no political structure external to CaCaCo's costs. CaCaCo is the structure of our world. There is no outside government to forgive its debts for the greater good, or even just to maintain overall system stability.

Compress the spring enough and it will explode loose.

Taken all together, CaCaCo serves as a kind of shorthand for the order of the world that has begotten our polycrisis, its own undoing.

The ways in which this world has been much better for some and much worse for others, though of great moral significance in understanding our own lives, are somewhat beside the point in apprehending our general global stuckness. CaCaCo's is currently the only world we have to work with. As it cracks up, corresponding reorganizations of violence are going to introduce a lot of instability and new or intensified forms of suffering.

Navigating panic at CaCaCo's disintegration will require both learning from the older worlds it violently supplanted and imagining new worlds after it.

The forces destroying CaCaCo, and threatening far more devastation still, are its own coiled tension, its long-deferred costs. They are the cumulative and necessary effects of producing CaCaCo in the first place. To shift images, these deferred costs are like deadly poison from agriculture-sustaining pesticides adding up over time in the food web, cumulative artifacts of the very processes that made and held a social world together now threatening it. The political economic machinery that could only be wrought by delaying these costs cannot, as they now fall due with increasing rapidity and intensity, contain their force. The technologies of CaCaCo, and this includes technologies of governance and activism and war as well as of scientific innovation and engineering and aesthetics, are not sufficient to incorporate their own deferred costs. Next worlds are inevitable.

CaCaCo itself is a good deal more complex than I've laid out here, of course, but these are the uncontroversial basics. The enmeshment of carbon-burning, capitalist political economies, and colonial violence-turned-law made our world that is wound so tight it is on the verge of exploding into chaos. Our CaCaCo world cannot solve problems that are themselves delayed costs of its construction. It is useful to understand carbon, capitalism, and colonialism as an assemblage not only because this offers insight into the development of "global modernity," but also and more because this clarifies what world it is that is falling apart—and how unstoppable the staggered collapse of this world is.

You can't unwind a tensioned spring.

And still. What we do now matters a great deal, both individually and collectively. Perhaps more than ever. Ours is a catastrophic era with little capacity for systemically addressing the troubles just now beginning to spring loose. How we live through and with and against that fact lays foundations for every future organization of human societies.

It may even be that, if we can apprehend the weight of our crises quickly enough, we'll reorient to avert some of their worst trajectories. Doing better starts with feeling how catastrophe is not merely pending but already underway. It starts with feeling the sense that we may be too late to do anything at all. It starts with feeling terror at unknown, terrific threats, feeling horror at the realization that, in fact, we don't at all know what to do next.

Panic is a name for this feeling.

WHERE ARE WE HEADED?

It's overwhelming to think we will not manage to act on our various crises in time. Most humans alive today are at least moderately likely to live out the deathly fate we've already mapped for thousands of other species: a nearish future of widespread hunger and starvation, grotesque rearrangement of bodies on the molecular level, automated and inhuman governance, the yawing void of nature robbed of relations, once-in-a-lifetime catastrophes piling each over the top of the last as we all just sort of circle the drain.

No one can confront this very real possible future and not feel an abyss fall yawingly away within themselves, which is why we mostly refuse to confront it.

To truly confront panic, we'll have to first surrender one of the most popular ways of refusing to live with it. That way is pretending we already know how to avert catastrophe.

The reality is that uncertainty and grave threat are at the very heart of the concept of a "crisis."[41] And, though crises are habitually misused by powerful people to shoehorn in their preferred ways of maintaining business as usual,[42] that doesn't mean there's no such thing as a crisis or that we shouldn't admit it when we are in one. When we are in crisis, we *don't know what to do* and yet *must do something*. But, precisely because of this urgency, we tend to want very badly to believe that *somebody*, at least, knows what to do. Even if not we ourselves, we want to suppose someone is working on it, has the right answers, knows how to unwind the coiled spring.

Take the climate crisis again. In the well-meaning FAQ with which Rebecca Solnit and Thelma Young Lutunatabua market their book *Not Too Late*, they exclaim, "The good news is: we know what to do! We know how to do it." [43] Though I align pretty closely with Solnit and Young Lutunatabua's slate of preferred large-scale actions, this claim is just not true. We have no plausible vision for how to accomplish the actions they present as solutions ("leave fossil fuel in the ground, build renewable energy systems worldwide, bring on a bunch of things from regenerative agriculture to design for energy efficiency to transit alternatives").[44] We don't know how to translate mass action into radically transformative policy in the hollowed-out competitive oligarchies of the rich countries.[45] We don't know how to pursue the recommended actions in ways that allow for equitable adaptation and quality-of-life improvements throughout the colonized world.[46] And we don't know how to change the core structures of CaCaCo without unleashing radical knock-on consequences.

Focus further in, on just one of these items. If by some extraordinary and unforeseeable political shift fossil fuel extraction were to cease tomorrow, billions would starve.[47] We don't have the "green" infrastructure necessary to maintain an agricultural revolution that allowed earth's human population to grow from two billion in 1928 to eight billion less than 100 years later—not in terms of growing food and not in terms of moving food around.[48] And yet, we *really do* need to not merely reduce carbon emissions radically, but also to be pulling carbon out of the air at scale, in ways we have not even invented yet. Not least, we *also* can't count on existing, CaCaCo agricultural systems to feed eight billion people in a rapidly heating world. They're already failing to do so.[49]

Equally, we haven't figured out how to procure sufficient raw materials for fossil fuel energy replacement worldwide. We're not even close to sourcing the "resources," still less to doing so in economically or environmentally sustainable ways.[50]

And all that's not accounting for capitalism's requirement of infinite growth, which means needing to replace not just this year's carbon spend, but this year's carbon spend adjusted for 2% inflation over the next 25 years, etc. Indeed, a much-touted ramping up of solar energy systems and electrification has, thus far and wholly in line with CaCaCo's core logic, expanded economic value by *adding to* rather than replacing carbon spend. Even as renewable energy use soared and production costs plummeted, governments and fossil fuel companies projected continued increases in coal production through at least 2030 and oil and gas production through at least 2050.[51] And that's just carbon! The full CaCaCo assemblage can't be unwound by agreeing to take the carbon out—if we can even manage to get there at all, which is itself doubtful.

This doesn't mean Solnit and Young Lutunatabua are wrong, exactly. We *do* know what sorts of changes we need to work toward to reduce carbon parts per million in the atmosphere. And we know carbon dioxide in the atmosphere (alongside methane and other greenhouse gases like CFCs) is the prime driver of climate change, our most visibly fast-developing crisis. Even more terrifying, we know that current environmental greenhouse gas levels commit the planet to at least 4°C of warming, possibly as much as 10°C as feedback loops operate.[52] That's human extinction levels of global heating, due largely to carbon emissions.

It's just that we have no real idea, within CaCaCo's organization of the world, how to actually decarbonize (still less, how to do so without making matters worse in new ways).

In part, this is because political economic structures are *also* human technologies. And we have no broadly shared idea whatsoever of how to get from the deadly CaCaCo assemblage to some other sort of political economic structure. Indeed, if we are fortunate to invent such pathways, they will come from billions of ordinary people panicking and then setting to work on designing new worlds entirely.[53] Economic and political elites and quasi-elites (including even professors like me) have some role to play in writing a new world, but the mechanisms whereby global humanity might be actualized enough to collaboratively shape the directions in which CaCaCo's stored energy explodes out must be—and will be, if we are very, very, very lucky—invented by terrified masses, not delivered from on high by beneficiaries of the present order of the world. Hence this book's insistence on sketching only possibilities. There is no full-scale map equal to the crisis.

It may in fact be already too late for panic to do any good. There may be no point to our lives, lived in the incandescence and explosively dying age of a general humanity that may not get its shit together in time to do any better. Who wouldn't feel panic at such a thought?

It's a rational response to an unbearable reality. The unfurling of CaCaCo's causal chains may well doom our species, along with all the other charismatic megafauna and a good portion of what's left living in the sky and beneath earth and ocean surfaces alike, to extinction.

If enough of us can manage to panic early enough, though—and make no mistake, early or late, panic at the ragged edges of a threatening and unknown world will come for us all—we may yet invent ways of being human together, approaches to humanizing that are usable in the hotter, darker days and nights ahead. We may have a chance at doing better than the worst. We may lay groundwork now for next possibilities after CaCaCo's dispersal to come. We may even, at long last, refashion ourselves as a truly global humanity.

Probably we won't. Certainly, we're not well on our way. But maybe we will. Panic, not hope, is a reasonable first emotional step.

Again, panic in the face of a world that is definitely falling apart is something we'll all feel sooner or later. The social and political question is what we do with that affect. How can we collectively navigate the feeling of being unequal to purposive movement toward the threateningly ragged horizons of CaCaCo's order? As our societies crumble, what will we do with our panic?

If panicking now is a pretty good idea (it is), that's not because the world we're losing has been so great for most people. It hasn't.[54] Rather, panic is the first emotional step in developing tools for humanizing. Averting the worst consequences of our gathering disasters will take work on a long-deferred dream of global humanity, strategies and ideas and attitudes for building a world that realizes the heterodox plurality of all its denizens.

This means taking some account of how not-past the past still is.

In point of fact, a world organized by a carbon-capitalism-colonialism assemblage has long been untenable for many, even most of its denizens. CaCaCo, as scholars like Kathryn Yusoff and Achille Mbembe detail,[55] is built on a machinery for extraction that localizes resource hoarding in some places and orderly forms of death and suffering in others. That's no less true for a blossoming "green economy" where child slave laborers lift cobalt in the Democratic Republic of Congo and indigenous people are dispossessed by lithium mining in Bolivia to serve American and European electric vehicle manufacturing than for a "traditional economy" that puts every oil-producing country in the "less-developed" world (from Nigeria to Iraq, Venezuela to Syria) under constant threat of military occupation, sanctions, or worse.[56] Panicking at an end does not imply that what came before was so all-fired terrific, nor can it guarantee that what comes next will be any better.

Still, panic's a start on humanizing, a first step toward becoming the global humanity we've long assured ourselves we already were and that we've never yet been. The goal of this book is to share tools for thinking and feeling, tools for living with panic on behalf of possible worlds-to-come.

We can, as Kathryn Yusoff urges in *A Billion Black Anthropocenes or None*, "alter how we think and imagine geological relations in nonextractive modes, to think about encountering the coming storm in ways that do not facilitate its permanent renewal."[57] Yusoff focuses on geology as a field of study and way of understanding the world around, beneath, and within us, but the principle holds more broadly. Here, I'm asking you to focus attention on an affect that for many people remains subterranean. The bet I invite you to join me in making is that learning to live with and through panic puts us in position to take seriously the enormity of our polycrisis— and so, to feel our way toward futures that make possible something other than disaster's permanent renewal.

A collapsing world looks different in Pakistan or Sri Lanka, where flood and famine have already intersected with or caused widespread social and institutional breakdown at the national level, than it does in South Africa or the United States, where civilizational failures still mostly show up as local phenomena. (Or perhaps that has already shifted by the time you read these words.)

From Johannesburg to the wealthy suburbs of Phoenix, the banks of Italy's drying Po River to sewage-swamped Jackson and ultra-leaded Flint to my neighbors on the still-colonized Navajo Nation, the question of water access haunts ever more households. Meanwhile, from hurricane-devastated beaches in Florida and Puerto Rico to flooded-out neighborhoods in Queensland or Auckland people watch helplessly as water reclaims its own. Matters are no less dire for victims of the latest chemical spill, residents of silent hollers where birds no longer sing or chatter, and whole jobless neighborhoods subjected to the further tyranny of AI-driven predictive policing. Much that was once dystopian science fiction is already today achieved reality, or nearly so. What progression in each of our many storms will tomorrow bring? How will we accommodate ourselves to a collapsing world, where catastrophes stack far, far faster than we can mitigate them?

The ever-accelerating climate and biodiversity crises, much like quantum leaps in AI capacity that give a majority shareholder class new ways of disposing everyday life (or the dimly felt reality that we are poisoned every day a little more by the novel chemical substances we ingest) together register that material reality is changing more rapidly than CaCaCo's political economic, engineering, and social technologies can effectively address. Deferred costs are falling due as crises. Crises are stacking to insurmountable heights.

At the same time, even most crisis solutions are pitched at levels that ordinary people and our systems themselves have no real way of acting on.

It's not just that policy prescriptions are wonkish, but that they are for the most part unactionable. Or, where proceeding in action, they solve last week's problems (at best) but not today's, and still less tomorrow's. Calls for complete system transformation, such as those U.N. Secretary-General António Guterres has made increasingly frequently and urgently,[58] are all but impossible to translate into day-to-day practice. As a system, CaCaCo cannot afford to heed such calls—there will never be enough value in this system to make good on all its deferred costs. As individuals and communities, we will bear these costs unevenly and with little capacity for forcing CaCaCo to change. We can at least know what's happening to us, though, can feel the impossibility of our situation fully and so begin work on what comes next.

In this space of disjunct, between CaCaCo's massively complex social structures and their ongoing deterioration in lived experience, *Panic Now?* offers a framework that everyday people can use for living in, with, and through an age of polycrisis. The next chapter, "Why Panic Now?", lays out four domains of human life that are in or on the edge of crisis—an AI revolution, a carbon emission-driven climate catastrophe, the human destruction of most wildlife on earth, and the still-unfolding disaster of proliferating synthetic chemicals with unclear properties.

We're headed for panic, more likely sooner than all that much later. Might as well get an early start and see where it can take us.

Chapter Two

WHY PANIC NOW?

To repeat, "panic now?" should be answered with a resounding "yes." The best time was twenty years ago. For anyone who hasn't gotten started yet, now is excellent, too.

So let's panic together a while. But I promise: by the end of this book, already in the next chapter even, we'll come to ways of navigating panic meaningfully. And if you haven't been for a walk in the forest or by a stream in a while, can I suggest getting out there? There's no way I could have written this chapter, while staying present to the awful world we are stuck building, without time on trail in the more-than-human places. Panic is not a replacement for loving the world, but a way into doing so very differently.

This chapter suggests four solid reasons for panicking, interwoven crises that will shape and reshape everything we know about what it is to be human and what it is to live a meaningful life: the AI revolution, climate breakdown, the sixth extinction, and the novel chemical crisis.

Any one of these would be a civilizational threat to CaCaCo, striking at the roots upon which it stands. Each is also an effect of CaCaCo, as though a great poisonous tree had so overgrown itself that its deathly boughs brushed over the root system and earth that gave it sustenance. On its own, each would press system integrity to the breaking point. Together, they render "business as usual" all but impossible for any serious person to imagine beyond the very near future.

These crises will cause most sentient life, including the majority of humans living today, extraordinary distress and difficulty in coming years.

And yet, their consequences are not wholly determined. They register the end of one world, but cannot in themselves predict the shapes of worlds to come.

It's worth noting, too, that other equally grave crises are afoot. But four is a good round number and just enough to bear thinking about. The point of this book is to think with crises long enough to panic wisely and well, not to elaborate on *all* the ways the world we know cannot be sustained. We can understand the crises of this chapter and others looming deeper in the shadows as dimensions of, to borrow a resonant term, a burgeoning polycrisis.[1]

For Cascade Institute thinkers Scott Janzwood and Thomas Homer-Dixon, polycrisis names a state of affairs where multiple intersecting matrices of risk and uncertainty collide. It is "any combination of three or more interacting systemic risks with the potential to cause a cascading runaway failure of Earth's natural and social systems that irreversibly and catastrophically degrades humanity's prospects."[2] The bottom line, for polycrisis, is a real likelihood of the world as we know it breaking down, through the intersecting and amplifying forces of multiple uncontained and uncontainable crises.

This framework is similar to that offered by economist Nouriel Roubini, who speaks of "megathreats." Roubini's megathreats are "severe problems that could cause vast damage and misery and cannot be solved quickly or easily."[3] Megathreats highlight the likelihood of a restructuring of our entire world order. They "will reshape our world. If you want to survive, do not be taken by surprise," warns Roubini.[4] And yet, for Roubini and most contemporary thinkers of polycrisis alike, though the world-to-come will be reshaped, its central coordinates (carbon, capitalism, and colonialism) will remain unchanged. A dark future will involve reorganized violence around this central constellation. Those who wish to survive ought not to be taken unaware, as there will be—as ever—winners and losers.

A lot of people who talk about a polycrisis are especially interested in how to make sure that CaCaCo's traditional winners and losers retain their respective positions. I am not.

Roubini, like Janzwood and Homer-Dixon, sees a great deal of uncertainty. But all three are pretty concerned with maintaining as much business as usual as possible. Their thinking of megathreats and polycrisis aligns with what is sometimes called the "Davos set," the group of wealthy and powerful people who attend World Economic Forum meetings in Davos, Switzerland. For the Davos set, polycrisis names a risk to CaCaCo continuity.[5]

This book starts from a much different understanding of "risk." CaCaCo *just is* breaking down. This is bad and will be ugly. But it's also a domain of new possibility. We're stuck breaking down, and we won't be able to avoid that. What can come next is what's most interesting.

The question is what the polycrisis of CaCaCo's crumbling will mean, and how we might live now to enable the building of better worlds in the coming ruins. With certainty, there will be a lot of (new and intensified forms of) misery and suffering in the next few decades. But there will also be a lot of new possibilities, possibilities we have not even imagined yet. This is not the end of all worlds, surely (probably?), just the end of one world.

As chapter one suggested, even a very badly formed world can be widely devastating in its staggered and then, at some point, explosive collapse.[6] But also, *every* new world has been built on the ruins of some other. How we panic today will determine to a large extent not simply an individual capacity to survive and profit, as Roubini and the Davos set emphasize, but what worlds we find ourselves collectively able to make a little further down the road.

Whether we call it polycrisis, megathreats, or something else entirely, CaCaCo is in the early stages of falling apart. Even if you are skeptical of this central position, I invite you to join me in considering it. What does it mean for you and your communities if I am right, if CaCaCo's spring is indeed tensioned to the breaking point, compressed by the weight of ever more deferred costs? This chapter explores some of the new system costs currently being deferred, as well as some of the old costs currently falling due. Together, they add up to ends of the world as we know it.

Between automated intellection, the climate crisis, the sixth mass extinction, and the novel chemical crisis, there's plenty to panic about—and yet, still time enough for panic to start us down a road to doing some good.

The brief sketches of this chapter are together a too-short overview of a horrifying future whose contours are already present. If we get lucky, taking them seriously may put us in position to avert the worst. If we fail to panic now, devastation so widespread as to be more properly termed annihilation is in the offing. The radical structural changes necessary to not merely build but outright *invent* new worlds start from collective attunement to the monstrous criminality of how we now are making a world.

The AI revolution is the newest dimension of our polycrisis, so I treat it first and devote to it a bit more space than to each of the others. Meanwhile, the general scopes of the climate crisis and sixth mass extinction are well-known, and yet many people don't understand the problems of scale they involve. This chapter treats the former partially in terms of how we have been trying to avoid panicking about it so far, and touches on the latter in terms of what it means for humans as one animal among many. The chapter closes by reviewing an old and well-established—and yet still badly understood and poorly mediated—disaster of CaCaCo ingenuity, the novel chemical crisis. Taken together, these and more dimensions of polycrisis are *why* we should panic *now*.

The question a judicious panic allows us not only to ask but together to begin answering is, "And then what?"

THE AI REVOLUTION

The years 2021 through 2023 saw AI development so rapid as to constitute the initial moments of a revolution. In this span, it became possible for virtually anyone to make a computer program produce a theoretically infinite stream of more or less human symbols (words, sentences, computer code, images, even video and "spoken" voices) at a relatively low cost.

On its face, that alone is not catastrophic. To the contrary, AI advocates promised (when not threatening imminent destruction by a machinic superintelligence) to solve all manner of intractable human problems: climate change, inequality, even the drudgery of email.

The devil was in the details. Or, really, in one detail: scale. Leave aside for now questions of what it *means* for societies to outsource decision-making to algorithms whose operation we cannot explain,[7] or of whether AI development can produce machines capacious enough to "see all 'round" CaCaCo's many wicked problems in human enough ways.[8] The AI revolution meant a radical increase in symbol-production. It was a revolution of scale. All of a sudden for many people, incomprehensibly much more symbol-production had become possible, at inconceivably faster rates and higher efficiency, with little real oversight by anybody.

Humans aren't very good at *disengaging* from symbols presented for our attention. Even when we ignore them, they get under our skin (that's the whole point of internet advertising banners). We're meaning-makers, whether we like it or not.

A great many of the new symbols being produced by machines—sentences and documents and pictures and movies—will be received by humans. (They are already.) We'll make sense of them when we encounter them. We can't help it. Plenty will displace other symbols, maybe displace symbols that are in some sense *better*. The already overwhelming welter of symbols, of information clamoring for attention from all sides, will grow exponentially worse. How will we respond? Meanwhile, all that machine production of symbols will displace many humans previously at work producing symbols (as in advertising, media, and other white-collar jobs).[9] The AI revolution is one dimension of polycrisis because it will change, by dint of scale, human relationships to symbol-production and -reception.

From a technological perspective, this revolution was driven especially by Large Language Models (LLMs) that drew on vast datasets and deep learning methods.[10] The core advance was in predictive generation of "tokens," next pieces of text or other symbols and marks that were statistically likely (but not *too* likely) to follow on from a given prompt. AI, in these years, produced discourse that for the first time felt authentically human to a wide range of audiences.

As I write in spring 2023, AI or automated intellection—and let us think of it as *automated* rather than *artificial*, that is, self-organizing rather than wrought or artificed, and as *intellection* rather than *intelligence*, i.e., a discursive product rather than the internal process of a conscious self[11]—is on the verge of being universally recognized as panickable. By the time everyone agrees it is time to panic, perhaps even before you hold this book in your hands, it's always a bit late. Still, better late than never.

In coming months and years, AI will radically reshape human meaning-making habits and processes, will shift the meaning of meaning itself. The exact unfolding of that will look uncertain for perhaps a few years yet, but panic is the right affect for getting at the magnitude—and risks—of the shift.

The symbolic architecture of human societies is changing faster than individual human minds, or even collective norms (much less policy and regulation), can adequately contain.[12] By contrast with previous waves of automation (and yet not wholly unlike them), what is being automated today is creation of something once supposed not only exclusively, but quintessentially, human: intellection products. Intellection products, from poems and pictures to reports and technical specifications to the code that underwrites all of digitally organized life, have typically been understood as results of human cognition. Indeed, for many people intellection and its symbol-products long seemed the very essence (for better or worse) of human cognition.[13] No longer.

The previous paragraph relied on passive voice, but of course *somebody* is doing the automating. It isn't simply happening, with no actors. Two primary groups are driving the AI revolution, one very publicly and the other more quietly.

Giant tech companies with overwhelmingly huge datasets, gleaned through ubiquitous surveillance of digital life, own the proprietary LLMs that have most captured contemporary imagination.

Led especially by Microsoft-backed OpenAI's Sam Altman, tech honchos hyped AI's ability to create intellection products through public performances of fear blended with excitement.[14] In that general big tech ambit, Microsoft (and others) swiftly rolled out versions of software that incorporated increasingly advanced AI "assistants." Alongside big tech, capitalist firms of every possible description pursued CaCaCo's basic logic as they began navigating AI: reduce production costs relative to the market value of their products. As it became possible to automate more slices of their work-product, they automated more slices of their work-product.[15] For just one of many instances, at the end of April 2023 IBM, one of the oldest and still biggest names in computing, announced a company-wide pause on hiring for positions that AI *might* be able to fill in the near future.[16]

Organized almost entirely by CaCaCo logics (and how would such scale occur otherwise in this world?), the AI revolution is massively carbon- and resource-intensive, accumulates value primarily for a majority shareholder class, and depends on violence-backed extraction and unequal ownership of spaces both digital and physical.[17] There is every reason to suppose that the AI revolution will impose extraordinary new costs on societies ill-equipped to contain these costs, which will thus appear as crises.[18]

And yet, the ways in which early panic about the AI revolution was publicly negotiated offer an excellent lesson in what *not* to do with our panic. If we want to panic wisely, we'd do well to tarry a while first with how we may have panicked unwisely thus far and, equally, have unwisely dismissed panic. Much of the AI-panic discourse has centered on education, and a brief history is instructive.

In autumn of 2022, massively well-funded tech startup OpenAI released a new interface for the then-current iteration of its natural language processing engine, GPT-3.[19] The interface was titled ChatGPT (perhaps hoping the ubiquity of chatbots, primarily in customer service applications, would render this new wonder market-soluble). For several months, academics and the general public alike became weirdly fascinated with one specific application of this interface: plagiarism and academic cheating more generally.[20]

Because ChatGPT could output English-language text that met common metrics for clarity and style, users newly aware of AI worried that students would put it to work in their places, outputting essays for K-12 and college classes alike.[21]

Subsequent months would show that this was an entirely realistic concern. But, it failed to get at what's most significant about the AI revolution. The concern-reaction about student writing, as such reactions will be, was quickly dubbed a "moral panic."[22] Critical media literacy scholars Nolan Higdon and Allison Butler, alongside others in cultural outlets ranging from *Inside Higher Ed* to *The New Yorker* to social media and academic articles, warned against overhyped AI concerns: "we are not panicking, and we do not think any educator should," because "ChatGPT is simply the latest tool in the century's long saga of academic dishonesty."[23] AI deflationism came into vogue. It was just like calculators!

For its part, after several weeks of demonstrating ChatGPT's power, OpenAI screwed the spigot down to a trickle. The interface, which after all costs real money to run novel commands through—primarily spent burning fossil carbon to generate electricity that powers and cools silicon-based microprocessing units, which are themselves produced at a staggering energy and greenhouse gas cost[24]—began returning increasingly stock replies to all sorts of queries. Before long, an enterprising young Princeton student announced that he had built an engine that could detect GPT-3 writing with great accuracy. The trick, 22-year old Edward Tian explained, was to look for both "perplexity" and "burstiness."[25] Meanwhile, OpenAI quickly began promising its own tools to detect AI-generated text, though the company cautioned that any such tool would by nature be "not fully reliable."[26] For a large chunk of popular discourse, generative AI's impacts had been reduced to cheating and, at least imaginarily, thereby resolved. No need to panic.

But the meaning of AI for society could not be so readily resolved as that. In other fora, coders, professors, office workers, marketers, and people in dozens of other professions quietly agreed that, whether through ChatGPT or other engines, they would be automating wide swathes of onerous tasks. A third group driving the revolution was everyday symbol users, if to a lesser extent. From business plans to environmental compliance reviews, GitHub documentation to videogame coding, departmental audits to letters of recommendation, journalism to, well, the professional version of college essays (articles and books), knowledge workers had seen the future and it was now. This vision was quickly validated by economists.[27]

Indeed, while a good portion of the chatterati was focused on whether or not to panic about one application of the AI revolution—academic dishonesty—the revolution was proceeding faster than could be adequately described in CaCaCo's legacy media.[28] The months of February and March 2023 alone saw the release of

- three new or substantially revised AIs by tech giant Google (its chatbot Bard, a Universal Speech Model performing automatic speech recognition on 1,000+ languages, and a robotics model PaLM-E that translates multi-modal symbolic inputs into embodied action on the world);

- Microsoft's GPT-based Bing Chat and its embedding of an AI titled Co-pilot throughout its vast empire of knowledge working platforms where humans have traditionally recombined symbols (from Excel to Teams, Word to PowerPoint); and

- alignment-focused company Anthropic's beta release of its "helpful, honest, and harmless" AI assistant Claude—explicitly designed to allay concerns about an apocalyptic future of hostile automated intellection.

And that's just the majors.[29] Oh, and OpenAI released the next iteration of its natural language processing engine, GPT-4, generally agreed to be the *new* most powerful AI ever publicly accessible. Among other things, where GPT-3 generated predictive text after having been trained on text alone, GPT-4 was trained on a wide variety of structured data sets. It could generate text from images and vice versa. (And more.)

Within days of GPT-4's release, OpenAI announced they would be pairing it with other existing programs, plug-ins ranging from the knowledge-focused (Wolfram Alpha) to the strictly commercial (Expedia and OpenTable).[30] This was to be the first step in a cautious rollout, in line with CEO Sam Altman's long-stated concerns about the disruptive, intensely threatening social forces that might be exerted by truly powerful AI.[31] Plug-ins didn't garner much enthusiasm in practice. Less than a month later, though, at least two open-source "autonomous AI agents" had been developed to interface with GPT-4 from without.

These autonomous agents, AutoGPT and BabyAGI, drew on OpenAI's engine to perform various activities in the digital world. Turning human-defined tasks into multi-stage processes that iteratively generated text, code, images, and more—while also performing internet searches and assessing its own work product—each allowed users, through chained AIs, to act on the world in ways they themselves could not foresee.[32] The results were astonishing. Suddenly, anyone with a fifty bucks in an OpenAI account and the willingness to overcome a couple small technical hurdles could create a website or incorporate and begin marketing a business or self-publish a book on Amazon, all without coding or really even understanding how any of the digital machinery they were using operated.

A person could tell a machine to do these things without themselves ever having thought through the book or business or website. The age of domain-general AI, a theoretically infinite complexity of symbol-production from a single prompt, had arrived.

Over the course of two-and-change months in spring 2023, the scope of what humans could do with machines—and what machines could do with machines—had broadened exponentially. Even setting aside the hype bubbling characteristic of CaCaCo's tech industry, any serious observer could see an AI revolution afoot. As you know better than I, this was hardly the end of it.

Troublingly, at first relatively few people asked what the near-term future portended by this explosive growth in AI capacity *meant*.

At one extreme of minimizing, educators and pundits outside tech focused largely on student cheating.[33] At the opposite extreme, tech conversations about the meaning of AI oriented toward the grandest of endpoints: artificial general intelligence, or AGI, and a threat of total human extinction.[34]

AGI has long been a focus of, even a monomania for, tech futurists. From *Star Trek* to *2001: A Space Odyssey*, the notion of artificial general intelligence, machines who are selves, limns human thinking of automation's promises and threats alike. For OpenAI, Anthropic, and other ultrahighly funded AI companies, developing AGI was their stated *raison d'être*.

A lot of people grew very concerned about where this was heading. There had emerged a real possibility, as was argued most intently, forcefully, and anticharismatically by Eliezer Yudkowsky (a veritable whirlwind of frenetic activity on Twitter), that true AGI would soon sound a death knell for the human species.[35]

In a very different vein, some disenthusiasts broadened out the focus to capture AI's astoundingly wasteful resource metabolization, further encoding or hardwiring of unjust social structures, and rapid intensification of an already deeply threatening surveillance society. Such concerns are not in error. But, it is possible to peer so closely at technological horizons that one misses other sorts of existential risk. No less promising and catastrophic than AGI and AI's many explicit costs are implicit costs of the AI revolution for human meaning-making writ large.

This is where it's helpful to have *automated intellection*, rather than artificial intelligence, in mind. What does it mean to automate "intelligence"? We don't even agree on what *intelligence* is in the first place.

There's little question that intellection—the reception and production of symbols that mean—is a core human activity. We humans do not merely have intellects, as a noun; we *intellect*, as a verb. What we think that thinking itself means has a lot to do with our phenomenologies, our understandings of *what it is like to be somebody*. At the very least, intellection involves the reception and production of marks that mean, symbols at work both within and between individual human subjects.[36] In an age where much formerly human intellection can be and is being produced by machines, it is precisely such understandings that stand in question.

Generative AI models all *automate*, or make machinic and self-organizing, something we long believed was particularly human. Their and our intellection products alike are bits of symbolic flotsam and jetsam that, once sufficiently accumulated, we call culture. AI isn't exactly the "artificing" of such intellection products, since as models have scaled up their creators have come less and less to understand how the iterative learning of natural language processing engines actually happens. And at the same time, these engines don't have relatively clear and singular goals: producing, say, an artificial flower that mimics a real one.

The intellection products generative AIs make, shy of AGI, are concatenations of lots and lots of smaller, recursively generated predictions. We don't have much evidence that they constitute (yet) a machinic culture or are intelligence (per se). And yet, as all those intellection products aggregate and are received by humans, they *will become* human culture. We just can't help making sense of symbols when we see them.

Of course, there's nothing intrinsically wrong with human culture's being shaped by nonhuman forces. Quite the contrary. The twentieth century and early twenty-first made clear to many scholars that much long supposed uniquely human (and then *at least* primate) wasn't.[37] Humans hardly hold a corner on intellection or cognition. Crows, ravens, and other corvidae, for instance, turned out to craft tools and actively reconcile after conflicts, and have paralleled great apes in performing social and physical cognition tasks.[38]

Still, the creation of intellection products—abstract marks on the world available for meaningful decoding—has continued to strike many humans as at least a *characteristically* human activity. This isn't to say we all produce and receive symbols in the same way, or even that it's such a great a thing to do. It's just that, whatever exactly it means (and arguing about what it means is part of what it means) intellection has continued to be a central feature of what human beings think being human entails, even long after it's been apparent that we aren't the only people in the world who do it.

Culture, in the broadest sense, is an accumulation of meaning-making moments in collective forms of behavior. As such, the who and how of culture-making matter very much. At stake is the meaning, if any there be, of our own lives. And, by the same token, the regularized forms of action that will and will not be available to us.

What and who are we regular humans, in a world where our usual intellection activities happen *for us* (on behalf of some of us), are automated (for the profit of a majority shareholder class)? *What are we for* when the production of symbols doesn't need terribly many of us, but we are unable ever to stop receiving them?

Answers to these questions remain substantially unclear.

In this connection, it's useful to think of the AI revolution as structured by at least three subcrises: alignment, disposition, and replacement. Each of these opens onto a future filled with not merely threats and opportunities, but a twinned certainty that the world will look very different and uncertainty about what that difference will be or mean. Each, moreover, represents fairly grave threats to the present political economic order of the world, threats that CaCaCo—which *needs* automation to reduce labor costs as energetic costs rise dramatically, but produces "surplus humanity" in the process[39]—is profoundly ill-equipped to resolve or even contain. An AI revolution is panickable along any of the three axes of subcrisis.

Generative AI (or any other AI) that is badly aligned to human users poses a wide range of risks—up to and including existential risks.[40] The replacement of human labor across multiple domains, if this occurs with any rapidity at all, is virtually guaranteed to be wildly socially destabilizing.[41] And the dangers of bad algorithmic disposition are increasingly well-understood, in the production and dissemination of "fake news," say, or the proliferation of "astroturfing" bots across all forms of social media.[42] Rather than detail all three, I want to drill down a little on just one of these: disposition.

Because alignment (especially with respect to AGI) and replacement (a near-inevitability if it is profitable) are vast sociotechnological issues that most individuals and small collectives can do little to negotiate, it's worth spending some extra time with disposition. That's not to say we *shouldn't* panic at the other two—we very probably should. But, fewer people are currently sounding the alarm at how we may be badly disposed by AI as such, over and above and beyond what we might call "bad content."[43]

Disposition is where automated intellection, both generative and otherwise, comes home to rest in and *as* individual human cognition. Since I was trained as a rhetorician, I'm especially interested in the persuasive force of symbols, how intellection products orient and organize not just our current ways of being, but our capacities for becoming new versions of our selves over time.

How AI disposes humans is, centrally, a problem of our capacity or lack thereof for meaning-making.

One thing rhetoricians know is that *nobody* escapes being influenced, disposed in one way or another by symbols. And not just by the content of symbols, but by symbol systems writ large. Humans are symbolic animals.[44] We each become who we are in discourse, remake ourselves and are remade by others many times over in the course of a life lived through symbolic exchange.[45] Our very selfhood is, in many ways, a rhetorical production, a lifelong process of influencing and being organized by others in symbols.[46] This is what it's like to be a human somebody (and probably a crow or dog or octopus somebody, too).

On the crass backside of this fact, there's a reason advertising and marketing are not only the infrastructural backbone of the internet as we know it, but also one of the highest-grossing industries in human history.[47]

But influencing one another with discourse, i.e., the products of intellection, is not merely a matter of coming up with arguments to persuade your parents to get a dog, or of being persuaded by your friends or an advertisement to try a new restaurant. It's just as much the background noise of "becoming somebody" in general as it is particular persuasive content, good or bad. For instance, the performative influence of gender norms,[48] national ideologies,[49] and iteratively reinforced habits of mind (rhetoricians refer to these habits and their accompanying beliefs, all together, as *doxa*)[50] are all just as important as the louder flashpoints of this or that battle in ever-ongoing wars of culture.

Being a symbolic animal in general is part of what it means to be human. And being a symbolic animal means being disposed by and disposing other symbolic animals, shaping one another and being inclined to act and make meaning ourselves by arrangements of symbols, by culture.

Generative AI is on the verge of becoming a new dispositif, a new mode of disposition, for human experiences of culture—and that's worth panicking about.

A *dispositif*, as political theorist Davide Panagia explains, is a kind of person-organizing assemblage of bits and pieces of culture. These assemblages reflect plenty of individual human intentions, but they do more than that. They are media that dispose us, in one way or another, simply by being the sorts of media that they are.

This is about more than just content, the things we see or hear. It's about the way media organize us at a still-deeper level. Panagia's aim is to "develop an account of media that looks to their dispositional powers."[51] If we can think of media as a dispositif, he suggests, we may be able to negotiate the ways in which we are being politically organized by different ways of ordering and receiving, making meaning of, the world.

The point is that we are disposed to be what we are by the kinds of media we live and make meaning through. When Panagia says media, he means not specific sources (like FOX or CNN) or platforms (like TikTok or even ChatGPT), but rather the plural of *medium*. Media are bigger technological assemblages that include and contain all the sources and platforms we think of as "media" in a more everyday sense. Ultimately, any given medium is a form of life. For nearly the whole of human history, symbol-production and -reception has shaped who and how we can come to be, and so what it is like to be somebody—and, in that, has shaped what meaning itself means.

Writing, in its various forms (from hieroglyphics to videogame design, shorthand to C++), is one sort of medium. Humans make marks that mean. Generative AI is, in its fullest development, not just an expansion of writing—humans may (or may not) set the intention, but the marks that mean are all made machinically. It is a whole new medium. It's pretty hard to know how to make sense of that.

Comprised of both material infrastructure and digital intellection products, the medium of AI disposes us toward not merely wanting or thinking, but actively *becoming* this, that, or the other. AI was a revolutionary medium, disposing us in truly novel ways, even before recent leaps in generative AI. But now it's obvious to everyone.

We find ourselves increasingly organized or shaped by the automated intellection products of this medium. That can cash out at the level of the content of thoughts (your racist uncle believes George Soros invented covid-19) and the content of actions (he's more likely to post meandering screeds or vaguely menacing memes on Facebook than he was a few years ago). More importantly, though, it cashes out at the level of forms of life and identity generally. Your uncle is becoming someone else entirely; the meaning of his life falls ever further away from your ability to make sense of it; he wants and feels and moves around in the world, but you no longer know who it is doing this wanting and feeling and moving around, or why.

What's important is that nobody's dominating anyone here, not exactly. Your uncle wasn't captured, forced to become someone else. But he also didn't sign up for it. Again, not exactly. He has become differently disposed.

His news feed shifted in accordance with algorithmic uptakes of his credit card usage, where he lingered in the grocery store, how long he hovered over a link before clicking, and millions more small intimacies of life captured as data.[52] For the most part, no one involved in disposing your uncle differently (hadn't he always been a little racist, anyhow?) wrenched him out of himself, plopped him down somewhere else. It's unlikely anyone even particularly wanted anything from him, besides his eyeballs on some advertisements.[53] But his life came to mean something different all the same.

And you think the same has not been true for you?

All that was happening even *before* the phase of AI revolution ushered in by generative automated intellection. Your racist uncle got worse back in the days when disposing a person some which way still required a fair bit of human labor power in the mix. And now, when it scarcely any longer does?

Dark predictions abound, foretelling how generative AI will shape us, at the level of the content of our thoughts and actions.[54] Many are surely correct.

We should be at least as worried about how the medium of generative AI will dispose us, arrange our ways of being and meaning and acting. What does a human life mean within the web of an AI revolution, where intellection products make a humanly received inhuman culture? What can it mean to "belong" to cultures made with machinic ultra-efficiency, on behalf of CaCaCo's biggest beneficiaries?

To what will the aggregate culture of automated intellection products dispose us? Panagia observes that, "like the practices of *dispositio* in classical rhetoric, the *dispositif*'s role is not that of transmission of meaning but of arranging moving parts."[55] Toward what wholes and whose ends will the AI revolution move us, we its parts and means who perhaps mean less than ever even as our lives are captured ever finely more by data harvesting apparatuses?[56]

From the algorithmic disposition of attention to the possibility of totalizing disposition by machine-generated symbols to the construction of human lives in environments shaped machinically to serve (i.e., "in alignment with") the preferences of CaCaCo's majority shareholder class, there is good reason to wonder *what most of us are even for* in an era of supercharged AI.

Nor is this an idle question. Given that international regulation of fuzzy, emerging threats on behalf of a general humanity has been defunct since at least the 1989-1992 interval, what's to stop the small portion of humanity that holds virtually all the cards from deciding that the rest of us, being unnecessary,[57] must fall by the wayside if their "longtermist" vision of humanity is to survive the climate crisis, sixth mass extinction, and novel chemical crisis? How might we find ourselves organized for the worse, in our own minds and in our ways of being together or seeing one another, along the way?

Might generative AI, controlled by CaCaCo's majority shareholder class, even dispose much of humanity to be more readily disposed *of* as the polycrisis unfolds?

THE CLIMATE CRISIS

That frightening thought notwithstanding, the AI revolution is in some ways least immediately threatening of our various emergencies. Sure, it upends the applecart of intellection, and does so for the profit of the few and with very little regard for the advantage of the many. And so yeah, it throws newly and more so into question all of human existence. Also, it costs a lot in carbon emissions, water, and other resources.

But what's new about any of *that*? It's this year's model of a standing crisis of meaning, and of maybe accidentally wiping ourselves out. More importantly, its deferred costs remain just that for now: *deferred* (though ever less so; hundreds of thousands, or more likely millions, of cognitive labor jobs worldwide will already have been automated by the time you read these words).[58]

The climate crisis, by contrast, is so novel it's changed how we understand geologic time. It is a cascade of delayed costs both coming due now and, somehow, still being accumulated all the same. The *intense visibility* of this is somewhat new.

The climate crisis will be worse soon, certainly, but it's increasingly clearly no longer just a problem for the future. It's here now.

French philosopher Yves Citton puts the point memorably: "So far, our various ecocides have proceeded too slowly and too inexorably to fit the point-in-time framework of a 'crisis.' That is what is now changing, and very quickly: our environmental destructions no longer threaten only our great-grandchildren."[59] As I write in spring 2023, vast swathes of central and southern California, one of the richest food-growing regions in the United States, sit underwater from snowmelt that has barely begun. A record high Sierra snowpack threatens not only those in the flood-and-mud zones, where landslides and coursing water alike loom large, but also the consumption patterns of the entire country. Around the globe, even though March 2023 was not subject to the "hot" climactic pattern known as El Niño, this was the second-hottest March in human-recorded history. El Niño would arrive a couple months later.

In April 2023, residents of Bangkok, Thailand were advised not to go outside as the heat index hit 54 degrees C (129° Fahrenheit)—a deadly level reminiscent of the Bangkok of novelist Paolo Bacigalupi's *The Windup Girl*. Except that Bacigalupi's novel is set in twenty-third century Thailand, not 2023.

And so on. You will be familiar with the instances closest to where and when you are reading from. These are early, early moments in a crisis that will, on the off chance of a best-case outcome, merely continue getting drastically worse for the next several decades.

Perhaps the tidiest indication that the not-just-a-megathreat of climate crisis is coming more fully into view has been widespread acknowledgment that we live today in a novel geologic era, an Anthropocene.

When chemistry Nobelist Paul Crutzen and his colleague Eugene Stoermer introduced "the Anthropocene" in 2000 as a term for naming the age of humanity's remaking of planetary systems, they found skeptical audiences.[60] Twenty-some years later, the term is inescapable.[61] (In fact, it refers to more than only climate change; but in public discourse the two have become synonymous.) For ecosystems from the burning Amazon rainforest to the melting glaciers of Greenland, Antarctica, and Nepal, from the aridifying American West to the heat-bleached Great Barrier Reef off the coast of Australia, there can be little question: ours is the age of human remaking of the Earth system writ large.

As I mentioned in chapter one, there are problems with "Anthropocene" terminology. For one, it assumes a globally shared anthropic cause for radically diminished planetary futures. I use Anthropocene since that seems to be, collectively, what we're going with. But let's not get confused and assign some vaguely equal responsibility to everybody. CaCaCo's global north beneficiaries, the consumer societies to which I and probably you too belong, have played a special role in producing our deathly new geologic era—and this necrotic Anthropocene's many human and nonhuman victims.[62]

We've reached a point in the climate crisis where long-winded screeds and extended descriptions of forthcoming catastrophe feel almost redundant, though.

You can see the early moments of global climate catastrophe unfolding around you. Even wildly business-as-usual media institutions like *USA Today*, long famous for offering the most anodyne and minimal possible version of news, have begun sounding the alarm. One recent headline, as I write in 2023, reads, "'We have already lost' in 2 key climate change signals, according to UN report."[63] From megafires licking at the edges of Los Angeles or threatening Greek heritage sites to back-to-back hurricanes and typhoons that leave coastal Florida and New Zealand alike devastated, climate change, as an appalled *New York Times* headline had it in the summer of 2021, is even coming "for rich countries."[64] By the logic of CaCaCo, this should be impossible. The entire system is predicated on the notion that risks can be distributed to those deemed less worthwhile while rewards accrue in the colonial core.

Instead, the very same august financial institutions that continue to finance fossil fuel development now also hedge their bets by reassessing risk from rising sea levels, fires, floods, aridification, and more.[65] It's getting harder to deny, even in New York and London.

There are still holdouts, of course. There are always holdouts. Not so long ago, one American president-to-be famously claimed that climate change was a Chinese hoax.[66] For decades prior to that (and still today), fossil fuel companies devoted a great deal of effort and money to persuading everyone (especially evangelical Christians) to disbelieve in the reality of climate change, with lasting success.[67] All the same, many audiences who were once ready to ignore the slow evidence of their senses can no longer do so. The actuality of the climate crisis has become virtually undeniable.[68] Inevitably, some turn instead to strategies for holding their own mounting panic at bay.

Refusal to really apprehend the climate crisis as a crisis for all of CaCaCo starts with a refusal to panic.

It is easy to ridicule a certain kind of religious certainty from outside, to mock Mormons invoking prayer as a primary strategy for saving the rapidly drying out Great Salt Lake, say.[69] But, at the end of the day, is the political naïveté of serious climate scientists like Michael Mann and Katharine Hayhoe (who insist that CaCaCo can save itself) really all that different?

Telling people not to panic because [insert your preferred deity or political party here] will save us is a form of denial. CaCaCo massively overdetermines the character of our polycrisis. The tensioned spring cannot be unwound. Our world *is* ending.

With that in mind, it's worth spending a moment with popular ways of keeping panic away. We can think of these as physical and political economic forms of denial. One sort of denial holds at bay knowledge of human-caused climate crisis as a basic reality. The other denies that it's the product of a certain kind of political economy, which in fact necessarily relies on the causes of the climate crisis (as discussed in chapter one) and so cannot "fix" this crisis.

Physical deniers simply refuse to accept the evidence of our collective apparatuses for making knowledge about the planet we inhabit. Climate change isn't real, or if real isn't that big a problem, of if a big problem is somehow not caused by human activities. Political economic deniers accept, and in many cases themselves have contributed to, our knowledge-making about the climate crisis. But they proceed as though equally empirically well-established realities about the political economy of CaCaCo could simply be wished away. Climate change is both real and really, really scary. But the CaCaCo world that produced and relies on and continues intensifying its causes at every single level can surely solve it. We just gotta believe.

The two positions map loosely with conservatives and liberals in the American political landscape, but only very loosely.[70] To hang flesh on the skeleton, think of them as conservative Christians and liberal climate scientists. What's important is to understand the ways they both—and so many more of us, too—*wrongly*, profoundly unhelpfully, hold panic at bay with just-so stories.

Holding panic at bay, when things really are falling apart, pretty much ensures horrific outcomes as matters worsen. The worst time to flee a sinking coastline forever is in the middle of a hurricane, alongside everybody else, all at once.

For a subset of Christians, and notwithstanding humanity's long history of lousy things happening to pretty good people, the catastrophic impacts of climate change seem literally unthinkable. Looking at those climate deniers from outside, one popular narrative ascribes their disbelief to belief in something else. A biblical Great Flood was accompanied by a divine compact. God promised never again to visit such destruction upon the earth. So, while things look bad now, they will surely improve! Or, conversely, apocalyptic end times are nearly upon us. Whatever happens next is God's will!

There may be real theological resonance in these views of Christian climate denial, but they miss the material reality of how, and how recently, many religionists became disposed to denial.

Recall that Christian voters strongly supported George H.W. Bush's climate action platform in 1988. As Robin Veldman shows in *The Gospel of Climate Skepticism*, climate denialism didn't just happen because of theology. Instead, Veldman's careful analysis of a key period of Christian media history demonstrates that, on evangelical-oriented television and radio broadcasts (and in novels and other media forms), "the coverage of climate change from 2006 to 2015 was heavily tilted toward skepticism." Indeed, a step further, the "mocking and dismissive coverage of climate advocates and advocacy that pervaded these programs powerfully conveyed the message that climate change was an issue that belonged to evangelicals' enemies, the secular elites."[71] Getting evangelicals to deny climate change (against some of their own earlier preferences for environmental stewardship) was a rhetorical achievement requiring ownership of captured airwaves and the articulation of friends and enemies. Far more than religion or religiosity, it was CaCaCo at work here.

So yes, Antarctic sea ice hit its lowest recorded extent in February 2022 and then again in 2023. If the increasingly threatened ice sheets of the Antarctic continent itself go, which they're prone to do faster than anyone thought they could,[72] the world could easily see three feet of sea level rise before 2100.[73] And yes, April 2023 sea surface temperatures were the hottest ever recorded, and hotter water expands.[74] Oh, and Greenland may be melting about one hundred times faster than we thought it was.[75] These changes will inundate nearly a billion coastal residents worldwide over the coming decades—and immiserate another billion or two for lack, in a tragic irony, of freshwater access. Also, let's be clear: "before 2100" does not mean "starting in 2100"; it means "starting now and getting ever worse."

But how do we get to the point of actually taking any of that seriously, like, in terms of action in the present?

What can it even mean to take the climate crisis seriously in our individual lives, when CaCaCo's machinery can only filter this crisis through global marketplaces? At the very least, it starts with understanding better what's holding us back from substantive action.

We often think that competing stories or political polarization are what stand in the way of climate action.

Religion allows people to hear grave details about the present climate breakdown and yet not tie these into projections about the future. The world to come has been assured in a particular way for them, and so the climate crisis *must not be* going to result in outcomes at odds with that future—accelerating glacial melt be damned. Accordingly, some of us may think, if it weren't for those pesky religionists and the fossil fuel company villains in the shadows behind them, we would all get on board with doing what's necessary. The "reality-based community" would take action, if we could only secure the necessary political power.

But all this isn't quite right.

Maybe more than anything, it's stories about friends and enemies,[76] and the way those stories shape our feelings as we process information, that help people avoid confronting the evidence of their senses.

Inaction is less about counterbeliefs and more just focusing on something—*someone*—else, whether enemy or friend.[77] Many coastal southeastern Americans, for whom sea level may rise by a staggering foot or more in just the next twenty-five years,[78] aren't so much locked onto theological promises about the future as they are reacting against keenly felt enemies in the present. Climate conferences, they have been told, aren't even about climate. They're about "absolute control over the way people live their lives, the kind of control that hasn't been seen since the fall of Communism. Only this time it would be exercised in the name of polar bears and penguins, not the proletariat."[79] An enemy indeed! Scorn, contempt, fear-of-the-other, and hatred are powerful antidotes against panic. More's the pity.

But, then, are matters really so different for serious climate scientists?

For some, surely, but the loudest voices (i.e., those most amplified by CaCaCo's cultural outlets) tend also to be farcical political fabulists. We hear consistently in the news from Michael Mann and Katharine Hayhoe (who both align loosely with the U.S. Democratic Party and urge a message of hope that CaCaCo can save itself if you vote wisely and keep on believing, and maybe do some protest marching). More rarely quoted are climate scientists like Rose Abramoff and Peter Kalmus (organizers with Scientist Rebellion, who urge climate scientists and others to use their cultural prestige to help ordinary people understand how extraordinarily dire our situation is and take immediate and drastic collective action).[80]

The hope many today insist we produce for them is an antidote against panic, but timely panic is a therapeutic dose of poison—a vaccine of sorts. Trying to force hope when panic is warranted is how political economic denialists, congenially and with the best of intentions, keep us all stuck in CaCaCo's death spiral.

Against all the evidence of any reasonable person's political senses, for example, Mann (with collaborator Susan Joy Hassol) was in 2023 still proclaiming that "the good news is that clean energy and other climate solutions are abundant and available."[81] For Hassol and Mann, "We can act with urgency to rein in the climate emergency and remake our civilization into one that respects the gift of a stable climate we inherited—one that we can pass on to our children."[82] This is the sort of thing that feels good to say and believe. It inspires hope, pushes panic back out the door and slams the window shut. Unfortunately, it's not very honest about either political or physical realities.

The reality is that nobody has a coherent vision for how to maintain the growth commitments of CaCaCo while *also* transitioning away from fossil fuels very, very quickly while *also* inventing new scalable technologies for undoing the harm we've already done to the biosphere (which would be required to claw back the "stable climate we inherited").

Still more, nobody has a coherent vision for how to force unwilling national governments away from marketism long enough to commit to binding global treaties on behalf of this technological vision of transition nobody's worked out yet. And let's not even start with the fiduciary structure of global corporate-state relations that has fossil fuel companies *still* suing to prevent climate action—and winning![83]

That doesn't mean we don't need to get off fossil fuels if we're to have any chance at all of avoiding the worst unfoldings of the climate crisis. We definitely do. But pretending we know how to, either politically/economically or energetically, is not truthful. It's helpful in holding panic at bay, maybe, but what if panic is what we need?

The Mann credo (and though I'm singling him out, it's more as a representative instance than anything else) is political hope. In a *Washington Post* op-ed in 2022, he writes (alongside Mark Hertsgaard and Saleemul Huq), "Understanding that we can still save our civilization if we take strong, fast action can banish the despair that paralyzes people and instead motivate them to get involved. . . . If citizens understand that things aren't hopeless, they can better push elected officials to make such changes."[84] Remember, "our civilization," the deadly mixture of carbon, capitalism, and colonialism I've been calling CaCaCo, needs all three elements to survive, to be "saved."

There's no saving CaCaCo from the climate crisis, because the climate crisis is literally what CaCaCo costs.

And yet, an insistence on continuity is the organizing conceit of Mann's 2021 book *The New Climate War*. There, what Mann calls "doomism" is supposed to present "a greater threat to climate action than outright denial."[85] Such statements, were the stakes not so horrifically high, would be delightfully naïve.

As everyone who's ever confronted an addiction knows, getting better doesn't start with insisting there's some relatively easy way out as long as everyone maintains hope. Getting better starts with acknowledging how unbearably bad things have gotten, and concomitantly that you actually don't know what to do next. And then you have to change everything.

Trying to avert panic with promises of CaCaCo continuity, unhappily, has become a normative position for an ever-larger subset of climate communicators.[86] Hope and trust in a liberal political establishment, for this climate realism that is political denialism, does the work that scorn and hatred did for CaCaCo's evangelical climate denial machinery.[87] The one is funded by grimacing fossil fuel interests. The other is funded by business-as-usual with a smiley face. Enemies and friends, friends and enemies.

Take Hayhoe's version of the hope narrative. Hayhoe is not only a climate scientist, but has made a genuinely admirable career of helping Christians to engage with the physical realities of climate catastrophe.

Like Mann's, however, Hayhoe's lens is always incrementalist hope. Even when acknowledging the need for systemic change, as in a *Time* essay titled "In the Face of Climate Change, We Must Act So that We Can Feel Hopeful," Hayhoe thinks of action itself as essentially continuity, not difference. We don't need to do radically different things, just make small changes. "What can you do? *Anything*. Recycle your yogurt cup after breakfast tomorrow," and etcetera.[88] Hayhoe's list reaches its apex at "Call Congress and demand a clearer path to net-zero."[89] A couple years later, in 2023, she urges glum readers of the IPCC's most recent summary of our ever-worsening state of affairs, "The science shows, and this IPCC report shows, that the solutions are at hand."[90] But "the science" in fact *doesn't* show that (as noted in chapter one). Nor does the IPCC report. The solutions are very much not at hand. Kind of obviously.

We do know what the problem is, and we do know some of what we're doing to make it worse. More carbon, more problems. We also have ideas about what we could do instead, though many of those are untested or outright magical thinking and others are completely incompatible with CaCaCo continuity. (Not that breaking with CaCaCo is a bad thing—it's just a very *different* thing from what Mann and Hayhoe suggest, with their small consumer actions and calling Congress and the like.) Solutions are anything but "at hand."

We simply do not know how to resolve the climate crisis in any way that would be even remotely equitable or globally just.[91] We almost certainly cannot resolve it at all with the political economic technologies of the current world. The difficulty with rosy pictures in a real crisis is that, almost by definition, they aren't empirically well-founded.

I'm not saying Mann, Hayhoe and the many others purveying hopeful stories about climate solutions are wrong about discoverable (though not yet discovered) scientific and technological possibilities, of course. I am noting that they're in profound denial regarding some empirically observable realities in both the current resource infrastructures and governance infrastructures, both national and international, of CaCaCo.

In the United States, for example, it's painfully well understood by political scientists that citizen preferences have, for the vast majority of the population, no correlation whatsoever with policy.[92] Moreover, the only electorally viable American political party to consistently acknowledge the physical reality of climate change (that's Democrats, for anyone keeping score) has, with equal consistency, failed even among party elites to produce, fight for, and win interest in truly significant climate legislation. To the contrary, they're part of the longstanding bipartisan consensus on the centrality of fossil fuels—i.e., carbon emissions, i.e., climate collapse—to "the American way of life."[93]

Worse still, large-scale climate legislation when it does come focuses primarily on stimulating new consumption—and is swiftly superseded by new fossil fuel investments.[94] Indeed, *new* investments in fossil fuel extraction and refining have grown rather than shrunk.[95] First and foremost, CaCaCo must be maintained. And this means that GDP growth must be maintained. Which means that, somehow, the nexus of carbon, capitalism, and colonialism as organizing assemblage for global societies must be guaranteed. But isn't the growthism this entails incompatible with solving the climate (or biodiversity, or other) crisis? Well, yeah, but . . . Just gotta believe, I guess.

If we commit to religious faith that the future will somehow not be devastated by CaCaCo's deferred costs, we're obviously sunk. So, too, for belief in the political economy of CaCaCo itself.

Our species' climate, also that of all the other species we know or can imagine outside of science fiction, is undergoing phenomenally rapid shifts. Oceans were heating, to take just one indicator, *twice as fast* in the fifteen years between 2006 and 2020 as they had been only fifty years prior.[96] Not only is the planet heating catastrophically quickly, but it is heating faster all the time.

And we did that. Mostly a "we" of the global north, of a wealthy colonial core that has hoarded a vast quantity of the earth's resources and had a greater direct impact on the planetary system than any other animal group we can find in the historical or fossil records. But, as the next section of this chapter details a little further, not only that "we."[97]

As U.N. Secretary-General António Guterres intoned repeatedly throughout the increasingly cataclysmic weather period of 2022 and 2023, it is not enough to tinker with CaCaCo. We cannot simply pursue some "biggest climate legislation ever" with our left hands while approving vast tracts of new oil and gas extraction projects with our right hands (as the Biden administration has done in the U.S.). "Investing in new fossil fuels infrastructure is moral and economic madness," per Guterres.[98] And yet, CaCaCo *runs on oil and gas.* Nor do we have the political technologies or the material infrastructure to do otherwise while maintaining anything even close to current resource consumption levels. Nor are we in the midst or early stages of anything approximating a planned or globally just transition away from fossil fuels.

You cannot dismantle the carbon infrastructure without dismantling the colonial global political system, which you cannot dismantle without dismantling capitalism. None of which anybody actually knows how to do (though degrowth advocates are at least *trying* to figure it out).[99]

This is the reality belied by injunctions to hope harder and simply invest in renewables. It's not that investing in renewables is bad or wrong, of course. It's just wildly insufficient.

To save ourselves, or at least a somewhat justly organized majority of global humanity, from the ravages of global heating and weirding beginning to unfold, we need—immediately, though late is better than never—to radically transform our modes of existence at all levels.

And we are exceedingly unlikely to accomplish rapid, radical transformation with the political economic technologies afforded us by CaCaCo.

As I concluded this writing, the Intergovernmental Panel on Climate Change (IPCC) had recently released its first synthesis report since the celebrated—and largely impactless—2015 Paris Agreement, a treaty that included no enforceable provisions and was immediately abrogated by nearly every major carbon-emitting country, and that also scrapped language from the equally toothless 1997 Kyoto Protocol, which had at least recognized the historical beneficiaries of CaCaCo as having greater emission-reduction obligations than its victims, but which also maintained the infinite economic growth goals and sovereign right to resource exploitation that had been enshrined as "sustainable" development at the 1992 Rio Earth Summit.

Before you read this book, the new synthesis report will have been presented at the twentieth-eighth Conference of the Parties (COP), held in Dubai, United Arab Emirates. UAE is one of the world's foremost sites of fossil carbon extraction. The IPCC has been producing (at once increasingly alarming and, necessarily, always scientifically conservative) reports for over thirty years. The 2023 report is duly terrifying.

Though projection models for global heating have grown increasingly sophisticated, and though the climate crisis is accelerating, with increasingly clearly catastrophic outcomes, and so the IPCC reports are ever-richer and ever-longer, the basic science on greenhouse gases as anthropic drivers of climate crisis has not changed much.

In the thirty years between 1992 and 2021, global GHG emissions rose by nearly 17 billion tons, or 45%, year over year.[100] In other words, despite near-universal understanding in 1992 of the role played by GHGs in forcing catastrophic global heating, the last thirty years saw GHG emissions per year nearly double.

No year during that period saw anything remotely like a drop in overall greenhouse gases in the atmosphere. To the contrary, though the rate of increase slowed and even dropped for global economic recessions, it jumped right back up with the stock market after each.[101] Global mean temperatures have risen correspondingly, as glaciers have melted and forests burned. The planet has accumulated as much heat in just the past fifteen years as in the—already themselves unprecedented—forty-five years before that. Most of that heat was absorbed by oceans, which are heating more quickly with nearly every new measurement. That, in turn, speeds up glacier melt and slows down the deep currents that maintain weather and climate stability for most of the planet.[102]

Nominally, all this has to change radically and even be reversed by 2030 or else we're screwed. Our entire organization of life has to change. The *New York Times*, mouthpiece for CaCaCo continuity, is one of thousands of capitalist outlets promising that instead techno-magic will step in and solve for decarbonization, any day now.[103] Obviously, we're screwed.

It's 2023 as I write, and whether you're reading this in 2024 or 2034, I'll wager that the overall concentration of GHGs in the atmosphere has continued to rise rather than fall from my time of writing. That's absolutely catastrophic. Catastrophic for life on earth, and certainly incompatible with the CaCaCo continuity promised by physical and political economic climate denialists alike.

As volcanologist Bill McGuire puts it toward the close of his justly acclaimed *Hothouse Earth*, "Because it is now going to be practically impossible to keep this side of the 1.5°C dangerous climate change guardrail, what we can be certain of is that climate change will be all-pervasive."[104] The "hothouse earth" McGuire describes in grim detail throughout the book is "a world in which lethal heatwaves and temperatures in excess of 50°C (122°F) in the tropics are nothing to write home about; a world where winters at temperate latitudes have dwindled to almost nothing and baking summers are the norm; a world where the oceans have heated beyond the point of no return and the mercury climbing to 30°C+ (86°F+) within the Arctic Circle is no big deal."[105] Perhaps you are already living in that world of fire, flood, staggeringly powerful weather events, widespread disease, waves of mass refugeeism, and substantive social breakdown.

Stay for a moment with that last piece. The climate crisis does not only mean suffering, death, desperation, immiseration. Equally and awfully, it means catastrophic social disintegration, civilizational failure.

Christian Parenti's *Tropic of Chaos* is perhaps the definitive text on how climate change sponsors social breakdown.[106] Near the outset, by way of motivation for the book, Parenti writes, "The negative-feedback loops that keep Earth's climate stable are increasingly giving way to destabilizing positive-feedback loops, in which departures from the norm build on themselves instead of diminishing over time. The Greenland and Antarctic ice sheets—which reflect large amounts of solar radiation back into space and regulate the flow of ocean currents—are melting at rates much faster than climate scientists had predicted even a few years ago."[107] CaCaCo's deferred costs are falling due faster, and faster, and faster than our social structures can account for. Anthropogenic changes in the earth system occur at every moment faster than the new plans of the previous moment can address.

Parenti writes from 2011. I write from 2023, twelve years later. If you like, at your time of reading, you can check out the latest studies of ice sheets in Greenland and Antarctica. You will probably discover them melting much faster than when Parenti wrote, or when I did.

If civilizations had epitaphs, CaCaCo's would have to read "Faster than Expected."

On a personal note, I was shocked, when I had opportunity to take a dip a few years back, to discover how *warm* the Arctic Ocean was in early July. Today, I am no longer even shocked by the threat of all-consuming megafire at my house each summer. We can get inured to just about anything, however terrible. In order to have a chance of actually transforming the world for the better, people have to refuse to normalize horrors—whether in 2024 or 2034. Panic is one way of starting to refuse the normalcy of the abyssal "faster than expected" with which CaCaCo is dying.

We are in the process of losing many, even most, of the ecosystem niches toward which humans and other species are adapted, and upon which the stability of the CaCaCo world—such as it is—depends. Our positive-feedback loops *will* exceed our civilizational capacity to adapt. The world we know, with all its damages and harms and hopes and possibilities, is ending.

That seems pretty panickable.

THE SIXTH EXTINCTION

It would be easy to mistake the sixth mass extinction for just an outgrowth of the climate crisis. The fact that I treat it more briefly here than the climate and AI crises maybe adds to that impression. It's more accurate, though, to say that the sixth extinction—a global biodiversity loss crisis—is the other side of the Anthropocene coin.[108]

Life on earth is in the early moments of a mass extinction event that parallels five others we know from the geologic record. Unlike the others, this mass extinction is human-caused.

Because CaCaCo logic requires that loss, to be cared about, be accounted for as cost (this book is not immune!), conversation about the sixth extinction tends to focus on "ecosystem services." And not for nothing. Human survival as we know it depends on vast ecological webs, including not only creatures large and small but plant life of every description, microbiomes, and stable relationships between all these. The literature on what we are losing in terms of ecosystem services is voluminous, and rightly so.[109] From viable soil and crop pollination to medicines and meaning, humans depend on the non-human world for our existence at every level.

But I want to focus on the *meaning* part here, since that's what CaCaCo counts out every time. What does it mean to live in the midst of a mass extinction we ourselves are causing? What is any individual human life *for* in such a context?

We live in a deadly geologic era made by humans. This making was itself made possible, to a large extent, via development of technologies that allowed a smallish chunk of us to burn enormous quantities of fossil fuels to produce work-energy, while conducting most of our business on a principle of speculative future value, with resources and land taken from others and claimed as our own—stabilized into a global system of nation-states that has codified CaCaCo as intrinsically unequal in perpetuity.[110]

Our necrotic Anthropocene has reorganized both the global carbon cycle and global distribution of resources. This was accomplished for the comparative benefit of most people in the global north via the extraordinary labor-power and extractive possibilities made available by projections of state violence throughout the global south (and previously unknown-to-Europeans parts of the global north). But not only that.

Beyond simply rearranging the climate of our habitat, CaCaCo humans (which we all are now, beneficiaries and extractees alike) have spent the last several hundred years destroying ever more of our habitats' other inhabitants. The looming end of earth's explosive biodiversity, at least

60

for the next few hundred thousand or several million years, is what the consumption capacity of some of us is turning out to cost everyone we share the planet with, human and otherwise.

Throughout our species history, of course, humans have had an extraordinarily deadly effect on other large land animals in lots of places and political economic systems.[111] But the way human-caused extinctions of all sorts accelerated during the last couple or few hundred years of CaCaCo is truly novel.[112]

One of the most gut-wrenching realities of the biodiversity crisis we have begun acknowledging as a sixth mass extinction is that, to date, it's mostly not even driven by catastrophic global heating.[113]

The climate crisis exacerbates devastation already accomplished. Before long, it will be a primary driver of loops of annihilation almost too painful to contemplate.

But thus far, the sixth extinction has been organized, more than anything, by changes in human land- and sea-use patterns over just the last one hundred years or so.[114] Those changes in land- and sea-use, associated with an exponentially increasing worldwide population of humans and correspondingly massive increases in resource metabolization enabled by the fossil capitalism assemblage,[115] belong to our species in the sense that nearly all of us participate in them. Again, this is not to say everyone's gained equally. To the contrary. An essential feature of CaCaCo has been its organization of land- and use patterns for the benefit of some (mostly in the global north) at the expense of others (mostly in the global south).[116] That's the colonialism of it all.

It's just that the patterns themselves really have changed nearly everywhere. What's worse, they seem nearly inescapable. Forget about the birds and the bees, on whom we depend for critical ecosystem services and who are dying like, well, like flies,[117] but who are different enough from humans to make many humans indifferent. We can't even stop killing off the creatures we find most charismatic, in the habitats we regard as most crucial.

Humans continue to devastate the lands of nearly extinct "orange people" (the highly intelligent great apes, orangutans) in East Kalimantan, Indonesia.[118] We poisoned China's friendly and inquisitive baiji or Yangtze River Dolphin out of existence with shipping pollutants and chemical waste.[119] And though much of the profit from such devastation travels to old imperial cores or concentrates with local members of a global majority shareholder class, it's not only the very wealthy or even, more generally, merely "we" of the global north doing the devastating.

A part of why really seeing CaCaCo straight-on feels so awful is that many of the individual people stuck directly destroying the possibility of nonhuman life have themselves been victims—or, at least, not primary drivers—of CaCaCo's global machinery.[120]

Globally, we (nearly) all play some role in an unfolding biodiversity crisis. In part, it's a function of our sheer growth in numbers (from barely two to more than eight billion humans in just the last hundred years), and in part it's the intensely consumerist forms of life inspired and forced by CaCaCo. The sixth extinction, much more than the climate crisis induced by carbon emissions primarily just from the wealthy world, indicts almost every human living.

And yet, this *still* isn't to say we're all equally to blame. As Kelly Hayes and Mariame Kaba write in *Let This Radicalize You*, "Most people are merely cooperating with the world as they understand it, either under the threat of violence or because they are navigating the illusions that were constructed around them."[121] We *are* all to blame for the sixth extinction, but not all equally so. To the contrary, "The people driving those conditions are a relative minority whose greed and violence does not define all of humanity."[122] And yet, even as Hayes and Kaba are surely right that "most people are simply being herded along,"[123] it's *also* true that there are no easy or ready ways off this carousel. Even what we should want to organize for is fraught with moral catastrophe.

Who can we become in confronting the enormity of a sixth mass extinction we cannot personally opt out of causing? What does it mean to participate in ending so much life on the only planet we know? Let's bring it down to the real level of individual tradeoffs—at least as assumed by CaCaCo.

In the current world system, how do you tell an impoverished palm oil plantation worker in Borneo that he will no longer be able to afford life-saving diabetes medication for his daughter because the teeming biodiversity of the Indonesian rainforest must be saved?[124] Of course, the rainforest *must* be saved. There's no question about it. But very few of our ideas about how to save it will assure him a living, and so his daughter life. Indeed, there are hundreds of millions—if not billions—of people just like him, working in industries that directly drive mass extinction. Can any serious person believe CaCaCo will support most, or even half, or really nearly any of them in transitioning to jobs that do not entail mass murder of our nonhuman kin?

There's a kind of cupidity, an intentionally obtuse false innocence, to supposing our current organization of the world, with its trillions of market-based moving parts, can be jerry-rigged to engineer some different outcome than the sixth extinction as long as we both (a) remain stuck in CaCaCo and (b) place a relatively high premium on human life.

The near-term implications of this fact are horrifying to contemplate.

Most images of the sixth extinction center sorrow. Starving polar bears wander the ragged edges of melting permafrost and slowly die of resource deprivation on lonely ice floes drifting the too-blue Arctic Ocean. Pelicans covered in black tar dot the blasted seaside and seagulls drown, yoked to some temporary food source by the strong chemical bonds of plastic rings around their necks.

The rhetoric and communication scholar Joshua Trey Barnett has written movingly of our being-moved by such moments (and many more, close to anyone's home) in a book titled *Mourning the Anthropocene*.[125] For Barnett, one of our greatest imperatives is to feel wholly and as a source of meaning the weight of suffering a human CaCaCo assemblage has imposed on the rest of life on earth.

We can become other to the deadly version of global humanity that is forcing a sixth extinction, but only if we "become capable of noticing ecological losses."[126] In practice, this means "acknowledging the impressions that these losses leave on ourselves and others, human and more-than-human alike" and so "responding to past, present, and potential losses in ways that fortify rather than undermine the conditions of earthly coexistence."[127] We need to feel more keenly and deeply the mounting losses of the sixth extinction. Not only this, though. We need to transform loss into care.

Earthly coexistence, for Barnett, involves new attunements to care— both care for others (human and nonhuman alike) and recognition of how profoundly *cared for* we are by the world around us. Ecosystems provide care, not "services." Our response, in turn, must also be one of care.

At stake in mourning the Anthropocene to this point of love is inventional capacity, the longtime payoff for studying rhetoric. In mourning global biodiversity loss in real time, we begin to inhabit "a world in which we (will) have loved capaciously" and, in so loving, have also come to "understand we are capable of shaping, if not determining, the conditions under which we live."[128] The work of mourning at play here is the work of love. In loss and love, we become capable of inventing new—less overwhelmingly deadly—worlds.[129]

It's a genuinely beautiful vision, and I think a useful one. But *are* we really capable, within CaCaCo at least, of inventing less deadly worlds?

Panic, recognizing that any less deadly world will come only with a great deal of new suffering, discontinuity, and disjunction, heads in another emotional direction.

In panic, we orient toward the future along an axis of impossibility, apprehending discontinuity. We blanch in the face of our own incapacity, unequal to the horrorshow we can see ourselves causing. This may start with mourning. It proceeds in the case of the sixth extinction through an almost but not quite cold-eyed, shell-shocked, stock-taking. How are things going with regard to catastrophic biodiversity loss? Terribly. How might they yet go? Still worse. Far, far worse. So much worse.

Sheer panic is the basis for any possible grappling with that future.

In her modern classic *The Sixth Extinction*, Elizabeth Kolbert details what is at stake. We have entered into one of the geologic record's own "times of panic," in which "whole groups of once-dominant organisms can disappear or be relegated to secondary roles, almost as if the globe has undergone a cast change."[130] CaCaCo commits us to deadliness, perhaps in the end ourselves to species-death as well.

In mass extinction events, Kolbert explains, "Conditions change so drastically or so suddenly (or so drastically *and* so suddenly) that evolutionary history counts for little. Indeed, the very traits that have been most useful for dealing with ordinary threats may turn out, under such extraordinary circumstances, to be fatal."[131] She sees this, at base, as a problem of symbolicity in general: "With the capacity to represent the world in signs and symbols comes the capacity to change it, which, as it happens, is also the capacity to destroy it."[132] There's something about being a symbolic animal, in Kolbert's telling, that makes humans especially likely to destroy our own conditions of existence—and so, too, everybody else's.

But, as this book has been showing (and as I return to discuss in chapter five), it's not just our general humanness doing the world in. It's the machinery of CaCaCo, a highly specific way of constructing global humanity.

Nearly twenty years before Kolbert, in *their* modern classic *The Sixth Extinction*, famed conservationist Richard Leakey and co-author Roger Lewin offered a remarkably similar view. The long sixth extinction is anthropogenic, a function of human intelligence (i.e., symbolicity): "The evolution of human intelligence therefore opened a vast potential for population expansion and growth, so that collectively the six billion humans alive today represent the greatest proportion of protoplasm on our planet."[133] Humans, Leakey and Lewin observe—back not even thirty years ago, when there were *two billion fewer of us, a quarter fewer than the eight billion we are*

now—became a globally ultradominant species during CaCaCo, expanding
and growing relentlessly in population. And this imposed costs on the rest
of life on earth. "We suck our sustenance from the rest of nature in a way
never before seen in the world, reducing its bounty as ours grows," as they
put it in one memorable passage.[134]

Though Leakey and Lewin, like Kolbert, present human-driven extinction as a function of humanity in general, there's no denying that it's
ramped up exponentially in the last couple hundred years. Think of extinction in terms of forests and wild grasslands, two of the habitats necessary
for much of the world's extraordinary variety of terrestrial life.

"Primitive" and medieval and other humans did lots of deforestation all
over the globe, as people often point out when pinning the sixth extinction
on general humanity. And it's true—they did! But it's been CaCaCo humans
who, in not even 120 years (from 1900 to 2018), reduced forest and wild
grassland/shrub cover from 75% to just 52% of the earth's surface—and
from 90% to 75% in the two hundred years before that (1700 to 1900).[135]
Note that Leakey and Lewin present "the destruction and fragmentation
of habitat, especially the inexorable cutting of tropical rainforests," as
"by far the most important" way in which humans drive extinction.[136] The
more of the earth's surface we capture for human use, the less is left for
our nonhuman relations.

In the thirty years between 1990 and 2020, roughly overlapping the
period between the two (distressingly similar) *Sixth Extinction*s, the world
lost 700,000 more square miles of forest. That's an area roughly the size
of Libya, a fifth the size of the United States, or three times the size of
France.[137]

Since we've *been* knowing how incredibly damaging deforestation is
(from the twin perspective of biodiversity loss and carbon emissions), afforestation projects have been a huge focus of global biodiversity preservation efforts and climate finance for decades. Planting trees is associated
with ecological consciousness and care for the world more than nearly
any other activity.

And yet, for decades CaCaCo afforestation projects have been so focused on short-term profitability as to have nearly no positive impact on
biodiversity—or even a net negative impact.[138] Vast new monoculture tree
plantations get seeded, countries get to say they are meeting reforestation
goals, and some companies profit. It may seem obvious that reforestation
and afforestation for biodiversity should center mixed native species of
trees,[139] but that mostly doesn't happen. Because CaCaCo selects for profitability, large-scale activities with a long horizon, like forest-rehabilitation

and -regeneration, regularly sacrifice their very purpose somewhere along the way.

Can we fix that specific problem? Sure! Probably we will. And what next deferred cost of CaCaCo's basic organizational structure will fall due, stymieing best-laid plans?

To make matters worse, with a hotter overall climate and more forests subject to megafire, it's getting increasingly difficult to even slow deforestation, much less reverse it. The money for doing it *without* making a profit, and thus actually successfully, hasn't shown up yet. Not even close.[140] Our nonhuman relations are suffering and dying accordingly.

We know better, and a good chunk of us are even trying to do better. We're throwing the best CaCaCo has to offer at the problem. And we're still killing off pretty much everybody else on the planet.[141]

A certain sort of catastrophe-denier likes to look at past predictions of disruption and devastation and, with a "ha-ha!" either spoken or implicit, note that they did not come to pass. For the sixth extinction as in many such cases, this is an ahistorical appeal to history—as though events were momentary bursts and not unfolding processes. We are now ten years on from Kolbert's modern classic, almost thirty from Leakey and Lewin's. The sixth extinction proceeds apace. Its contours grow worse every year.

Who *are we*, in all this, we destroyers of worlds?

Like any really serious catastrophe, the biodiversity loss crisis is not the work of an instant. You can point out some of its worst villains, but a lot of it boils down to—and requires—most people just sort of shuffling along the paths laid out for them.

The sixth extinction is a global necrosis or deathliness unfolding across time, baked in a little more each month and year that CaCaCo's patterns remain relatively stable. Leakey and Lewin wrote in 1996, Kolbert in 2014. As I complete this book in 2023, one-in-eight bird species (of which there are roughly 11,000 around the world) is threatened with extinction.[142] Across the vast, mostly unpopulated land mass of the United States alone, a staggering 40% of all animal species and 41% of ecosystems risk extinction.[143] Past mass extinctions have seen the end of about 75% of existing species globally each time. We are not on track to do better.[144]

Perhaps it is time to panic now?

THE NOVEL CHEMICAL CRISIS

If the geologically sudden loss of countless species—whole ecosystems evolved over hundreds of thousands and millions of years—is the end of something old, CaCaCo's introduction of hundreds of thousands of new substances into the physico-chemical world is a horrifying novelty.[145]

Today, the talk is of per- and polyfluoroalkyl substances: colloquially, PFAS. Often labeled forever chemicals, they're in our water, in the food we eat, suffusing our bodies and causing untold damage.[146] This novel set of substances, introduced about 70 years ago into Earth's geologic record by CaCaCo ingenuity, is simultaneously an all-purpose solution to a variety of quasi-problems and a general disaster. These carcinogens and endocrine disruptors, present in manufacturing of all sorts—from frying pans to fast fashion to firefighting foam—may well be at the root of widespread difficulties with human conception.[147]

It is almost poignant that our species, which has wildly overpopulated the earth relative to CaCaCo's strategies for resource mobilization, could off itself, in the style of 2006 dystopian thriller *Children of Men*, through self-incurred inability to procreate. But while it's true that no competent discussion of the polycrisis can ignore human population numbers, there's no cause for celebration in our growing and involuntary inability to reproduce.

Happily, a solution is on the horizon. Already, we are finding cost-effective ways to neutralize PFAS in tap-water.[148] And who knows what innovation will be next? We humans are nothing if not prolific reorganizers of chemical bonds, especially with the wind of capital's need to be invested at our backs. And so, the siren song of techno-optimists greets each new fix with a refrain redolent of George W. Bush in those heady early days of the two-decade American war in Iraq and Afghanistan: "Mission accomplished!"[149] Tally all the missions "accomplished" and they make an impressive heap.

More glumly, turn the problem around and ask what's going on, exactly, that we keep needing to mitigate novel harms introduced by a century or so of Blitzkrieg raids on the periodic table. After all, PFAS is just the latest in a long string of novel chemical structures that turned out, after being heavily marketed and incorporated into global supply chains at all levels, to do more harm than good.

Before we learned to think of PFAS, we talked of BPAs.[150] Earlier still, it was DDT. Each was introduced as a problem-solver, a kind of miracle substance. Each, in turn, came to serve as an emblem of manufacturing hubris, a site of grave concern—only for the lesson to be forgotten entirely with the next wonder substance.

DDT (dichloro-diphenyl-trichloroethane), for example, was first synthesized in 1874, but its use as an insecticide wasn't recognized until 1939.

Within a matter of years, this incredibly helpful novel chemical was being produced at scale and put to use around the world. Its ability to kill insects without immediately harming humans or other charismatic species made it perfect for mitigating the impacts of everything from malaria-carrying mosquitoes in the tropics to the Colorado potato beetle. Today, many younger people (in the U.S.) have scarcely heard of it.[151]

In part, that's because Rachel Carson's 1962 *Silent Spring* brought DDT into the public imagination with the same overtones of horror, shock, and dismay that PFAS is beginning to evoke now.[152]

In warmly open-hearted but also chillingly matter-of-fact tones, Carson described DDT as one driver of a world where spring no longer means songbirds. No chatter and hum of new life. And in that silence, a blossoming evil both moral and intensely practical.

Songbirds, Carson suggests in *Silent Spring*, are ambient markers of the world's aliveness for even we often dull humans. In discussing the sixth extinction, I touched on the fact that birds have been dying in ever-increasing numbers for decades now—for reasons that range from virus transmission intensified by industrial agriculture to shifting human land- and sea-use patterns to global heating and its sequelae. Indeed, the loss of "wild bird mass" is part of what we refer to when we speak of the sixth extinction.[153]

But early on, before mass extinction processes had become widely obvious, Carson asked people to think of birds as victims of a very specific sort of catastrophe: the novel chemical crisis.

She invited readers to imagine a world in which "on the mornings that once had throbbed with the dawn chorus of robins, catbirds, doves, jays, wrens, and scores of other bird voices there was now no sound; only silence lay over the fields and woods and marsh."[154] In that "fable for tomorrow," the loss of songbirds registers a far broader loss of life, of the livingness of the world itself. Worse still, "No witchcraft, no enemy action had silenced the rebirth of new life in this stricken world. The people had done it themselves."[155]

The people doing it themselves are us. Most at stake in the novel chemical crisis is the way human inventiveness in CaCaCo proceeds at a pace life in general cannot accommodate. Guess how consumer behavior fits into that. We're going too fast for the world, for our own selves.

Carson traces DDT's and other pesticides' pathways through rapidly dying webs of life. She speaks more generally of a world in which "the chemicals to which life is asked to make its adjustment are no longer merely the calcium and silica and copper and all the rest of minerals washed out of rocks and carried in rivers to the sea; they are the synthetic creations of man's inventive mind, brewed in his laboratories, and having no counter-parts in nature."[156] The problem she highlights isn't novelty itself, but the scale and speed of chemical synthesis. Webs of life adapt slowly, for the most part. As Carson has it, "Given time—time not in years but in millen-nia—life adjusts, and a balance has been reached."[157] The living world takes time to adjust to novelties. Life's intricate, adaptive development is slow.

By contrast, as with the rest of the polycrisis, the ever-accelerating pace with which CaCaCo humans throw new chemical compounds at the living world beggars belief. And not just belief. Physical and social-technological adaptation as well.[158] Carson writes, "For time is the essential ingredient; but in the modern world there is no time."[159] How absurd to suppose we humans—biophysical bodies and adaptive technologies that we, too, are—would be exempt from the realities of life itself!

Already in 1962, in the United States, 500 novel chemicals were ap-proved for use each year.[160] As a result, "For the first time in the history of the world, every human being is now subjected to contact with dangerous chemicals from the moment of conception until death."[161] Novel chemi-cal synthesis continues apace today. In the seven years between 2016 and 2023, for instance, nearly 5,000 new compounds were submitted for EPA review. Just over 4,000 were reviewed.[162] A dangerously underfunded and politically embattled Environmental Protection Agency chokes beneath the pile of novel chemicals to be assessed each year. Despite plenty of goodwill and even a legislative mandate (2016's federal Toxic Substances Control Act), the resources for long-term, truly large-scale modeling of novel chemical effects are wholly outpaced by the speed of novel chemical synthesis and a strong preference among CaCaCo elites that *not too much* governance happen.[163]

Carson's condemnation of what I've been calling CaCaCo remains scar-ily relevant: "This is an era of specialists, each of whom sees his own prob-lem and is unaware of or intolerant of the larger frame into which it fits. It is also an era dominated by industry, in which the right to make a dollar at whatever cost is seldom challenged."[164]

The United States is hardly alone in this. Globally, production of novel entities (including both chemicals and plastics) has increased by a factor of 50 since 1950; it is expected to triple that again by 2050.[165] Thus far, some-where in the neighborhood of 350,000 new synthetic compounds have been introduced to the living world, many in contexts with few environmental protections at all.[166] The chemical industry is CaCaCo's second-largest manufacturing industry, synthesizing ever more compounds for use in ever more industries.[167] And like carbon emissions, once out in the world, novel chemicals do not stay where they are put.

Instead, traveling through the riverine systems and larger water cycle that sustains all life on earth, novel chemicals and plastics end up *everywhere*.[168] Chemists themselves are increasingly sounding the alarm: we are "outside the safe operating space for the planetary boundary for novel entities."[169] Even in unspoiled Antarctica and atop the highest glaciers of Nepal, PFAS comes down in precipitation. Rainwater around the planet is now, for the first time in human history, fundamentally unsafe to drink.[170] Which new entities will we notice next? How will they disrupt the basic coordinates of life?

Much like for greenhouse gases and the climate crisis, the underlying forces shaping this reality are not newly discovered. We know there is a problem, but seem powerless to collectively act. That, too, is not new.

Even in 1962, when *Silent Spring* brought well-established concerns about DDT to public light in the most powerful way, the concerns had been bubbling for a couple decades (including in Carson's own writing since at least 1945). The powerful place in the world *and* relative ineffectivity of Carson's extraordinary text together offer an important lesson about how "speaking truth to power" gets captured or spoken over or ignored by CaCaCo.[171] In a world organized to a very great degree by material, physical forces, there is a tendency to expect a lot more from words than even the very finest words can offer.

Those who know Carson today know her because *Silent Spring* is one of the most socially effective books written in the last century.

It played a key role in the eventual establishment of the Environmental Protection Agency, and in the banning of DDT both within the United States and (to a lesser extent) worldwide. It continues to provide a touchstone for new conversations about dangerous chemicals—but, also, we *continue to have to have* those conversations, and they continue to go badly to a very large degree.[172] As famed biologist E.O. Wilson writes in the afterword to a 2002 reissue of *Silent Spring*, "The battle Rachel Carson helped to lead on behalf of the environment is far from won. We are still poisoning the air and water and eroding the biosphere, albeit less so than if Carson had not written."[173] Indeed, seen in terms of the nearly unchecked propagation of novel chemicals over the 20 years since Wilson's afterword, the battle seems to be going worse than ever.

Rachel Carson offered a beautiful and harrowing vision of human impact on the world. She shaped not only decades of discourse, but had real and material effects on human behavior. She is credited with almost single-handedly ending the widespread use of DDT. And yet, we have not really quite done even that.[174]

As I write in the spring of 2023 it is all too possible to walk miles in the vast ponderosa forests that surround me in the mountain southwest with scarce a songbird to be heard. Where are the dark-eyed juncos and nuthatches who once called these woods home? To which of our crises is their absence, this quiet forest, due?

The industrial machinery of CaCaCo releases novel chemicals in effluents and gaseous emissions and the breaking down of plastics at rates we cannot keep up with accounting for.[175] Those chemicals disperse and aggregate in the food web, accumulating in living creatures of every sort. We know what a few of them do.

As for the rest? Or how even to screen for them, if companies choose not to report production data to regulators—as happens with incredible regularity, globally? We've little idea. Yet.

Carson's motivation for writing *Silent Spring* was not only concern for birds or pesticides. It was foresight, recognition that "allow[ing] these chemicals to be used with little or no advance investigation of their effect on soil, water, wildlife, and man himself" would prove disastrous.[176] But advance investigation, or at least *too much* advance investigation, runs counter to CaCaCo's organizing logic of cost-deferral. And what we do not investigate in advance, we habitually fail to recognize until too late. The novel chemical crisis, which CaCaCo cannot simply "fix" because it is completely aligned with the cost-deferring and -externalizing logic whereby carbon, capitalism, and colonialism have assembled a world, is today still scarcely recognized as such.

Anyone looking can see that worse outcomes are around the bend. We can be sure of it. We cannot yet say what they are, is all. At best, perhaps, we can follow Indigenous scholars like Max Liboiron in developing new relations to the lands where we live. Liboiron asks, "Where are plastics in the various land relations around you, Reader? What can plastics teach you? What is a chemical where you are?"[177]

I can answer Liboiron with a nod to the contested history of snowmaking with treated wastewater at my local ski resort, Arizona Snowbowl. Occupying the upper reaches of *Nuva'tukya'ovi* (Hopi) or *Dook'o'oslííd* (Navajo/Diné) or the San Francisco Peaks (settler), Snowbowl's wastewater-snow distributes trace amounts of hormones, antibiotics, and other pharmaceutical compounds across the entire watershed.[178] How might those build up?

Or I can point to the way plastic refuse along the interstate or blown from wind-savaged recycling bins on the residential street at my house flows into Pumphouse Wash, which traps it along drying-up banks as winter snow finishes melting out. The wash runs at least a trickle year-round across from the house where I live, carries microplastics down to Oak Creek and, much later, the Sea of Cortez. We can, and should, answer Liboiron's questions.

But this won't change the for-now inexorable logic of a machinery that combines extraction with cheap energy with the accumulation of capital in speculative investments. A CaCaCo version of "we" will continue synthesizing novel chemicals undeterred by our own foreknowledge that doing so will prove catastrophic at least some of the time, just as undeterred as we are at scale by the obligation to care for earthly co-existence and ecological relations.

Such is the character of polycrisis across its many domains, not just the four sketched here in outline. Individually, we can change (up to a point). At scale, our world system cannot be reformed.

CaCaCo's deferred costs are not happenstance, but integral. As such, CaCaCo cannot account for these costs. Its overall existence as a social-technological or political economic assemblage requires that costs remain external, eternally deferred. So, my local negotiation of the costs, while meaningful and even transformative for me as a person, can have no real impact on the larger structures of CaCaCo—not fast enough to avert much of what is worst, at least.

The physical world exceeds human technologies. Some costs, like those of the novel chemical crisis, will fall due and be collected whether we agree to pay them or not.

As with the AI revolution, the climate crisis, and the sixth extinction, the ways in which CaCaCo organizes human ingenuity in synthesizing novel compounds throws up a lot more—and far, far bigger—problems than this civilization can solve. When seen in terms of deferred costs (a different perspective than that suggested by more common, and more immediately morally compelling, criticisms of present harm), CaCaCo's polycrisis can be understood as imposing failure on the very system those costs enabled.

Public conversations haven't much emphasized that the novel chemical crisis is a global, quasi-universal phenomenon, a singular and encompassing and ongoing catastrophe. In one sense, it isn't. Liboiron's point is in part that the crisis of pollution, which literally *is colonialism* in his telling, is ineliminably local, cashes out in the particular harms that define our relations to place, to Land. But the novel chemical crisis is certainly also, in another sense, *generalized*. All our really serious crises are.

Which means that, thus far, we've barely scratched the surface of our overwhelmingly troubled global futures. I've outlined a few dimensions of the polycrisis that eats CaCaCo from within, but even this is just a back-of-the-napkin sketch. A world is ending. The tensioned spring that bursts toward its end cannot be unwound. We panic.

And then what?

Chapter Three

MUST WE REALLY PANIC?

Phew! Those last couple chapters were pretty rough. The concrete realities of our polycrisis are devastating, our stuckness in CaCaCo almost more than can be borne. By contrast, the sensitive reader may find this chapter's theoretical and historical arguments for panic easier going. I certainly do.[1]

There can be relief, appropriate relief, in realizing it's okay to panic. This chapter is about some general lessons we can take from panic.

It's worth remembering that no one says or hears "don't panic" unless *somebody* is already panicking or on the verge of it. Douglas Adams puts the point amusingly when introducing the eponymous *Hitchhiker's Guide to the Galaxy*. In his classic sci-fi comic novel, at first glance the *Guide* "looked insanely complicated, and this was one of the reasons why the snug plastic cover it fitted into had the words DON'T PANIC printed on it in large friendly letters."[2] Later, a little after the destruction of Earth to make way for an interstellar express route, Adams' hapless protagonist Arthur Dent picks up a copy of the *Guide* on board one of the Earth-destroying spaceships. "'I like the cover,' he said. '"Don't Panic." It's the first helpful or intelligible thing anybody's said to me all day.'"[3] In Dent's case, it was too late for panic to do any good. His planet was already gone. He was stuck in an alien spaceship, about to be dragged all over the universe. "Don't panic" was pretty good advice.

For us, though, there may still be time for panic to do some good. I give a lineage of panic in this chapter that helps clarify its uses.

But first, in the face of the polycrisis outlined in the last chapter, what sense should we—we who are neither Arthur Dent joining an imaginary Vogon death fleet nor supersemigenius CaCaCo billionaires on actual

Earth—make of the injunction *not* to panic, which flies increasingly fast and furious all around us?

Suppose we could heed that injunction, arrest the biopsychosocial processes flowing through us as panic, regulate hearts and minds alike. Where would the panic go?

In a sense, this is the question for every affect or structure of feeling. The literature on blocked feelings that come to rest within us, contorting body and soul around them, is voluminous.[4] So, too, the literature on how affects flow through us, catch us up in political and social movements, reshape us individually and collectively and, along the way, remake the very world.[5] For panic, though, the question is especially fraught.

Chest clenched and tight, a frenzy of sensations flying behind the eyes, our next move hopelessly uncertain in the paralyzing matrix of more vectors than can be analyzed, risk's heavy hand closing darkly over every horizon, we are panicking. And then what? Let's say you somehow don't panic. What are you supposed to do instead?

Proscriptions against panic tend to come bundled with prescriptions for hope. An astonishing number of even naked predictions of civilizational collapse hinge on selling hope. I discussed the political economic denialism of some hopeful climate scientists in the last chapter. To really drive home the absurdity of that don't-panic-do-hope matrix, consider also the hope-peddling of billionaires.

CaCaCo's biggest beneficiaries, people like Elon Musk and Jeff Bezos, have optimism to spare. When we hear from billionaires in the media, hope is always in the air (even when they talk about crises they find very concerning). So, when Microsoft co-founder Bill Gates—one of the richest people in the world and, increasingly, a hoarder of farmland[6]—says of the climate crisis, "The amount of change, new ideas. It's way greater than the pandemic. And it needs a level of cooperation that would be unprecedented," you can bet things will end on an upbeat note.[7]

In this case, interviewer Anderson Cooper claims, "You're talking about changing everything in the economy. I mean, every aspect of it."[8] Gates clarifies, "Yeah, the physical economy."[9] That clarification—"the physical economy"—underscores the key feature of CaCaCo hope: *system continuity*.

The way we make cement and electricity should change radically, but the ownership and investment structures that facilitate these should remain the same. Addressing crises means innovation, new technologies, changing the physical economy. If you're a billionaire, what it does *not* mean is changing the political economic system itself. For Gates' worldview, the capitalism and colonialism parts of CaCaCo should be just fine without the carbon bit. The transition will be tough but doable, even inspiring. Chapters one and two of this book laid out some reasons why people should find this self-serving vision dubious—not just morally, but as a practical horizon for the polycrisis.[10]

In our time of staggered collapse, when most of the globe's population is either *already* subject to the stacked weight of climate disasters or will be within the next decade-and-a-half, there's something farcically out of touch about millionaire Cooper plumping billionaire Gates for optimism.

"But you are optimistic?" Cooper asks.[11] "If people think it's easy, they're wrong. If people think it's impossible they're wrong," Gates replies. The interview ends on a soaring note from Gates: "It's possible. But it'll be the most amazing thing mankind has ever done."[12] What is "it"? Decarbonizing CaCaCo without changing its basic political economic structure. Hopeful, indeed! But perhaps the hope of CaCaCo's biggest beneficiaries doesn't serve the rest of us all that well?

Perhaps Cooper and Gates (who, for one of many instances of minimization, imagine a future with hundreds of thousands of climate refugees instead of the billions anticipated by more serious thinkers[13]) aren't speaking seriously at all about the climate crisis, much less the still-larger polycrisis? Perhaps the same is true when Elon Musk talks about the AI revolution, or Jeff Bezos about the sixth extinction?[14] Perhaps the hope CaCaCo's windfall-receivers urge for the rest of us is, in essence, about nothing more than keeping business as usual running for as long as possible?

There's nothing wrong with hope, of course. Hope carries people across some pretty dark valleys. But hope also doesn't need salespeople. In common idioms, we can see it clearly. The English expression "hope springs eternal" and its more dour German equivalent *die Hoffnung stirbt zuletzt* ("hope dies last") register a deep understanding that, as yet another expression has it, where there's life, there's hope. Anyone *selling* hope, this intrinsic stuff that abounds wherever life is, may be performing some sleight of hand.

In the case of our polycrisis, the press apparatus of CaCaCo has settled on hopeful terms as the tonal bookend to every story.[15] Once you notice it, like a gas-powered leaf-blower a few doors down, it becomes almost impossible to ignore.

And so here we are, at this point in the arc of popular stories about the polycrisis. Hope is a heroic achievement, panic an understandable but still somewhat shameful moral failing. Well enough, I suppose, if more hopefulness about CaCaCo's ability to pay off the deferred costs falling due is what's needed. But is it?

Aren't there times when panic really is just the ticket?

A TALE OF TWO PANICS

Before getting into the etymology and collectivity of panic, the way it might lead to new attunements and even a sense of wonder, the wild personhood of the world and possibilities it opens up, let me offer two anecdotes. They're from the same road trip.

The first night was sleeping in the still-closed Alaskan camper ("It raises! It lowers!") on the enormous boat of a rustbucket chevy truck I'd picked up for less than a song.

Dogs and I in the camper somewhere far from human habitation in the silent desert, camper still lowered because I'd been too weary to ratchet up its creakingly ancient mechanism when we'd finally arrived, as far from anywhere as I could reasonably get. Woke in the night to use the restroom and made a bracing discovery: The camper door opened just fine from outside in the closed position, but on the inside no doorhandle was accessible. That was tucked somewhere high behind the lowered upper shell.

But fine, right? It's a hassle, but you can crank the thing open, wind out its metal joints with the lever. Yes, except I'd snugged the camper shut from outside as well. I didn't trust its exterior latches to hold the hoary thing closed while driving, and had looped ratchet-straps over the top, clamming it tight on the truck bed.

I was well and truly stuck. In the middle of desert nowhere, where sun would bake me and Sonny and Xmas alive the next day. No cell service, no one to hear me scream. And I desperately needed to pee.

Panic's sharp rise is familiar to almost anybody, though there's no universal description. For me it's a tightness, a sense of being constrained, closed in on. Grave danger on the horizon, a feeling of overwhelm, taut muscles with nowhere to go, short, sharp breaths. Like a guy who's trapped himself in an unopenable tin can in the middle of a desert.

I peed in a jug. I'm not proud (or ashamed). And then I went back to sleep.

There was no need for panic, so I made the decision not to. I'd still be trapped in the morning, but I'd be thinking a lot more clearly then and able to see a little, too. With nearly no sunlight entering the camper, it'd be hours into daylight before we'd even start to get cooked. We'd surely figure something out before then.

Within half an hour of waking, I'd managed to crowbar enough distance between upper and lower shell of the camper to get a long screwdriver to the outer door handle. We were out and free. And to be clear, I don't think there's anything special about me here. Anyone who managed not to panic would have done more or less the same.

That's the case against panic.

* * *

The second night was driving up a long grade from California into Arizona, on Interstate 8 near the border with Mexico.

That same '79 crew cab chevy I bought for four hundred bucks and dropped a new very old engine into for a few hundred more had, no surprise, mechanical issues. Least of these, but requiring constant vigilance, was that between burning and leaking it went through a quart of engine oil every thousand miles or so. Which was hard to track, the odometer being broken.

I felt the engine rumbling differently. Not the constant thrum of an obscenely fuel-inefficient V-8 dragging seven thousand pounds of steel and rust and rubber up a hill, but a more uneven grinding. It was definitely time to add more oil.

Middle of the night again, vehicles whizzing by at 80, 90, 100 miles per hour in the darkness. Wire fencing stretched tight for hundreds of miles parallel to the highway, somewhere on the other side of it an international border, mixed-surface shoulder dropping slightly to gravel and scrub, and us—me, mid-sized Sonny and big Xmas, a laptop with the only copy of my half-finished PhD dissertation, and that deathtrap Alaskan camper—level enough on shoulder and scrub.

Dumped oil down into the crankcase, but I'd run the truck too hot for too long. A thick line drizzled onto the exhaust manifold and burst into flame. Red and yellow leaping in the engine bay, hot wind from the autos racing by, and I felt full-throated, no-turning-back, it's-on-now panic.

Desperate to make that impossible feeling go away, I rushed to find leashes, bundle the dogs out of the truck, grab my computer, hope for the best. We'd have to go forward on foot, walk along the fenceline, figure out some way back to Indiana (in case it's not obvious from context, I was not long on money, as broke as most grad students or a little more). The thoughts rushed through, hyperaccelerated by the heartbeat they were trying to outrun. Clearly, this was a time to panic.

But it wasn't *just* panic. It wasn't, that is, panic moving directly into the action that chases panic's thoroughgoing unbearableness away. Instead, somehow, for whatever reason, I stayed with the feeling a little longer, didn't just set off in whichever line of motion would make it go away, didn't act.

And remembered I had a fire extinguisher in the cab.

I think most anyone who remembered the fire extinguisher would be able to grab it, more or less intuitively work the controls, put the fire out. In seconds, thick white powder choked the flames, dusted the engine compartment. And then standing there, on the side of the road in sudden darkness flashed through by headlights, thinking about how much worse it could have gone.[16]

A sublime occupation of two times at once. The burning truck, the burning world, the fire put out. The vast, receding theater of a sky far greater than the thin, pale dots spotting it and the yellow flashes raging by me alike. Something like wonder.

Obviously, panic was necessary. Necessary but not sufficient. If I'd done nothing but hope, I'd have lost everything. It wasn't a question. But if I hadn't been fortunate enough to stay with the panic, tarry with it for whatever reason, I'd have been hoofing it with my hounds, a couple thousand miles from home, no money and no truck, no good options. Who knows where things could have gone from there.

Us, we went home.

Panic can be attunement to unacceptable risk, uncertainty, the likelihood of devastation. It can be inducement to desperately necessary action. Felt fully enough, it can be a starting point for something else entirely.

When you don't have a fire extinguisher handy, though, and it's not just your own little household you've got to organize, the question of how to panic wisely is far trickier.

Before arriving in chapter four at reflections on panicking wisely about our polycrisis, it's useful to understand more what panic itself *is* and *means*. At the very least, panic is a useful way of feeling distressingly unsure about a risky future.

ETYMOLOGY OR COLLECTIVITY

Etymologically speaking, panic starts with Pan, a minor Greek deity or demigod. *Panikos* (πανικός), or "of Pan," designates in Attic Greek a fear response to the meaning-rich but untranslatable echoes, whistles, and stirring wind of hills and valleys outside town walls, the realm of Pan.

Fully stated, panic is *phobos panikos*, the fear of Pan. Its victims are, above all, armies. Camped between cities in the night, they are subject to falling into panicked disarray at the small sounds of the more-than-human world.[17] Equally, panic designates the wild—random-seeming to shepherds—disunion into which herds of goats and flocks of sheep are wont at times to fall, their cries echoing from every hillside and commingling with the sounds of the hills themselves, no predator immediately in sight.[18]

Surely, goats and sheep know something of wildness that shepherds do not?

Today, panic is a mood for navigating CaCaCo's burgeoning polycrisis. Our lifeways are the cause of the end of the world that sustains them.

The question is how we may learn to panic wisely, with *phronēsis*, prudence or practical wisdom.[19]

Panic fear or *phóbos panikós* contains in its very way of experiencing the world a kernel of wisdom.[20] Panicking, the army in the night correctly apprehends something of a devastation to come. Panic is a liminal or in-between mood, in which armies and herds of goats alike sense their own demise and fall apart. They collapse early and avoid the rush.

Panic may thus, a little surprisingly, serve as precursor to infrastructurally novel possibilities. It opens space for new sorts of worldmaking. That's not to say panic is always and everywhere good, of course. No more so than anger or joy or sorrow or hope. Like all these others, panic has its moments. It might even be *necessary*. But it's certainly not enjoyable.

For me personally, phenomenologically speaking, panic starts with something like a rapid heartbeat and shortness of breath. I feel constricted, closed in on. My vision narrows. I *have to* do something. But what?! It's no fun at all.

For whatever it's worth, you're more likely to suffer from an anxiety disorder—including panic disorder—than any other mental health condition.[21]

Whether you do or don't, you've almost certainly experienced the physical state of panic at one time or another. The American Psychological Association's most recent edition of the Diagnostic and Statistical Manual (DSM-V-TR) describes a panic attack as "an abrupt surge of intense fear or intense discomfort that reaches a peak within minutes," and that includes at least four of the following symptoms: palpitations, pounding heart, or accelerated heart rate; sweating; trembling or shaking; sensations of shortness of breath or smothering; feelings of choking; chest pain or discomfort; nausea or abdominal distress; feeling dizzy, unsteady, lightheaded, or faint; chills or heat sensations; paresthesias (numbness or tingling sensations); derealization (feeling of unreality) or depersonalization (being detached from oneself); fear of losing control or "going crazy"; and fear of dying.[22] If relatively few people suffer from panic attacks per se, virtually everyone has experienced some of these dimensions of panic.

Our experiences of panic are embodied apprehensions of a threatening world. Often, though, they aren't well-tuned for the immediate circumstances.

From a clinical perspective, "The fundamental and protective emotion of fear occurring at inappropriate times (where there is nothing to be afraid of) is a substantial problem in psychopathology."[23] Fear interrupts the body as panic, occurs in us *as us*, dislocating experience from the present moment. And this seems to be a transcultural phenomenon. In *ihahamuka*, for instance, Rwandans reliving trauma from genocide feel shortness of breath, gasp for air, fall to the ground.[24] In panic, our bodies literally close down to the future, often lungs first.[25] Small wonder that we think of panic as a bad thing, a state to be avoided or, when traversing it proves unavoidable, exited expeditiously.

But, as with most feelings, there's more to the story than just how the feeling feels. The point of tracing panic back to Pan and all those Greek armies falling apart in the night is that doing so gives us access to the richness of this unavoidable affect.

Panic is a state of being to which we're helplessly subject and from which we've much to learn. Learning from panic starts with thinking about what it means to be "of Pan." And Pan, again, is a liminal figure *par excellence*.

Perhaps most important of all is the way the god Pan marks, for the ancient Greeks, entry into symbolic experience—meaningful words, sounds, and gestures—of something outside culture.

Pan begins appearing throughout fifth-century Greek artifacts and textual fragments as variations on a common theme, "a theme that announces the liminal figure of the Arcadian goatherd, with his characteristic interaction of fear and desire, of animal and god, under the sign of music and the dance."[26] Never wholly at home among the Greek gods, who nearly all are humanoid as Pan wavers between goatlike and wholly goat on hind legs walking,[27] Pan is subordinate to the rest of the pantheon. He is the "henchman of Zeus, servant of Dionysus, submissive if need be to Artemis, 'dog' of the Mother, somewhat clownish companion of the great Aphrodite," and "we have also met him acting the devotee of pastoral Hermes or Hecate of the crossroads."[28] Not much of a god at all, then, and yet he had a whole cult—an ancient Greek religion—of his own.

Neither human nor animal, deity nor mortal, but both and on both fronts, Pan preserves Arcadian wildness in the heart of the great city Athens. As Philippe Borgeaud puts it in his definitive study, Pan "grows to maturity in a thankless place, a place of abandonment or rejection, but also a source of beginnings, a place for an originating presence."[29] The mood or affect that Pan induces, above all in the armies constantly traversing the ancient Greek world, is one of fearful disarray: "Pan works upon the sense of hearing and makes it phantasmal; under his influence, nothing is taken for something—but this nothing (this echo), as the myth of Echo shows, is not really just *anything*: it derives in the last analysis from that otherworldly music, those faraway harmonies of the syrinx that lead the dance and the song of the nymphs."[30] The panic that grips armies in the night is at once nothing at all and earthly premonition of death and also a divine something, an echo of joyous harmonies.

And small wonder, for Pan is in fact a god of peace. Indeed, "the very first panic was an episode in the war between the gods and Titans. Pan, foster brother and ally of Zeus, put to flight the partisans of Cronos and thus used his destructive powers to clear the ground for the construction of the Olympian order."[31] Those armies who submit to panic, to read the Athenian mythology a little against itself, do so to clear the way for new order. Their deathly order collapses that new life may emerge. Are we consumer hordes, we lockstep armies of CaCaCo's deathly continuity, not a great deal like the child-eating Cronos and his cronies? What different orders might our panic make possible?

Pan is habitually associated with war, but rarely warlike himself. In one of the odder episodes of Greek history, he earns a temple in Athens after the runner Philippides or Pheidippides reports being accosted by the reproachful god while returning home from a mission to ask Sparta for help repelling the Persian army. Philippides, as ancient historian Herodotus tells the tale,

"According to the account which he gave to the Athenians on his return . . . fell in with the god Pan, who called him by his name, and bade him ask the Athenians 'wherefore they neglected him so entirely, when he was kindly disposed toward them, and had often helped them in times past, and would do so again in time to come?' The Athenians, entirely believing in the truth of this report, . . . set up a temple to Pan under the Acropolis."[32]

Pan, the source of panic, secures a place of worship in Athens only by wheedling with a messenger running through the wild places (above Tegea, in the vicinity of Mount Parthenium). His temple is established at a cave by the Acropolis. A wildness at the outermost edges of settled human experience insists on being heard. And a worship-place for that wildness, that only-sort-of-a-god, is built in the heart of Greece's greatest city.

So liminal a figure is Pan that, in the *Laws*, Plato would exclude his dances from the body politic entire. In Plato's stringent interpretation of what can properly belong to the city, his delineation of the components of meaningful collective life, Pan aligns with a category of "'Bacchic' dances and the like, which (the dancers allege) are a 'representation' of drunken persons they call Nymphs and Pans and Sileni and Satyrs."[33] The dancers are by their very nature unreliable witnesses, per Plato. Such dances "resist all attempts to label them" and so have no place in communal life.[34] The statesman, accordingly, "may ignore [them] as outside his province."[35] There is no place for the in-between in Plato's orderly city of laws.

And yet, Pan *did* have a temple at Athens. He *was* incorporated into the ritual and so also political life of the city, labeling difficulties and all. And where there's Pan, there's panic.

As noted, for the Greeks panic appeared first and foremost as a military problem. Borgeaud describes the strange and threatening admixture of disunion and collectivity inspired by Pan's fear:

"Panic brings disorder. The solders may leave their posts and must be kept still. Aeneas advises that the men be ordered to sing the paean and keep still wherever they are. Better yet: if the alarm is raised at night, tell each man to take his arms and sit on his bed; anyone who gets up will be cut down like an enemy."[36]

In this curious description, the danger to an army is that "the victims of panic are in the grip of the imagination, which is to say, of their worst fears."[37] Captured by fear, soldiers in the night are likely to cut one another down, supposing their friends their foes. The best response, per ancient chronicler of panic Aeneas Tacticus? Make everybody sit on their beds. Sing a collectivizing song. Nobody move.

You can panic alone, of course, but from its inception "panic" has designated an at once deconstructive and collectivizing affect. What's at stake in most injunctions against panicking is not only the discord it sows, but at least equally its collectivizing force.

Today, panic's collectivity calls to mind a classic image from dystopian fiction, film, and television: cars lined along a freeway, filling up the shoulders, windows broken and interiors burned out or moldering green or both. Such images register something we know in a deep and ancestral way. When we all fall apart all at once, few of us survive.

Hence this book's titular focus on timing. Panic now? How about now? Or maybe now?

Where things go most horribly wrong, we have all panicked at once. But not only that: *all too late*. Long after it could have been fruitful, we become together the catastrophic collective subject of panic. We are divided in a war of each against all and yet, at the same time, become a vast, heaving, miasmic totality. One martial response is to get everybody to sit still. "Don't panic!" Good advice for poor Arthur Dent.

For the ancient Greeks, the problem was that panic formed the *wrong sort* of collectivity. The Greek world, though we like our pastoral images of it and our carefully curated understanding of peaceful Athens the seat of culture and birthplace of democracy, was riven by near-constant wars.[38] The orderly army, subject to discipline and coordinated as a collective body across vast distances and with little in the way of long-distance communication technology besides runners like Philippides, was subject to disarray. There was always a danger that armies might break down and reform as the collective subject of panic. Literally, move in the wrong directions.

But what if the army was itself the wrong direction, was the wrong sort of collectivity in the first place?

Think again of the dystopian film's lifeless highway filled with hulls of cars that once held a panicked mob. Can we not imagine this very same image registering mass collective abandonment of automobile and car culture alike, not the beginning of horror but its end? The empty vehicles are lined in orderly rows. Perhaps their inhabitants parked them there, needing neither dead highway nor deadly automobile any longer, to keep these out of the way of a richer sort of life. Perhaps they panicked in time, and it is only we who imagine that panic always comes too late to save anyone. Perhaps the empty hulls are remnants of an orderly collective exit from the deadly order of CaCaCo. Perhaps *we* are the wrong direction.

Given what we know of Pan, isn't there something odd in our imagining panic's collectivity to be necessarily that of a devastation? Have we really earned our cinematic assumption that all those empty cars going nowhere on the vast plain of an eight-lane freeway crammed to bursting had been filled with people who burned to death or died of a virus? The bet of this book, and it is a historically well-grounded bet, is that panic means something more than that.

One of panic's central destinations in ancient Greece was anything but the deadly disarray of a civilization crumbling in on and against itself. That was happening already *without* the panic. That was the constant war bit.

By contrast with military order, panic led to a way of being together at the troubled intersection of city and countryside. It was Pan's liminality, the wildness installed at a cave near the Acropolis (literally, the "high point of the city") and flourishing in many more throughout the countryside, that made this possible. For the Attic cult of Pan, gathering for rituals in caves around wooden panpipes that resembled and in a sense *were* wind whistling in the trees, the panic of the goat herd was transmogrified into another sort of collectivity.

Outside the city, but still of it, cults of Pan and of the nymphs offered ancient Greeks a way to make human meaning of a nonhuman world that, in its strange otherness, could never be domesticated.[39] The nonhuman world could be loved. We could be its goat-like lovers, adoring it in song. We could carry it with us, *as us*, with panpipes and dance and returns to caves. But it could never quite be tamed.

Functional collectivity, the kind that goes somewhere useful with panic, doesn't just happen. We organize symbolically around key sites of meaning that exceed our very grasp.[40] Often, as with Attic Greek incorporation of the rural god Pan into the city of Athens, at the center of those sites of meaning is something that's a little more than we can handle. We bring the wildness into our fold, even worship it, but it continues to resist domestication.

And that's okay.

The panic of the goat herd becomes the panic of the goatherd becomes Pan, heard in a place of goats, becomes the liminal collective dance of the devotees of Pan, heard echoing across the Acropolis from a cave in the center of the city.

ATTUNEMENT OR WONDER

To panic, then, is to align—as an individual in a group of humans—with something beyond human ken, or at least beyond the city walls.

Panic is an intermediary affect or mood, a way of being-with the world that is more-than-human. A great deal of human thinking (today, especially under the banner of a theoretical trend called posthumanism) acts as though the non-human world is more or less benign, genial enough to human interests that we become our best selves when we align with it. The etymological roots of panic suggest a different story.

Panic is an attunement with the more-than-human world precisely in its unbearable, threatening otherness. We *are* small and insignificant, even in an era of global history our species has so thoroughly reshaped as to make naming it after ourselves (the Anthropocene) basically reasonable. In panic, we feel this threatened smallness right down to our bones. And it feels terrible.

What possible use can such an attunement have? What use, indeed, does any attunement have? It is a way in which we share a frequency with "the music of the spheres," with a world shaped by harmonies that exceed us.[41]

Attunement is how we are when we are *with* the world. We are always in the world, of course. Where else would we be? And so, by default, we are always with the world. But we are not always *with* the world, resonating to the frequency of all that is around us. More often, we charge through the world pretty heedless of what surrounds us, filled with our own CaCaCo purposes, pursuing preferences, seeking to bend life's disorder to our wills or else escape it entirely, retreating to the fantasied refuge of our own minds and devices. In attunement, we shift not merely gears but modes of transport entirely.

All of which re-invokes the question: In panic, what are we attuning to, and why does it matter? Must we really panic?

On the other side of panic lies something like wonder. Under the right, which is to say the wrong, circumstances (stuck within the tensioned spring of CaCaCo, say), it's pretty darn hard to get to wonder without panic. We need to feel deeply the *impossibility* of the CaCaCo world we inhabit, need to feel that impossibility as an icy blast from the future rushing in to chill us. Panic opens the door to a not-yet-arrived-but-also-not-avoidable end of our world. The otherness of the world we feelingly attune to in panic, if we are but willing to live through the first blast of fear and anxiety and even terror, reintroduces itself to us as extraordinary, beyond compare, rich with life.

The glint of mountain lion eyes up a hillside in the dark opens onto a full silhouette, inspiring terror, panic. "I have to get away!" But if I remain, call out to the lion—"I see you! My species is trouble but we mean you none! We are here, Zada and I! We are here! We see you!"—I will encounter something on the other side of panic, something that matters in a raw and undigestible and absolutely vital way. But only if I've been willing to stay with the panic, allow myself to be held by it.

Just there, where the world is beyond compare, where it exceeds our capacity for sense-making and rebuffs every attempt at comparison with the world we've known before, we can come together as the collective subject of panic in wonder. Zada the dog and I stand close, ears up, looking and smelling and listening toward the limestone outcropping above. We are here. The lion pads out of sight. They are here, too.

Where panic gives way to openness onto the world in its alterity, we feel awe or wonder. This destination for panic, in the Greek world, dots the wooded hills and caves of Arcadia with Pan's pastoral cults. Wonder at the world beyond the city walls takes pride of place even in the Athenian metropole.

Digital artist and philosopher Jenny Odell, in a lovely book titled *How to Do Nothing*, articulates the sort of wonder I have in mind. Describing what happened when she stopped always doing something, began instead to pay attention to the birds around her, she writes,

"Over the years, my continued attention began to dissolve the edges of the checklist approach. I noticed that certain birds were only in my neighborhood during part of the year, like cedar waxwings and white-crowned sparrows. In the winter, my crows came by less often. . . . Even if they stay in the same place, birds can look so different not only throughout their life but during different seasons, so much so that many pages of the Sibley guide have to show different ages, as well as breeding and non-breeding versions, of the same bird. So, there were not only birds, but there was bird time."[42]

As Odell continues, she runs through different bird contexts and forms of individuality, the nonsensicality of the general category "birds" itself. "There were simply too many relationships determining what I was seeing . . . This context, of course, also included me."[43] Attunement to Pan's dominion, even within the city, can beget a fuller awareness of one's own place in it all. Not for nothing, the growing sense of wonder and relational fullness running through Odell's book began with panic.

How to Do Nothing sets out from the all-consuming attention economy. In the midst of our digital optimization, "a certain nervous feeling, of being overstimulated and unable to sustain a train of thought, lingers."[44] A shortness of breath, perhaps. A sense of being closed in on by a world that streamlines our attention and surveils us at every moment. Echoes of the AI revolution's dispositif. The wonder Odell builds out from that initial panic is lifegiving, and it does not deny the otherness of the nonhuman world with which she finds herself in ever-closer relation. Quite the opposite. Wonder discovers a livelier world altogether, on the other side of a world's ending that panic first intuited.

On this note, consider also Rachel Carson's small tract on wonder. Between 1951's expansively beautiful *The Sea Around Us* and 1962's terrifying *Silent Spring*, which did so much to curtail the spread of DDT and introduce appropriately panicky questions about novel chemicals into popular consciousness (and upon which she worked for nearly two decades), in 1956 Carson wrote a long essay for *Woman's Home Companion* titled "Help Your Child to Wonder." Expanding this essay into a book was a central concern of the latter portion of her too-brief life, but time ran out.[45]

Carson's posthumously published *The Sense of Wonder* mostly details her rich, vivid exploration of the nonhuman world with her nephew Roger. For Carson, wonder is an emotion children especially excel at, a freshness of perspective and due recognition of the extraordinariness of the world surrounding us. It is available to us all. "The lasting pleasures of contact with the natural world are not reserved for scientists but are available to anyone who will place himself under the influence of earth, sea, sky, and their amazing life."[46] To find wonder, we have but to place ourselves under the influence of the living world.

One might suppose such a definition borne of long, contemplative, and peaceful reception of the world around.

And yet, Carson wrote this essay at the white-hot peak of her research for *Silent Spring*. Filled with horror at the rapid disappearance from the world of not just songbirds but all sorts of living things, she averred, "Those who contemplate the beauty of the earth find reserves of strength that will endure as long as life lasts."[47] Such contemplation is not opposed to panic at the ways CaCaCo twists and warps the beauty of the earth, but was in Carson's own life entwined with it. Wonder is not an evasion of terror, panic, fear. It is what comes alongside and after panic, if we will but attune.

The tortures inflicted by DDT and other novel chemicals on the living world, which Carson was mid-stream in exposing when she wrote *The Sense of Wonder*, surely inspired such lines as "One way to open your eyes to unnoticed beauty is to ask yourself, 'What if I had never seen this before? What if I knew I would never see it again?'"[48]

It is almost unbearable to see in mind's eye the towering ponderosas around my house swept by fire, the beating wings of adversarial ravens and hawks side-by-side as they desperately flee a fast-moving wall of flame roaring up too-dry canyon walls from below the Mogollon Rim. This hasn't happened yet.

But if I refuse to see it, hold panic at bay by hoping it just won't happen, I'll never know how happy the trees are after a good winter in these times of dying. I won't feel their radiant greenness holding me. I won't be able to listen rightly to what the birds are saying when they chatter happily, grabbing slow-moving insects from the air above the well-filled wash on a cool pre-summer evening.

This is a time of extremes. No honest person can long deny the cataclysmic swirling of CaCaCo's deferred costs. No person who denies our polycrisis will ever really know the world around them. Love, like pollution, can be generalized; but if it is not local, it is nothing at all. Alone in loving this world, the dying lands we inhabit, do we have any chance at all of building something other than just more shit companies in the coming ashes.[49]

All through her work on *Silent Spring*, Carson was mapping out wonder.[50] Wonder is where panic goes next when it arises as attunement to a collapsing world, and when we stay present with both it and the bits of world nearest us.

GAIA OR ACTION

Panic at an ending can lead to wonder and love of the world around. But wonder at what, more generally? Wonder in relation with what living—monstrous, beautiful, more-than-human, personable, threatening, loving, even divine—world? Wonder, and then what?

These are the questions *Gaia* asks.

Philosopher Isabelle Stengers' *In Catastrophic Times* details a sense of Gaia as the otherworldliness of the world, or the world as an Other, at the point of climatological, chemical, and biodiversity crises.[51] Throwing an AI revolution into the mix, with its looming threat of hostile more-than-human intelligence, only underscores the point.[52] In a future that is liable to go very, very badly for most of us, the question is not how to "avoid terrible ordeals" but rather how to become "capable of surviving these ordeals without sinking into barbarism."[53] We begin to answer that question by grokking the world itself differently.

To apprehend Gaia through a sense of wonder, on the basis of panic, as a vast, living, sensitive, even touchy organism, is to be goaded into action—action on the world and action on ourselves.

For Stengers, realism about the polycrisis means acceptance that CaCaCo is circling the drain. Things will go badly; we should panic. But this isn't to say we should throw up our hands and do nothing. The very opposite.

Even in our catastrophic times there remains space for political action. It's just a question of what sorts of action are meaningful now.

There's not time to work up to seizing the machinery of production and hoping the state fades away, maybe, nor is there time for a slow, reformist march through the institutions. The polycrisis does not afford long-horizon, continuity-based visions of politics. The terrible face Gaia turns to us says we will not slowly resolve CaCaCo's crises. The time for pretty stories about how the moral arc of the universe bends is over. CaCaCo cannot be reformed on behalf of justice, and not just because it's at odds with the very idea of justice in its basic logic. More than anything, there simply isn't time. The deferred costs are falling due already.

Political action today should focus on how we may dispose ourselves and one another differently, not to "fix" CaCaCo but on behalf of truly alternate futures. How can we become other to our own selves in attunement and so alliance with Gaia—even and especially in times that are and will be broadly catastrophic?

We will not prevent the staggered collapse through which a CaCaCo world ends. But we can act now, today, in ways that align us differently with Gaia.

We can act to open space for new living worlds in the coming ruins of this old and necrotic one where we for now remain stuck. Panic's political stakes are located not just in the present, but in a catastrophic future anterior, a time that "will have been." What can new organizations of resource metabolization now *have made possible* in times of rebuilding to come?

Political action aligned with Gaia means learning to become, as Stengers' sometime-collaborator Bruno Latour puts it, the peoples of Gaia.[54] I get into some specifics about that in the next chapter, but first let's look at the big picture, the theoretical goal.

Why must we become countrypeople of a living Earth beyond countries and human bonds, become peoples we have not been before? Because the peoples we are now, ordered by CaCaCo, cannot persist. We are peoples of a failing civilization, a world that will be ever more in tatters for ever more of us for (probably) the rest of our lives. What are the stakes of becoming the peoples of Gaia? At the very least, we can say they are high, higher even than when Latour wrote:

"At the present moment, in mid-2018, [we] . . . are wondering with unconcealed anguish whether it will be possible to avert another August 1914, another suicide—this time worldwide and no longer just European—of nations, under which such a deep depression has been dug that they will all plunge headlong into it—with enthusiasm and delight. And this time no one will be able to count on the belated support of the United States."[55]

Just a year and change later, CaCaCo's desperately bad management of the covid-19 pandemic would demonstrate that "global humanity" does not have the necessary resources to save itself from even fairly routine problems. In 2018, Latour could present the polycrisis as a question. Today, it is what we have instead of a horizon.

The institutions of our world will not save us from their own deferred costs. They will not even save themselves. The question posed by Gaia, there on the other side of panic, is what we can do now to leave better artifacts for worldbuilding in times of radically diminished resource access to come.

Stengers frames this in terms of political struggle that will change who we are. She says we should today work on constituting "'resonance chambers' such that what happens to one group makes others think and act, but also such that where one group achieves something, what they learn, what they make exist, becomes so many resources and experimental possibilities for others."[56]

This is partly about solidarities between different sorts of political action groups. And it's partly about broader intellectual responsibility, a sort of epistemic or symbol-receiving activism. If, for instance, I want to be shaped by the political struggle of a vast wave of strikes and riots through which, for months, millions of everyday French people fought their own state's efforts to immiserate all but very wealthy older people, I'll need to look beyond the *New York Times*.[57] The core media institutions of CaCaCo (and their proto-fascist opponents, outlets like Newsmax and One America News Network) aren't going to be my most reliable guides to popular struggle against CaCaCo's desperate business as usual.[58] Aligning with Gaia, at the level of figuring out what's even happening, means taking CaCaCo-aligned sources with plenty of salt.

But Stengers' point goes deeper still, to the core of who we are.

We have to learn to act with and on and for one another as co-constituent elements of a far larger living organism, a world that exceeds the deadliness of CaCaCo.

Whether working at a grand scale, organizing for things like climate-adaptive public energy grids and AI regulation, or a small one, pulling plastic from your local waterways and preserving wildlife corridors,[59] action in Stengers' sense is only sort of for this world we currently inhabit. Political action in alignment with Gaia organizes not just the world, but *us* differently. Along the way, what we do matters some, but how we do it matters as much or more. To align with Gaia within the scope of the polycrisis is to design possible futures for after CaCaCo crumbles (whether we accept that we are doing so or not).

Action of the right sorts, which I talk about in the next chapter as judicious ways of panicking, makes us a different "we" in the present. The results of political action can partially improve matters in the time that remains for CaCaCo. But what matters most in the context of our general stuckness are the sorts of future collectivities and visions of possibility that action now enables.

We will not save CaCaCo. But neither are we free to desist from meaningful tasks within it (whatever we take those to be).

Laying new foundations for better worlds, worlds that might be built in the hotter, darker, more difficult future that is coming for us all, is the end-goal of appropriately panicked action. In learning to become the peoples of Gaia, we make good on panic's promise as a basis for collectivizing wonder and self-remaking action. "*However precarious or small it might be* each achievement matters. None will suffice to appease Gaia, but all will contribute to responding to the trials that are coming, in a mode that is not barbaric."[60] Political action inoculates against our worst selves, the "we" who want to feel like nice people but who also will kick others away from the sides of CaCaCo's few and inadequate life rafts as times worsen and resources for our habitual consumption dwindle.

In all this, then, let's not lose track of Gaia themselves. Who or what is this Gaia, who cannot be appeased and yet who offers us a horizon for becoming less barbaric?

The Gaia of Stengers and Latour derives in part from that of chemist James Lovelock and biologist Lynn Margulis. The basic idea is simply that the entire planet is a living organism. That's not a metaphor. For Lovelock, "The composition of the earth's atmosphere and the temperature of the surface is actively maintained and regulated by the biosphere, by life, by what the ancient Greeks used to call Gaia."[61] *Gaia* is a way of understanding the entirety of Earth—including us humans and all our many machinations—as a colossally interwoven being, much more living than not.

As the world of and beyond CaCaCo and all its crises, Gaia appears in consciousness as a Thou, somebody we owe something big.

The word names the world as an other to whom we are obligated and whose vicissitudes we cannot afford to ignore, with whom we are in relation in some way. A world that, as Stengers puts it, is *touchy*, hypersensitive.[62] This living world-system, of which we are but one element, appears to us now and again as a whole: as Nature, or Planet Earth, Starship Earth, the harmony of the celestial spheres. Apprehended through the self-reflective insight to which panic leads, it is Gaia.

Gaia, whose lifely organization we threaten now at every level, turns their gaze within and upon us, strange and terrible. We attune in panic with that Thou. Gaia erupts into conscious experience *as a world* far more powerful than our designs, ill and wonderful alike. That this other inspires no less fear than wonder has much to do with our own behaviors and with an unworkable fantasy of collective control over the nonhuman world.

For a lot of people, for a pretty long time, it got to looking like global humanity (or at least the global north bits of it) would be able to avoid payment on the deferred costs of things like "the American way of life." The risks associated with this all-consuming way of life could be managed, distributed. CaCaCo is nothing if not a risk-distribution mechanism.

For a few short decades, at least since the fall of communism and the rise of "sustainable development," most of us in the global north (and an allied majority shareholder class around the world) have supposed that, while we cannot quite control the tides, some of us can determine pretty well who will fall beneath them and who rise above. Plenty of people have grumbled about it, but nearly all have acquiesced to there being *somebody in charge* who more or less knows what they are doing.[63]

We can protest and ask them to do different things. We can type in all caps on social media, berate our friends for not voting or for voting for the wrong people or for voting at all. What we can't do is imagine a different world. We can't even quite believe this one won't, more or less and as long as we're lucky and as long as we live in a CaCaCo beneficiary country, look out for us, sort for our little stakes in it. Even those who are assiduously critical, as long as we've been acquiescing to the general social technologies of the CaCaCo world—going to work, doing our thing, "living our best lives"—have pretty much assumed the basic risk-distribution machinery would work well enough for us.

As chapter two suggested, all that is changing. What becomes clear in the boundaryless flow of novel chemicals, the ubiquity of data harvesting and AI disposition of lives, in global weirding and the genocide of human and nonhuman relations alike, is that nobody can manage how risks are being distributed now. There is no *management* of deferred costs that fall due with colossal interest. Gaia is calling in their loans. The shit company is going under.

Why panic now? Because there's so much to panic about, especially for people who assumed bad things would mostly be happening to other people. Increasingly, Gaia reminds us all of the unmappability of a world onto which panic opens relation.

I've been working with financial metaphors here, but Gaia is not exactly a creditor standing outside of humans. No more so than an entire body stands "outside" of a gallbladder or a cancerous cluster of cells. Metastatic as we may be, even CaCaCo's deathly version of global humanity is bodily, corporeal, within but also a part of Gaia. At most, we are moments of a whole (and, in point of fact, we are very different sorts of moments from one place to another, not just global south to global north but within our larger societies, people to people). This is where new, Gaia-aligned forms of responsibility become possible for us.

Because if moments, then motions. And if motions, for a symbolic creature like the human, then actions. And if any thinking about actions at all, well, I'm sorry, but there's no way around it—plans. There's no opting out of some agenda-setting, even after we admit that CaCaCo's risk distribution mechanisms have gone haywire (after having always been haywire). We're gonna be doing some worldmaking. The question is, "What sort?"

In *Designs for the Pluriverse*, anthropologist Arturo Escobar lays out a beautifully capacious answer to that question. His vision is of worldmaking as open-ended, intentionally pluralistic planning or design.

Action on and within Gaia is unavoidable. But our way of doing and designing has been deadly and badly thought through. We find ourselves, when we apprehend Gaia through our panic, to have been running along heedlessly within the scope of the Mayan "*pachakuti*: a profound overhaul of the existing social order, not as a result of a sudden act or a new great synthesis of knowledge or novel agreements, but of an expansive and steady, albeit discontinuous, effort to permanently unsettle and alter the established order."[64] In that great cycle, most of what we humans of CaCaCo have been up to has been more cancerous than not for Gaia, on the whole. In our necrotic Anthropocene, we are the orderly gallbladder and its metastatic unsettling alike.

But the very organization of the CaCaCo world is radically at odds with remedying the damage done. From within this space, can we really hope to map different futures differently, we who are disposed by CaCaCo? Isn't designing better futures just the same old shell game of risks and deferred costs? And isn't that farcical when the deferred costs falling due are not merely owed to human (and dehumanized) creditors, but to the planet itself?

What could it mean to re-form ourselves as peoples of Gaia, different sorts of motions within the pachakuti or return of time?[65]

For Escobar, becoming less metastatic can only happen once we've apprehended CaCaCo's unviability going forward. It all starts with relations.

Not all worlds will end, but *a* world most certainly will. Escobar's vision foregrounds the development of possibility within this framework of impossibility. For a different sort of worldmaking, "relationality involves more than nondualism" and "reimagining the human needs to go beyond the deconstruction of humanism (still the focus of most posthumanist thought) in order to contemplate effective possibilities for the human as a crucial political project for the present."[66] If we're really serious about attuning to and so acting in alignment with Gaia, as I discuss in the next chapter, we'll need at long last to get serious about humanizing.

We don't get to not be the sort of animal we are, whatever exactly that is. We can definitely become what we are a lot differently.

Design, in this connection, is anything but the certainty or forcedness we often associate with that word. To the contrary, it starts from recognition that *another world is possible*.[67] Not merely possible but, as CaCaCo collapses, inevitable. This recognition invites responsibility.

Design can be speculative, based on the assumption of discontinuity, rather than just another mechanism for disposing bodies and minds from above, securing acquiescence within CaCaCo. Design for a pluriverse organizes itself around relations, gaps between the places where we've gotten stuck in the current world and openings for worlds to come. Such a vision of design is collaborative, between different humans and between humans and nonhumans and between humans and the biosphere itself.

This is design as a covering term for all the ways we "make visible the notions of the good life emerging from [people's] own experience *in their place[s]*."[68] Escobar's vision of design involves drawing out, in alignment with Gaia, what people (human and otherwise) already value in the places where we are, over and above and beneath and beyond our stuckness in this failing CaCaCo world. Design, planning, laying out schemes and dreams: these sorts of symbolic actions are not pieces of life we humans seem readily able to jettison. But we can do them very differently.

We can learn to design speculatively, on the basis of exactly those sorts of relations CaCaCo most excludes. Where, in our own places, does Gaia becomes apparent to us? What sense of a good or meaningful life aligns with the biosphere, aligns with forms of relation that CaCaCo cannot burn or plow under or extract or monetize?

On the other side of panic, of a desperate reckoning with how bad a pass we really have come to and how much worse things are poised to get, is worldmaking as relational design, action with and for Gaia.

Where collectivity and wonder come together on the terrain of attunement to Gaia, new possibilities for action emerge. Ultimately, if panic is to go somewhere useful, it has to proceed in collective action that does not lose the sense of wonder. Tempered by a kind of awe at the otherness of a world coming ever still into being, panic's attunements bring us to shared work with all Gaia's peoples. To real plans for that speculative work.

If we panic in time, if we become together in political actions knotted around the tight density of our panic, we can feel the beauty of a world that is not ours to shape and, yet, which we will have shaped. We can become together the peoples of Gaia. At one moment, perhaps, that may mean purposefully all walking away from rush hour at once, leaving empty cars to fill empty freeways forevermore. Perhaps, in new attunements on the other side of panic, we can even design plans for what may come after CaCaCo—and begin acting on them.

So, must we really panic? Well, we will. And if we will, then we'd better do so as soon and as wisely as we possibly can. Also, we probably *should*.

Chapter Four

From Panic To Practical Wisdom

This is a book about panic as a starting point for developing what the ancient Greeks called *phronēsis*, practical wisdom, for the polycrisis.

There is a time and a place for panic and, so, wiser and sillier ways of panicking. In the last three chapters, I asked you to stay with me and panic a while, and then to tarry with the bigger question of what panic is for, where it goes. When we let ourselves stay with this difficult feeling, it sometimes leads, through wonder and action, toward wisdom. Even and especially as CaCaCo continues breaking down.

So, I've been suggesting that panic's destiny need not be incapacity, that taking panic in stride is crucial in facing up squarely to the way one world is ending. But how exactly can we panic wisely? What would that even mean?

This chapter weaves together four dispositions that panicking wisely can shape. Twining with dimensions of the polycrisis to which this book as a whole responds, these ways of being oriented toward action are solidarities, disruptions, novelties, and archaisms.

This how-to chapter isn't quite a "how-to," though. Wouldn't it be nice if taking the polycrisis seriously meant we knew for sure what to do next! Unfortunately, I don't.

The pay-off for reading arduous books about the contemporary world is usually that you get to imaginatively identify with policy makers and business leaders, people standing at the levers of power. Or else you get to imagine yourself an organizer or a revolutionary, someone working in concert with others to address grave wrongs, to bend the universe's moral arc toward justice or seize power from villains and usher in a new order. Both identifications have their uses.

But the situation this book describes is one where all those people, besides the first group's being questionable alter egos anyhow, are themselves stuck within CaCaCo's logic of deferred costs. Those costs falling due is causing CaCaCo's collapse. You should definitely try to do things, but you won't fix *this* world.

Well, I think you won't, at any rate. Ruling *anything* well and truly outside the domain of possibility is virtually impossible.

Certainly, plenty of people won't want to take what I've said here to heart, or just will remain unpersuaded about horizons. Those who feel themselves called to fix the CaCaCo world, as long as they direct efforts to the less villainous sorts of tech innovations or to organizing for justice or truly radical transformation, are doing necessary work for building next worlds, too. Even if they don't think that's what they're doing. As I said at the outset, no book can be for everybody.

The suggestions here are really just some ideas for regular people to try out in their own lives.[1] They're strategies a person can practice for inoculating themselves against those who presume to know. If humanizing is to become possible, starting now and continuing in the ruins of the CaCaCo world, we're all going to have to get a lot more comfortable with not knowing what happens next—and with taking action anyhow.

As matters worsen, though, plenty of charlatans will pop up with The Answer. It will be tempting to believe them. The less willing we are to stay with panic, to see it through to what wisdom comes after, the more tempted we will be.

Learning to panic wisely is a vaccine against comforting—and false, and deadly—certainties. CaCaCo *is* falling apart. We can be certain of that much. But the promise, "If you just do X, then it will be okay (or will not fall apart, or will fall apart for other people but not for you, and etcetera)," is a false one. Nobody can promise you outcomes in a disappearing world. I certainly don't.

How incredibly uncertain our horizons are (barely hinted at in chapter two's discussion of polycrisis), how devastating CaCaCo's breakdown is likely to become as it proceeds, is what makes panic appropriate in the first place.

The four tools for humanizing discussed in this chapter are ways of thinking and feeling and acting I've found on the other side of sheer panic my own self. I hope they can be useful to you. No guarantees, but perhaps these dispositions can even help us locate some fire extinguishers.

That said, let me acknowledge a crucial limitation of scope. My goal is to develop tools for humanizing. Accordingly, I don't focus on the many and various technological inventions—from carbon-capture-and-storage, the less supervillainy sorts of geoengineering, and material science innovations, all the way to degrowth and other sorts of radical political economy—it will take to get any grip at all on our acceleratingly catastrophic planetary trajectory.[2] Rather, the focus here is on how we might become peoples who can, in the very world that has formed us badly, collaboratively begin designing better next worlds. How we may, for ourselves and other living creatures, align with Gaia now, already, before it all falls apart.

Humanizing well enough to build better worlds after CaCaCo will involve plenty of technological innovation and social experimentation. Books about both abound. The focus here is narrower. Though intimately bound up with those larger questions, I've been trying to figure out how regular people might dispose ourselves differently.

How can we become, moving on from and with panic, peoples of Gaia, the sorts of peoples one would *want* to have shaping new worlds? How can we do that now, in the time of CaCaCo's crumbling?

Ultimately, as I discuss in the closing moments of this chapter and throughout the next, we need to start humanizing before CaCaCo staggers much further into its catabolic (ever-increasingly resource-metabolizing, consumptive into death) collapse. That won't save CaCaCo, but it will create more space for different *next*s.

The panicky wisdom with which this book is concerned, panic at the end of an inhumane world that is collapsing, should serve as inducement to humanizing.

SOLIDARITIES

Panic can get us to collectivity, as its etymology suggests, but not all collectivities are created equal.

Most of what's worst in human history, including CaCaCo's massified black hole of resource consumption itself, has been collective.[3] From the suprarational orderliness of the Nazi death machine—as Hannah Arendt put it, Nazi officials "prided themselves on belonging to a movement, as distinguished from a party, and a movement could not be bound by a program"[4]—to the crowd surging over itself and trampling its members at the gates of a soccer stadium, to the righteous pile-on of a digital mob that emerges with miasmic unconscious force, and back to those dystopian rows of burnt or moldering cars stretched to the horizon on an abandoned freeway, collectivity has plenty of ways of going wrong. And plenty of those involve panic.

But collectivity also goes right. In the Attic cults of Pan, there is a fierce, wildly musical love for the very nature that has been denatured by the Athenian *polis*. In the labor unions that gave us child labor laws and the weekend, for whom "an injury to one is an injury to all," we find a classic example of collectivity going right. The way of being and feeling that motivates such collectives and gets practiced in them is solidarity.

In their striking introduction to *Solidarity: The Past, Present, and Future of a World-Changing Idea*, Leah Hunt-Hendrix and Astra Taylor highlight that solidarity is nothing without practice and risk. It starts with "conceiving of ourselves as intrinsically bound in relations of mutuality and care that span generations" and, through this expansion of our senses of self-interest, ends in taking strategic risks together, "creat[ing] new communities across social distinctions, class divides, and militarized borders."[5] We imagine ourselves differently, more deeply related to one another, than we have in the past. This imagining sponsors new forms of action, of community. We become willing to take risks together by dint of relations we may not have recognized before. New possibilities arise.

If we are to do anything but shuffle along for extended decades of climate genocide and social unraveling, we will have to discover rather a lot of solidarity, rather quickly.

So, what is solidarity, exactly? Better to ask what it's for. Solidarity is about connecting, in imagination and action alike, with others we are not supposed to be connected to—in projects of shared liberation or creative possibility.

When we act in fellow feeling with others, near or far, in order to transform deathly structures of life, we exercise the sort of solidarity I mean here. Solidarity habitually starts with a panicked sense of how bad things are, but it does not end there.[6] You go to a union meeting because work conditions are damaging your body and spirit. You don't know what to do about it. Together with coworkers, including some people you don't usually get along with or maybe even like, you invent new possibilities.

The whole point of solidarity is to open up new routes of possibility. In *Seeing Like an Activist*, political theorist Erin Pineda presents this in terms of "*imaginative transit*—the process of thinking and traveling across boundaries and disparate contexts."[7] Solidarity is how we connect with others we *aren't supposed to be connected with* in this world, in the service of designing new worlds. It's a medium for making new possibilities exactly there, at the panicked, angry, hurt, helpless sites of being-harmed by the structure of a world.

The world I'm talking about through this book is that of CaCaCo writ large. It's deadly, and it's also falling apart.

Pineda's drilled down into a substratum of resistance to CaCaCo's business-as-usual that most everyone recognizes as a key period of solidarity.[8] She studies transnational civil disobedience in the latter part of the 20th century, and especially the U.S. civil rights movement, as a deeper form of imaginative transit than many realize.

Looking at how activists in the United States "linked their dissent to that of anticolonial activists and tied the context of Jim Crow to a wider world of global white supremacy,"[9] Pineda opens up a new way of understanding civil rights. Civil rights themselves are globally communal; they necessarily transcend borders.

It's common to think of the civil rights movement in the United States without much reference to people acting to change the rest of the world, however. At most, Americans may think about connections to domestic Cold War politics, the wars in Korea and Vietnam, or more occasionally, global communism. What Pineda shows is that civil rights activists explicitly and self-consciously worked to dismantle white supremacist social structures in the U.S. by learning from anticolonial activists abroad.

Solidarity, in this view, is inventive action that moves across CaCaCo's rigid national and racial boundaries. It is what Latour's people of Gaia do that others do not.

Solidarity is a way of cashing out in practice, in moments of learning and working together, Stengers' sense of political struggle as collective self-making along new lines. As such, this is a disposition toward *making new worlds possible*. It is a refusal to think and act as though the way the world has been carved up thus far is natural, necessary, or even entirely real. This includes holding space for one another, maintaining a sense that *we* could yet be other than we have been thus far. Hunt-Hendrix and Taylor put a key implication nicely: "Solidarity means not writing anyone off completely, not throwing anyone away."[10] In ongoing, volitional processes, we can decide again and again to be a *we* that doesn't exist yet. This is a disposition we can practice.

Solidarity is imaginative transit across real boundaries that makes new possibilities exist. It is a simultaneously imaginary and real sharedness that allows people to build new horizons.

The world has seemed to be one sort of way, indeed, *has been that way*. Its constraints have been our own, its limits imprisoning any "we" that could speak and make its presence felt. And then, something changes. We change. New worlds become sensible through attunement to the world-making that others, maybe people far away, are doing in response to constraints much like our own.

Think of the keywords of civil rights rhetoric. As Pineda notes, "when SNCC Chairman John Lewis spoke about the 'serious revolution' being waged in the South in his own March on Washington speech, he stepped beyond domestic borders to frame the fight for enfranchisement and human rights here at home in terms borrowed from South Africa."[11] What did Lewis urge? "'One man, one vote' is the African cry. It is ours too. It must be ours."[12] In practices of solidarity, we allow ourselves to be shaped by the struggles of others. We reimagine what is possible for us, here, based on what someone else has done, over there. Not only that, but we *become* this reimagined new "we," transcending old boundaries.

"One man, one vote" is today, for most Americans, one of the slogans most closely identified with the civil rights movement. The civil rights movement (partial though its achievement was, in the end) was a large-scale practice of solidarity—not only between Black Americans, or between Black and white Americans, or between Americans of all races, but between Americans and South Africans, Ghanaians and Americans, peoples seeking civil rights and resisting the deadly white supremacism of CaCaCo logics the world over. These are the peoples of Gaia, or at least a basis for becoming such.

But solidarity's unification across difference should not be taken for the erasure of difference. To the contrary, as political philosopher Nathan Rochelle DuFord argues, "solidarity functions in its most democratic way when it is open to conflict."[13] Imaginative transit that binds us with those we are not supposed to relate to only works, only actually binds, if it's for real. Conflict is an essential element of being for real.[14]

We will habitually fail to find consensus. We will disagree, at times strenuously and painfully and about very important things.

What solidarity asks of us is not that we achieve unicity of vision or even action, but rather that we engage in processes of imaginative transit. We have to remain willing, workingly willing, to connect with people we are not supposed to be connected to, take strategic risks together on behalf of new social imaginaries.

This starts with taking seriously real failures of our social order. It starts with panicking enough to feel how very much we need each other. Solidarity is "a way to build society in its wreckage."[15] It is a disposition we pick up after we have met and walked a while with panic at CaCaCo's inability to reform itself (in time).

Solidarity is co-participation with people we cannot wholly agree with in the national movements for racial justice that animate both Pineda's and DuFord's accounts. Equally, though, it begins with smaller acts.

We can come together with neighbors we do not like to begin building a local power grid or wireless communication mesh, for instance, seeking shared freedom from some of CaCaCo's deadlier entanglements and ever more fraught failure points. This may begin simply with stepping outside the next time the power goes out. "You okay over there? Any idea what happened? Need anything?"

Whether in an immediate location or across vast distances, solidarity is imaginative transit toward relation with those from whom we might suppose ourselves cut off. Quite at odds with the algorithmic dispositions that hold so much of our attention in digital space, where we fixate on irreconcilable differences and enmities, we develop the disposition toward solidarity in recognizing shared vulnerabilities to a touchy living world. Where Gaia is, you are, too. And me as well. We are here.

Through solidarity, other worlds become possible, as member organizations of the World Social Forum have been trying to tell us for the last two decades and more.[16]

And yet, as suggested already, CaCaCo excludes from power or incorporates into itself every attempt at reform. The tools of this world cannot readily be turned to construction of the next.

And so, more than nearly any other disposition, each new moment of solidarity produces experiences of failure. Often, the sensibility of failure comes—incorrectly—to shape our later assessment of solidarity's effects. We can see that our great moments of solidarity have come to dust in the end, and though the thrill of living together with others in the direction of another world remade us, we evaluate the movements and masses and moments in which we've participated as having failed. This is a cognitive error.

Solidarity doesn't remake the world directly. It makes making other worlds possible.

As I finish writing this book, the Writers' Guild of America has begun an open-ended strike. Across film, television, and related creative media, writers are withholding their labor for the common good.

Those making a relative fortune and those barely scraping by alike have heeded the call—"Pencils Down!"—from Brooklyn, NY to Burbank, CA. Against the efforts of some of the wealthiest corporations in the world to separate writers in the East from those in the West, or the writers' rooms of late-night television from screenwriters on big-budget blockbusters or indie flicks, members of the union announced, "All of us, or none of us."

The companies responded: "Very well, then—none of you." A key point of contention in all this was the role of generative AI in entertainment.[17]

The writers asked for guarantees that AI use on projects covered by any bargaining agreement would be clearly regulated. They wanted assurances that AI wouldn't be used to write or rewrite literary material, wouldn't be treated as source material in its own right. The entertainment corporations countered by offering annual meetings to discuss advances in technology. Countered, in other words, with less than nothing.

Will Amazon, Netflix and Hulu be allowed to outsource symbol production to OpenAI, Anthropic, and Google? Are they doing so already as you read this book? What role will there be for writers, actual human beings who write, in the "writers' rooms" of the very near future? How will you be disposed if the writers lose their strike?

Picketing the offices of massive entertainment platforms like Amazon and Netflix, WGA workers seek solidarity from passersby and the world at large. They ask those who write or engage with what's been written, anywhere, in any capacity, to recognize a site of shared political struggle. What world, they ask us, do you want to live in? As symbol-makers? As consumers of symbols?

Do we not *want* to live in a world of human stories in all their humanness, or is the good-enough intellection production of AI really good enough, no matter how it disposes (of) us? WGA East member-negotiator Greg Iwinski expresses the concern with generative AI, which is germane both in what it means for anyone else who produces symbols for a living and what it means for all of us who consume others' symbol production: "The threat of us being replaced is not that [AI is] going to match our quality. It's going to be that our bosses aren't going to care."[18]

As you read these words, the WGA has long since won or lost its strike. Most likely, the strike secured higher pay and better working conditions. Equally likely, it failed to preclude some uses of generative AI to replace human writers. Perhaps in the end it assured these creative industries, at least, of finer human oversight of machinic writing. Or perhaps not even that. The solidarity of collective action's worldmaking, regardless of any concrete experiences of failure to change the world along the way, is lasting.

For years to come, around the world, ever more of us will find ourselves asking, "What symbolic production must remain human? Why?" When we ask these questions, that we still *can* ask these questions will be due in part to the processes of solidarity lived out by the striking writers of the WGA.

Solidarity puts us into question, and it opens onto uncertain horizons. This is its charm and its risk.

There is no guarantee that practices of solidarity will pay off. When I step onto the porch and call out to my neighbors in the darkened night, perhaps there will be no reply. My coworkers may not want to organize with me. Many fights, good and noble fights, we will lose.

At stake is an open-ended kind of exposure, an orientation toward being-together that rhetorician Diane Davis calls "inessential solidarity" and Yves Citton calls *"sharing our incompleteness."*[19] For Davis, inessential solidarity names the way that being somebody at all is, from the start or even before the start, about being-with and being-for other somebodies. We are for-others. They, in turn, are for-us and for-one-another.

Solidarity is inessential, it has no essence. And yet it is the basis of every human (and more-than-human) experience. That I am anyone at all is only in response to your call, there in the impossibly dark night. Solidarity is the groundless fundament of all somebodiness, the relational character of being itself.

At the same time, solidarity is also a specific disposition we can take up and consciously practice. Indeed, to get in touch with the sort of creature that we are, we must actively pursue imaginative transit across borders. And yet, practicing solidarity is a hard choice to make.

There really is no way of knowing that even conscious commitments to one another, acts and avowals of solidarity, will go anywhere at all. As Davis puts this, the decision to solidaristically aim for justice "would necessarily take place as a tentative gesture, offering itself without clarity or certitude, both as a test and an invitation."[20] No promises, just possibilities that may or may not even be possible. Seen thus, solidarity is about choosing to be together with unexpected others in zones of risk, seeing who *we* might yet become there.

And what could induce us to take such a risk, to extend this tentative and uncertain gesture? What can motivate our imaginative transit across boundaries? What better than panic, felt and held close, at the end of some world.

A pressing question, then, for anyone who has begun to panic (wisely) at the polycrisis is what new solidarities to invite. With whom are you more closely connected than you might have thought? What strangers' struggles, as you look around the world right now, may in fact be your very own?

DISRUPTIONS

At the level of effects, "even for wealthy countries," the climate crisis ought to be our surest source of solidarity. Once it's in the air, that carbon is weirding *everybody's* globe. Indeed, as bad as things already are, we've barely begun to be disrupted—even by the heating associated with previously emitted greenhouse gases, much less those to come as we continue failing to end CaCaCo early.[21]

There is no "outside" to the disruptions of this crisis that is even more fully planetary than were the world wars of the twentieth century.[22] We're all going to be experiencing some pretty awful consequences in the near future, including a lot of people who don't yet believe they will. From fire and flood to pandemics and crop failures, not only the global south but also most of CaCaCo's historical beneficiaries in the global north are in for uncertainty and suffering and radical social disruption. Not just in 2050 or 2100, but kinda more now.[23]

So, the climate crisis should induce solidarity. Instead, though, its disruptions serve most easily as new sites for fostering discord. Discord and hard friend-enemy distinctions, in place of solidarity's imaginative transit, are set to allow CaCaCo's biggest beneficiaries to wring a few more years of "as usual" out of "business."

One of the clearer ways CaCaCo's unraveling has already begun is in terms of mass displacement. But, even when we say it, we mostly don't quite know it.

In the current order of the world, migration is hard to grasp as *we-making*, even when (like now) it should be pretty easy to see as *everyone's shared concern*. People tend to apprehend migrants as "outside" wherever they are, trying to get "in." From outsider to enemy is a pretty short imaginative step, and one autocrats and oligarchs are good at disposing people toward taking. In response, many well-meaning people declare their personal support for migrants even as their more friendly-voiced political avatars pursue roughly the same border policies as the more outwardly vicious strongmen.[24]

The reality is that there's no way for mass displacement to *not* be disruptive. This is something most people will have to reckon with, sooner rather than later, whether they remain where they are or become part of a vast new swathe of humanity on the move.

Most of us are just not that good at recognizing scale, though. So, we miss that when millions more people than usual are on the move (i.e., right now), something bigger still must be afoot. Because millions is only the beginning. It's no exaggeration to say the coming century is likely to see billions of people driven out of lost zones of habitability as the earth's atmosphere continues superheating.[25] Again, that's starting now (or, more accurately, a few years ago), not later.

Part of why it's tough for people to recognize mass migration as a unifying force, and why it's easy for strongmen to seize on this disruption to deepen friend-enemy thinking instead of solidarity, is that CaCaCo's world is already a pretty difficult place to move around in.

For the majority of human history, people's movement mostly depended on resource constraints rather than organized systems of violence. Sure, there were wars and revolutions and new religions and all the rest to determine how a given stretch of land and society would be organized, but a lot of the time when people didn't like a form of social organization, or their crops failed, or a volcano erupted, or they deforested a region and hunting suffered, they just went elsewhere. For many thousands of years, you could get a whole new world without especially having to fight over the old one (though there seems to have been plenty of that as well).[26]

A globally integrated system for *preventing* people from moving around freely has been a CaCaCo achievement. It's hard today to envision truly mass migration because our very sense of "normal" rests on the overwhelming majority of people around the world not being able to move freely.

And yet, except for these last couple hundred years of CaCaCo stuckness, and in a few longstanding (usually imperial) systems that popped up elsewhere in history, most of global humanity had neither ultra-complex, highly integrated social-material worlds nor the intense fear of disrupting these, of throwing them off kilter. Most of the time before now, when people didn't like where they were, they went somewhere else. Most of the time, nobody stopped them.

That doesn't mean nobody ever tried to control the flow of people between places, of course. People have been trying to stop each other from moving around for millennia (often, small groups of people trying to stop everybody else nearby).[27] But today's global humanity, organized into rigidly defined peoples in map-lined places, CaCaCo humans who cannot go other places without permission from multiple authorities, takes that to a whole 'nother level.

That's largely but not *entirely* an ill-starred feature of CaCaCo.

Migration, especially mass migration away from settled ecological niches, really is disruptive for everybody in a world as densely populated as our own. Indeed, everywhere humans have ever gone, we've disrupted ecological niches. In that, we're like any other species moving around.

But for the majority of human history, there weren't that many of us. Outside of a few large empires, disruption was more frequently something humans did by arriving somewhere new or leaving somewhere old than something that *happened to* long-lasting, socially complex sites of civilization when others arrived. For many pre-CaCaCo polities, the political consequences of people leaving were clearer than those of people arriving, and the notion that people "vote with their feet" still has an almost mythic force when we think about human social organization. Though less true than it once was, that idea enjoys a rich afterlife in political science literatures on exit, voice, and loyalty as ways of navigating deep disagreements.[28]

And yet, few people today *can* vote with their feet. On the one hand, the world sees more migration than ever before (281 million people, or about 3.6% of the human population, lived in 2022 outside their countries of birth).[29] On the other hand, each of these people requires permission—sometimes from a whole host of different entities—to move around. And that's not always only a bad thing (though it most often is).

The complexity of human movement became clear in a hurry to people from CaCaCo beneficiary countries during the covid-19 pandemic, when much of the world closed borders. It has always been clear to anyone born in a CaCaCo extractee country who does not travel by private jet.

Your birthplace's location in CaCaCo's global hierarchy of humanness determines the comparative valuation of the "people" you belong to. This, in turn, determines the value of your passport and the difficulty with which movement, especially the long-term migration of "exit," will be possible for you. A world of rigid, militarized borders is a world in which you can only sort of leave wherever you start from. Or, you can leave, but you can't necessarily go anywhere else.[30]

Throughout the CaCaCo centuries, reaching a fever pitch by the end of the twentieth and beginning of the twenty-first, ever more of the world's spaces have gotten organized by stasis, fixity.[31] You belong somewhere. You are not welcome somewhere else.

If you're a regular person today, you can't just go wherever you want (especially but not only if you hold a global south passport). Going wherever they want is for the extremely wealthy, to whom borders only occasionally apply.[32] By 2023, it had become virtually impossible—both intensely dangerous and logistically baffling—for most people in most parts of the world to travel across more than two national borders. In such a context, truly mass migration between countries and regions of the globe is hard for most people to wrap their heads around.

And yet, it is in fact happening. People are fleeing places in ever-greater numbers. In 2022, in Mexico alone over 444,000 migrants were detained as they headed north through the country.[33] In 2023, U.S. Border Patrol was filling unofficial refugee camps just inside the southern U.S. border with people from all over the world.[34] People are in fact *trying* to exit, are desperate to vote with their feet. CaCaCo, however, responds to such efforts with violence.

As the climate emergency renders ever more highly populated places inhospitable or outright uninhabitable, the simple fact is that mass displacement is on the menu. You can only degrade densely settled ecological niches but so much before their inhabitants leave. And notwithstanding creepily racist fear-mongering about migration patterns already, there's no denying that it *does disrupt things* when large bodies of people move on their own recognizance across and between administrative, organizational lines.

The question is how to sustain disruption.

CaCaCo's mapped out an unjust world of relatively settled borders—literally defined along old colonial lines, from the treaty-designated reservations of Indian Country in the United States to East African civil wars that trace justification for territorial sovereignty back to just a few years of Italian colonization. This world, where those in the global south are more immediately subject to the climate crisis's ravages than CaCaCo beneficiaries in the global north, has always been deeply unjust. Now, it is no longer stable.

(Also, it was never stable. But now that's more obvious.)

As anyone who's lived in a smallish city that suddenly became popular can tell you, scale changes things. People can move around faster than anybody is willing to or knows how to or even *can* build infrastructure for. The place you know was one thing, then it got hot, and now you can't afford to rent your same apartment, traffic's a disaster, and the coolest forest trails are all chock full of nuts. This is small-scale migration.

As the climate crisis renders ever more portions of the globe uninhabitable and, long before uninhabitable, dangerous and unpromising, ever more people will be on the move. Some will be desperately broke, others dripping with wealth.

To get at just how disruptive all that will be without giving fuel to the fever dreams of ethnonationalists is hard. So, think for the moment only in intra-national terms, as climate migration *within* U.S. national borders.

As Jake Bittle details in *The Great Displacement*, the coming decades will see millions of Americans permanently leaving the places they come from.[35] In parts of the country, like the increasingly fiery mountain west where I live or the Gulf and southeastern Atlantic coasts that will see a foot of sea-level rise (or more) in just the next 25 years or so, many smaller towns will empty. Burned or flooded out, blown away like arable topsoil in the Midwest, or crowded out by coughing, sneezing hordes in the densely populated BosWash corridor during the next pandemic, or maybe fleeing chemical spills in Ohio or Indiana, millions of people in the United States are going to be looking for somewhere else to go—permanently—in the near future.

Some will be displaced before disaster hits them, most after. CaCaCo is exceedingly unlikely to pony up the trillions it would cost to accomplish geographic climate adaptation in a humane and orderly way. Moreover,

"Even with an adaptation initiative of adequate scale [which we won't get], it will be impossible to save every place. There will be coastal bayou towns that will wash away, small riverside villages that succumb to the current, beautiful mountain towns like Paradise that will burn in raging wildfires. . . . No amount of political intervention and investment can stop that from happening, and thus for many Americans climate change will look like letting go of their old ideas of home."[36]

One supposes, contra the city-dwelling Bittle's assumptions, that it won't just be small towns in visibly risky locations either.

How long, and for how many people, can Miami remain habitable? How about the greater Washington, D.C. bog? What happens when a truly big hurricane hits New York and New Jersey, a super-super-Sandy? Who wants to stay in Oklahoma City or Omaha during the new dustbowl, with unsurvivable wet-bulb temperatures in summer to boot? And that's just the loss and leaving side of the equation.

The question Bittle barely touches, because it is a question no one can answer yet in much detail, is where all those Americans who have surrendered their old ideas of home—who may easily be you or I—will go. And what will happen when we get there.

How, for instance, will machine learning and ubiquitous surveillance be used to keep us where we're put, in the refugee camps of the future? What roles will there be for us in a world where much of the intellection production we'd bring to the table has already been automated? Who needs us, when we get to wherever we end up?

This is the sort of disruption we have to learn to sustain. Regardless of whether you're on the move or able to stay put, failing to sustain displacement's disruption will put a rapid end to the project, however unrealized thus far, of global humanity.[37]

Short-sighted people can close ranks pretty fast against outsiders once they feel stability threatened. Still worse, paradoxically, when stability is not just threatened but virtually certain to be lost. People fearing for their capacity to metabolize resources in habituated ways are all too often on the lookout for someone who will promise to name an enemy and protect them from change.

But the scale of disruption—from the climate catastrophe alone, to say nothing of the rest of the polycrisis—will make ranks-closing and wall-building either meaningless or else genocidal (or, more likely, both). What can you do now to avert the genocidal, or at least to refuse it in the places where you live?

Learn to sustain disruption.

It's easy to suppose oneself a decent person, empathetic to those in need, but how far will that carry you when a destitute forest-dwelling person lights the fire that nearly burns down your city, kills countless of your forest kin? Will you remember the decades of divestment in public infrastructure that put him, a fellow person, down and out on a dirt road that happened to be near you? Will you take it upon yourself to ride or drive forest service roads looking for illegal fires? And then what? What *should* you do? How *can* you sustain such disruption when it's not a few dozen people making do back there in the woods, but a thousand or ten thousand?

And you who live in the "smart" supercity, are you any better? Will you not cluck when my home burns, wonder why *those people* choose to live *there*? Do you not already, as though you didn't know that the world has never been an infinite free play of choices? How will you react when I and all my neighbors move to your neighborhood, piling in ten families to a storefront? How will you feel about implementing AI tools that police us (and dehumanize us) effectively enough to keep even awareness of our presence from your doorstep?

Even a very small emotional disruption, like mourning our Anthropocene through solidarity with the (human and nonhuman) people most immediately affected by it so far, can be difficult to sustain. How much harder when all of us come to join you where you are?

It is, as art-punk band The Mekons put it nearly forty years ago, hard to be human—and increasingly so.

And but let's be clear: there's no amount of humanizing that can avert CaCaCo's staggered collapse. Keep in mind, after all, that I'm talking right now just about the climate crisis and one of its many outcomes (mass displacement), not the rest of its outcomes and not the rest of the polycrisis.

Still, sustaining disruption is a wise bet on doing something that maintains decency in places of panic. This starts with keeping honest track of what's actually happening, while it's happening. But this is hard.

Anthropologist Michael Taussig describes evocatively the real difficulty of not losing track of our own wise panic in the ever-renewed flow of nor-malcy. Discussing the lead-up to and then aftermath of 2011's Hurricane Irene in New York, he writes, "Each day people are more skittish; another pulse is beating, yet within a couple of months nobody remembers."[38] The stakes are high. Let's hope we don't forget them, don't further normalize the already abominable as it careers into a moral abyss.

For anyone who doesn't want to end up surprised and horrified to find themselves signing up a little down the road to support local autocrats with big plans for keeping their corners of paradise clear of undesirables, the time to practice sustaining disruption is now.

But we can't really *sustain* disruption unless we stay a while, as in chapter two, with the extremity of the polycrisis we are in. And that starts with panic.

For a certain frame of mind, it is tempting to think that solving big problems like the climate crisis can and should be an orderly, incremental process. You put your shoulder to the wheel, move it a little way. The next person comes along and does their part, too. It's not glamorous, but it's effective. Given time and consistent commitment, you can move the very world on its axis.

You take the carbon emissions problem, and you address it in this box over here. Next to it is another box for methane emissions, and another beside it for nitrous oxide. All those greenhouse gas boxes go in one big box, and then you've got another for "transforming the physical economy." That one gets stacked on top of "a just energy transition," which somehow always gets left at the bottom. Once you've got those problems in those boxes, you take the climate displacement or mass migration problem and you address it in that box over there. But now you've got to run out and get more boxes. Because, as chapter two indicated, this batch doesn't even set you up to make real headway on the climate emergency alone. And there's a whole polycrisis beyond that.

In our catastrophic age or period of polycrisis, both time and consistent commitment to work on melioristic reform are and will continue to be lacking. More generally, there's little reason to believe that incremental change has an arc—now! suddenly! after not doing for decades!—that runs to solutions for our accumulating and interweaving catastrophes.

Nobody has a theory of change that will help CaCaCo save itself from what CaCaCo costs. There's a lot of disruption of business as usual baked into the structure of business as usual, and not in the "creative destruc-tion" sense capitalists like.[39] More just in the destructive destruction sense of too many people on the move.

To add oil to that fire, there is no one crisis that cannot (as suggested by the entwining of four—and merely four!—in this book) both domino into and be superseded in our attention by another. Each crisis impacts the next, and is eclipsed by it in our (pretty meager in the first place) processes of political will formation.

So, defenders of incremental progress may have been right about some prior stage of world history (that's a question for historians), but they can get no purchase on the polycrisis. Patient work at a single issue, cashed out over decades, will avail us little now.

There is no issue (not carbon emissions, not novel chemicals, not the eradication of wildlife, not even automated intellection) that has time for incrementalism. There's going to be a lot of disruption to pay.

The question becomes, then, "What disruptions can we sustain?" And, equally, "How can we become people who sustain disruptions equanimously?" As the CaCaCo world's deathly order is disrupted ever more, by both its own deferred costs and people hoping to change it by, say, blowing up pipelines, what dispositions allow us to resist the coming barbarism? How can we sustain mass displacement *also* when we are immediately threatened by it (or are the threats to one another)?

Sustaining disruption is, at heart, about seeding possibility for something other to both the barbarism of continuity and the barbarism of acceleration. This is different than common invocations of resilience.[40] It is a disposition that makes new things possible, if not now then later, by holding a kind of loving space for the end of a CaCaCo world.

If the end of a world is panickable (it is), the alternative—totalitarian efforts to force continuity or wild and dangerous bets on accelerating collapse—are more terrifying still. Some of those alternatives look at first blush, though, like the very thing I'm talking about.

A corporate HR emphasis on developing resilience, for instance, encourages us to become the sorts of people who sustain disruptions to the norm.[41] But here, a return to the norm is assumed. We move fluidly into online meeting spaces, for instance, when a pandemic makes face-to-face communication intrinsically hostile, threatening. As viral loads decrease, or the sun comes out, or most of those who were going to die do, or our leaders agree that the economy needs us out and about, we return to usual habits. We get back to normal. We have "bounced back." We were "resilient."

But to what norm, what habits, what world?

Resilience in popular culture (trauma psychologists tend to mean something different by the word) assumes large-scale social continuity. It is something you or I practice, an individual way we respond to troubling events or moments. When the world itself is collapsing, though, resilience is the wrong framework.[42]

Sustaining disruption is both a psychic and a practical stance. It's not a bad idea to plant a garden, pursue better relations with one's neighbors, even install grid-free solar power for those who can afford it (or pursue a solar collective with others who live nearby). All these can help a person sustain disruptions in a more than momentary sort of way. You'll be able to keep food and medications cold if the power goes out for weeks or months, for instance.

Still more, though, what staves off the coming barbarism is our attitudes to disruption, identifications with it even. We can practice accepting the ways in which disruptions will be more and more ubiquitous in coming years.

Mass displacement, for only a single instance, will change everything about CaCaCo's normal. Whether you're leaving or receiving, it'll be the end of a world.[43] With practice, though, we can learn to sustain such disruptions.

I'm drawing on two competing senses of the word "sustain" here.

On the one hand, to sustain something is to tolerate it, bear it, survive it. We sustain injuries, are bloodied but not broken. On the other hand, something sustained has been given sustenance, preserved, lent duration in the world. Sustained power outages might go on for weeks, even months. Climate displacement is a decades-long process that has barely begun, and yet already overwhelms infrastructures for both intra- and international migration. How will we sustain that? How will we sustain ourselves as these subcrises of the climate emergency unfold over time? What "we" will be given sustenance, by what local and communal dispositions?

These are questions for CaCaCo's process of staggered collapse, questions that need answers before their time arrives, questions a person can come to through panic's practical wisdom.

As such, they are intimately connected to the more intentional sorts of disruption suggested by Andreas Malm in *How to Blow Up a Pipeline*.[44] Malm's title isn't just a provocation. It's a serious suggestion. Given that an enormous amount of policing technology is already being poured into trying to prevent even relatively minor activist disruptions,[45] it's worth staying with Malm to think about how to *sustain* disruptions instead.

CaCaCo's staggered collapse hinges on the continuities enabled—and then, disabled—by carbon-burning.

When Bill Gates, Anderson Cooper, and self-described "decarb bros" imagine decarbonizing, they think about transforming the physical economy. That is to say, they assume the continuity of other social (and physical) structures associated with capitalism and colonialism. They take for granted, in other words, that you can pull the carbon out and they will still be kings. CaCaCo can become CaCo + renewables.

As chapter one highlighted, this is a wildly unrealistic assumption, both physically and in political economic terms.[46] Not only do we not actually know *how* to decarbonize while sustaining most of the world's population or *whether* this is in fact technologically feasible, but there's little reason to believe doing so can happen fast enough and justly enough to halt the self-accelerating global system collapse processes currently underway. It's just not profitable, not well-aligned with the short-term imperative of returns on capital speculation. You can't unwind a tensioned spring.

And yet, it's absolutely true that we do need somehow to get off carbon. Moreover, lots of people are working on ways of doing so. It's just that CaCaCo's self-appointed best and brightest aren't leading the way. Or when they *are* leading the way, as Malm puts it,

"The commitment to the endless accumulation of capital wins out every time. After the past three decades there can be no doubt that the ruling classes are constitutionally incapable of responding to the catastrophe in any other way than by expediting it; of their own accord, under their inner compulsion, they can do nothing but burn their way to the end."[47]

Malm's aim is to help people see ways of accelerating the process of CaCaCo's self-destruction—before solutions for maintaining CaCaCo get worked out, both because they *never will be* and because they *shouldn't be*.[48]

So, when Malm asks, "When do we start physically attacking the things that consume our planet and destroy them with our own hands? Is there a good reason we have waited this long?"[49] there's no despair implied. But he does mean that we need dispositions other than hope and resilience.

Malm urges people to consider accelerating the collapse of the physical infrastructure for carbon-burning, in the hope that doing so will provide an impetus for truly transformative change (in time to avoid the very worst).

A complementary orientation, starting with panic, leans toward sustaining disruptions. To sustain disruptions of the sort Malm champions is not necessarily ourselves to cause them (though that's his primary emphasis, it's not mine). Rather, it is also to frame them in a spirit of solidarity.

For example: If activists sabotage a natural gas pipeline, how will I heat my house in the extreme winter cold induced by global weirding while also holding fast to my understanding that they may, in fact, have been right to do so? How will I reject, accepting with equanimity this disruption of my rhythms of comfort, the intensified policing and surveillance that are fascism's handmaidens at such moments?

How will you sustain the disruption to your motion when Extinction Rebellion protesters block the freeway? You're just trying to get to work, aren't you? Can't they find some other place or way to protest? Why are they disrupting *your* life?

But won't your life be far more disrupted when that freeway is washed away by floods, or when it empties out forever? Perhaps those activists are onto something? If they can "Just Stop Oil," even a little bit, mightn't we *all* have more less awful choices about how to live just a few years from now? Aren't you better served by their disruptions than by those Bill Gates and the decarb bros and AI mavens will serve up for you, replete with autorenewable subscription charges in automatically increasing increments, as the polycrisis deepens? Perhaps the one can forestall some of the other?

Probably not. But we who are not ourselves ready to blow up a pipeline must align, becoming together the peoples of Gaia, with those who are.

The people Malm's book calls upon are not only those who *will* blow up pipelines. Equally, his book is for an audience who would be receptive to that disruption, would recognize the disruption's value in making the present—wholly unviable, necrotic, genocidal—order of the norm impossible.

This is especially clear when Malm urges against fatalism. Against despair, and with utter realism about the damage already done, he writes, "the movement knows that it faces a giant salvaging operation: safeguarding as much space as possible on this scarred planet for human life to survive and maybe thrive and, in the best case, healing some of the wounds from the past centuries."[50] These are the stakes he asks us to keep in mind, both those who blow up a pipeline and those of us who learn to sustain such disruption.

I am not myself willing to assassinate an Exxon executive or a Nestlé board member, and I can't and don't countenance murder. But I understand how someone would get even to there as the systems of violence that undergird "normalcy" get mobilized against ever more of those who were "normal people" before. The reorganizations of violence to come will take stochastic turns; their contours are for now still unclear. That they will come is not.[51] And so I am prepared to weather subsequent fluctuations in the price of gas, both logistically (because I panicked early and sought means of transportation and mutual aid to avoid being wholly stranded in what is, after all, a certain future of oil and gas price shocks) and morally or conceptually. The murder distresses me, but I see a way to "temporize the essence," to place it in proper worldly context even as I do not affirm it.[52] Indeed, not only do I not affirm it, but I feel strongly that there is *no world* in which such violence is morally justified without remainder.[53]

And yet, the oil executive and water privatization company board member are themselves blowing up this world.

The disruption of "normal" that is the rest of our lives now, the radical change that is climate genocide and untold suffering and mass displacement, is *their preferred* disruption. The radical who assassinates them hopes to change all of our preferences. Which of these disruptions can I better sustain without losing my capacity for humanity?

If I can sustain these disruptions, perhaps I will not be as receptive when my neighbors come to demonize people from Phoenix fleeing an extended power outage in a heatwave. Perhaps I will temporize the essence, too, when my home is threatened by the fires of the homeless. Here comes everybody.

It's only a matter of time before it's you and I on the move as well.

There will be no humanizing in the world coming already into being for a person, for peoples however local or small, who cannot sustain disruption. Our challenge is to become such peoples.

NOVELTIES

One nice way to think about preparing to sustain disruptions is through the lens of "community defense." Community defense sounds martial, and it can be,[54] but that's not the essence of it. A lot of community defense is more about novel social forms.[55]

Take a group like Jackson, MS-based Cooperation Jackson.[56]

Cooperation Jackson is a local movement, a network of worker cooperatives and a community land trust in and around Jackson, Mississippi. The group's aim is to build a "solidarity economy" that radically reorganizes everything from supply chains to farming practices to collective self-determination.[57] But it's not just that. Cooperation Jackson is about preparing the concrete possibility of another world. It is "a vehicle specifically created" to "advance the struggle for economic democracy as a prelude towards the democratic transition to eco-socialism."[58] There's a long-arc vision here.

Cooperation Jackson's got all sorts of concrete projects going on, with a particular focus on worker-owned businesses and permaculture farming.[59] But it's worth staying a moment with the intermediate-range vision that moves, through community defense applied to the shaping of state and local policy, toward the longer arc. As organizer Kali Akuno puts it, Cooperation Jackson is working to "develop a new transformative culture":

"In order to reinforce the development of this new culture within the present confines of Mississippi and the overall capitalist world-system, we have to harness the power of the Black working class and utilize it politically to eliminate the structural barriers blocking the 'legal' development of the solidarity economy . . . One of the main things we have to eliminate are the Mississippi legal statutes that presently restrict cooperatives to farming, businesses, utilities, and credit unions. We have to create a new legal framework and paradigm that will enable any form of productive endeavor to become a cooperative or solidarity enterprise."[60]

The mid-range goal, in other words, is to tear down legal structures that hinder development of cooperatives (worker-owned businesses) across all sectors of the economy. To do so requires remaking the state from within (a project Cooperation Jackson has undertaken with electoral politics). Their emphasis isn't mostly on the state, though: just enough to clear way for designing alternative futures. This isn't your grandpappy's revolutionary leftism.

Cooperation Jackson orients, on the one hand, toward immediately usable community defense projects and, on the other hand, toward removing elements of the state apparatus that obstruct collaborative development of novel social forms.

A core aspect of Cooperation Jackson's immediately practical work to make a new world possible is collaborating with various local organizations to form cooperative, worker-run businesses of all sorts. It helps Black-run businesses, in a historical stronghold of chattel slavery, in the capitol city of the poorest state in the richest country in the world, to work together on developing a new social order that can be raised up in CaCaCo's coming ruins.

Now, on the one hand, a person might say, "We don't have time for all that!" And they'd be right. But Cooperation Jackson's is the sort of experimentation with novel social forms that works regardless of whether it "works" or not.

That is to say, what Akuno and his collaborators in Cooperation Jackson are working on is a sort of novelty that gains rather than losing value when everything else falls apart. As CaCaCo crumbles, there's going to be a lot of unclarity about what happens next. Not just, and maybe not visibly for a while yet, at the grand scale of nation-states and international agenda-setting cliques like the G7. More at your local level, in your neighborhood. Indeed, in a lot of neighborhoods, "even in the wealthy countries," the world is already ending.

So, the time to experiment with social forms that can build better worlds in the ruins of this one is today. And the right sorts of novelties can help in sustaining disruption as well. But to get there means panicking wisely enough to act now—in ways that aren't already laid out in advance.

When the city of Jackson's extended and ongoing water pollution crisis came to a head in fall of 2022, Cooperation Jackson stepped up. They coordinated with others to make water deliveries to the 160,000+ people struggling without potable water for nearly a month. As importantly, they followed up on the emergency with a new theory and a new practice.

Beginning on the grounds of the Fannie Lou Hamer Community Land Trust that Cooperation Jackson stewards, the group set out to build "community based water catchment, treatment, and delivery systems" that could scale cooperatively across neighborhoods.[61] The plan was to treat their own water system as proof of concept, ultimately creating "a critical mass of these systems at various community centers and to network them to be able to address future water crises."[62] As I write in spring of 2023, they are midstream in scaling the concept. This, changing practice to sustain disruptions and then revising theory and strategy to accommodate the new practices, is what the oft-invoked and rarely defined word *praxis* means. It is a form of practical wisdom.

If it sounds like I'm urging something like prepping when I talk about Cooperation Jackson as a community defense organization, well, I am. Literally, you're reading a book about preparing for collapse. I'm not sure how much clearer I can make it.

But prepping in the way that Cooperation Jackson does looks solidaristic rather than individualistic. Recall by contrast the economist Nouriel Roubini, who in chapter two we saw urging attention to megathreats as a strategy for securing competitive advantage in a period of civilizational failure. That's not the goal here. Rather, like Stengers, Cooperation Jackson invites us to construct novel social and material arrangements to sustain disruption *now* as a way of resisting the coming barbarism.

In a world of diminished resource availability, nothing is deadlier to others—more barbaric—than insisting that one's own resource consumption remain uninterrupted come what may. And yet, even sustaining disruption entails *some* continuity. Novel social forms represent one way of squaring that circle.

The end of one world does not mean that no next world will arise. Too, any world's dying is more process than event. A focus on novel social forms lets us work on building next worlds as CaCaCo's falls to pieces.

But let me acknowledge again, very directly, that there's no averting CaCaCo's worst consequences without an awful lot of technological novelty. Most of whatever's developed won't be implemented swiftly enough to serve most people even in the beneficiary countries, and most will be withheld from a global south that *must* remain disadvantaged to preserve capitalism and colonialism even as the carbon mix shifts. Still, new tech will be part of the picture for ameliorating the fallout from CaCaCo's ongoing failure. Even (perhaps especially) as this deathly system's long-deferred costs eat up its capacity for resource investment in new schemes of the grand variety, there *will* be geoengineering of one sort or another. Probably of the worst sort,[63] but perhaps of wiser sorts, too. There will be new approaches to harvesting "waste" heavy metals from solar-powered desalination. There will be PFAS-eating microbes or lazer treatments and various schemes to pay—and arm—indigenous land stewards safeguarding traditional lands. Some of those will even scale moderately well for a while.

All that, though, is mostly for the rulers of the world to hash out, the big *Is* whose grand tragicomic drama will brook no interruption before ending in blood. We are not them (for now). And their world is ending anyhow.

What can the little *we* of global humanity, still in its plural infancy, do for now? Practicing solidarity and sustaining disruption are crucial, but alone very little. It's all very well to become people who can survive things falling apart, but without some *other* novel trajectory, what's the point? The novelties I'm interested in here, novelties on the far side of panic, concern ways of thinking, feeling, and living available to regular people today, in the places where we are. They are ways of designing possible futures together.

Our question has to be: What new forms of living together can we make right now, which might prepare ground for other sorts of worldmaking in a hotter, darker future?[64]

It's a question that takes shape for each dimension of polycrisis differently. How can we—today—navigate the nexus of an AI revolution that changes the nature of work and meaning-making at the very same time as we live through the dying out of our species-companions across the earth? What social forms could possibly be novel enough to help us make sense of an unprecedented change of climate that reshapes our societies even as new chemicals restructure the webs of life passing through us and constituting our own lives at every level? What should we be aiming for, in our novelties?

I'm deeply skeptical of anyone who claims to have answers in hand to such questions.

And yet, just as the would-be masters of the universe will have their novelties, so too will the rest of us. Of that much, we can be certain. The challenge at hand is one of collaborative invention, in the places where we are.

What remains to be seen, then, is the extent to which tomorrow's novelties will reflect the same deadly old paradigms as yesterday's. Or, less analytically and more responsibly: How do *we* begin designing other futures in the midst of a necrotic and denial-structured present, perhaps at times through the very technologies (both social and material) with which we also seek unsuccessfully to remediate, contain, and transform the long-deferred costs of CaCaCo's past several hundred years?

One way of getting at these questions is through the various novel social forms Cooperation Jackson is building. Their sort of organizing, which is sometimes called prefigurative politics (because it acts out in the present a world that does not yet exist) requires one sort of imaginative transit.

A very different, wholly unnovel, sort of imaginative transit comes when we identify too neatly with CaCaCo's technological innovations. Though a more emotionally satisfying sort of story than the one this book offers, there's (ironically) nothing new at all about listing out all the great new tech coming online. That's a big part of how we usually avoid panicking. For instance, both left-activist and right-apologist books would at this point lay out a few of the big recent inventions that seem truly fabulous, novelties birthed by need (both social and physical technologies). Seeing a growing array of technological possibilities might produce a sensation of wellness, comfort. "Ah! We *are* fixing things!" And yet, that old familiar feeling would be a lie. We are not fixing things, and we will not.[65]

The—open, standing—question for each of us is what parts we can play, in the communities where we are, to design next worlds. By what maieutics might we help in birthing other worlds even as this CaCaCo world around us is dying?

There's no universal answer to that. Without question there will be many smaller, more local novelties we *make amongst ourselves*; there already are.[66] Even as CaCaCo thrashes through years or decades of dying throes, there will arise and deepen spaces between and among us that attune to what might yet happen next.

Some of those spaces will be new social forms, made in committed projects like Cooperation Jackson's. Other novelties will be smaller still.

Take waste. (No, take it.) While the shit company has been driving life on earth out of business, it certainly doesn't follow that its failure will be the end of human waste and wastage. But we can come to see discard in ways that don't foreground waste. CaCaCo relies on "waste" as part of its core logic. Externalities (like chemical waste or PFAS breaking down in the water supply), which turn out to be deferred costs (like involuntary infertility and hormone disruption), are necessary for making this world. But, as we're beginning to realize, what goes around does indeed come around. CaCaCo's many and various deferred costs, in falling due as a polycrisis, are laying waste to the version of normalcy most of us know.[67]

In the future, we'll have to be a lot more careful about how we distance ourselves from what we take to be waste. We can start now.

Max Liboiron and collaborator Josh Lepawsky's *Discard Studies* offers a truly novel vision—of "discarding well" as the basis for radically different social forms than CaCaCo has accustomed us to regard as normal.[68]

Discard is not optional, but it need not be careless. In a sense, the deathliness of our present order is precisely the consequence of not taking seriously what we discard, assuming that whatever we do not keep flows away as waste, an externality. As Liboiron and Lepawsky argue, "for systems to hold together, to subsist and persist, they *must* discard."[69] Our "waste" is never external to us, but intrinsic to who we can become. Flushed away as an externality, it returns as a deferred cost.

Whether understood as externalities or deferred costs, the forces laying waste to a familiar world today are discard effluvia of that very world's construction. Waste encompasses no less the carbon dioxide trapping sun energy at earth's surface, left in the air after we burn carbon fossil fuels, than the skills and training and relations that led to a career as a software developer or writer or graphic artist rendered redundant by a revolution in generative AI. Most evocatively, perhaps, waste is plastic and chemical waste: novel entities slowly breaking down as they pass around and around in the global hydrological cycle, radically reshaping human and other forms of life as they go.

What's wasted doesn't disappear. What's discarded is never gone. The point of discard studies, as a domain of scholarship, is to make novel forms of knowledge about waste—and so to live differently, as and where we are. Maybe I should start composting dog poop in my backyard, use it to feed a couple apple trees?

Instead of asking what's recyclable, for another instance, the discard studies Liboiron and Lepawsky lay out encourage us to think about why *recycling* in particular comes to dominate our thinking about how to waste wisely or discard well.[70] What are the existing infrastructures and social forces that allow us to continue producing, in their example for that question, novel chemicals like BPA (a known endocrine disruptor) in ever-greater quantities, shuffling it through paper recycling (because BPA coats, among other things, vast reams of paper receipts for commercial transactions) and into everybody's bloodstreams? How does this way of discarding shape our current and near-future possibilities?

Badly, as we know from chapter two. But and then what? What are we to do with such knowledge?

For Liboiron and Lepawsky, the point of discard studies is to allow us to ask new questions that open up different forms of social relation. Ultimately, "instead of a certain list of objects, discard studies starts with a question: What must be discarded for this or that system to be created and to carry on?"[71] What we discard determines who we can be.[72]

So, what could it look like to build societies, from the ground up, during the ongoing process of CaCaCo's staggered collapse, around discarding well? What might it look like to build them even in future wastelands?[73] On a far smaller level, what does it look like to begin discarding more wisely now, as and where we are?

For Liboiron and Lepawsky, discarding well requires "dealing with *systems*, not *symptoms*. Two key aspects of systems are the infrastructures and norms that support those systems and make them dominant. Plastic bag litter on a street is a symptom of a system of disposability that produces plastic packaging but also supports recycling that cleans it up: both modern litter and recycling are symptoms of disposability."[74]

As our current "waste management" systems break down (and they will; Jackson is more harbinger than outlier) with what do we replace them along the way? If I am terrified by how novel chemicals are restructuring my body's own relation with itself (I am), what novel systems can I help build—where I am, with the capacities available to me—to relate differently with CaCaCo's zombie system of disposability and waste that shuffles them into my bloodstream? Maybe it's time to discard activities that involve a lot of packaging and receipts?

The practice of this disposition places us in different relations to what's discarded. We can decide what to discard a lot more wisely, not to "save the earth" but to become peoples of Gaia. How can novel social forms help us to account for "waste" in fundamentally different ways and, so, to become different *wes*? What can I invite my neighbors to think and feel with me when floodwaters back up the sewage all around us?

These are questions any given "I" can only ask about and with some newly becoming "we." No *I* alone and no universal *we* can answer them on behalf of all global humanity.

Following on the theme of solidarity, perhaps the most important novelties associated with panic about the novel chemical crisis (and all the others) are social arrangements we can begin to make.

Because sure, at its worst panic's social novelty is, again, the stampede. At its best, though, it is the efflorescence of imaginative transit and social experimentation with which the 1950s, 1960s, and 1970s navigated panic about the atom bomb and CaCaCo's longstanding failures of racial democracy, or the cults of Pan with which Arcadians and other Greeks held on to wildness and radical freedom even as they found themselves folded into the structures of a Hellenic civilization centered on the slave-states of Athens and Sparta.

Prefigurative politics, building novel social forms as a way of anticipating and calling new political possibilities into being,[75] didn't cash out very effectively as a twentieth-century politics. People tried it plenty, and it didn't "work." There just wasn't a causal mechanism that could get this sort of (intrinsically pretty local) anarchist politics to change the massive, ultra-complex societies of CaCaCo. But that was back when people were (rightly) trying to change *this* world.

Panic Now? is a book for people who might be ready to lay foundations for next worlds. This one can't be reformed (in time). It's on its way out.

Prefigurative politics were indeed a bit too starry-eyed as a strategy for changing CaCaCo. But once we've panicked seriously enough at this world's ending, they start looking like just what we need to start designing the next.

Practicing novel social forms—from the highly elaborated community defense and worldmaking of Cooperation Jackson to simply thinking together with those close to us about how and what we discard—is part of how regular people can collaboratively design for new worlds even as the future continues getting hotter, darker, and weirder. Prefigurative politics are practical invention of new futures in a world that is breaking down.

ARCHAISMS

But newness, in turn, gives way. We create novel social forms, then panic afresh at an end that keeps on, after all, approaching. Efforts to avert the worst are as naught, time and again. Indeed, the newest thing of all—this mass extinction we've begun, perhaps only the sixth in several billion years of Gaia—is death incarnate. Shaken, we turn back to older habits of thought and practice, to archaisms.

Archaisms start with the question of the archaic: What even is it?

"The archaic" is one of those phrases without any single, clear referent. What's archaic is old, of course, but *exactly how old* and *which old things* depends a lot on who's using the term. It's definitely older than merely "old" but equally definitely shy of "eternal," and can be positively valenced (apprehended with a kind of wonder) or negatively (shunned as the mis-begotten past). The bottom line is that what's archaic is old in a way that has to do with the origins of some world.

For Germanist and intellectual historian Paul Bishop, introducing his edited volume on the matter, the archaic is "autonomy without agency: it is the world as it brings itself into being."[76] Bishop draws on French philosopher Bertrand Vergely to further elaborate:

"Each of us has a sense of the world-as-a-world-brought-into-being, inasmuch as to mature and grow old is 'to approach the great mystery of existence,' or 'to get back in touch with its originary radicality, with the originary absolute,' as the poets show us. Nostalgia, says Vergely, is not a regression, but an advance into the mystery of life, in which beauty approaches us."[77]

Let's bring that down to earth a little. We inhabit a world that has come from somewhere. As stable as it seems at any particular moment, it was some newness before we got here. Any given world has its sources, its points and processes of origination. And there is beauty in these, which we apprehend in the nostalgia with which so many move toward individual ends of life.

Archaisms, seen in this light, are something like practical dimensions of origination. They are those pieces of the past we can see and can see behind us and beneath the architecture of the present world, and so can apprehend (in a way that is sublime, both beautiful and terrible) as worldmaking.

To turn to archaisms is to pick back up worldmaking practices or habits of thought and action. These remnants of older worlds served, in their time, as the very origins of our own. Panic disposes us to look backward for worldbuilding inspiration. We might turn anew to old ceremonies, for instance.

More generally, we turn with nostalgia to remnants of older worlds when our own is unfulfilling, unsatisfying, or—as today—partway through ending. There's nothing new about that. But CaCaCo in its maturity, in its globally achieved fullness through the late twentieth and early twenty-first centuries, is more than a little skeptical of archaisms, especially of the wondrous variety.[78] Indeed, I'm suggesting archaisms here as part of how we may become peoples of Gaia rather than peoples of CaCaCo precisely because there's something about this world we live in that's unusually hostile toward the archaic. Embracing archaisms is one way of preparing for the end of a CaCaCo world.

The CaCaCo era we called modernity was suffused, oozing at every pore, with novelty. While we definitely need to do things differently to make way for new worlds after CaCaCo's end, even novel social forms and modes of relation won't save us. Nor can giddy techno-optimism—that mania for the new whose victims hang hope on every development in every realm, from the latest twitches of motion toward cold fusion to political novelties like the indictment of a former U.S. president—tether a person to the ground of pragmatic possibility. We need more than just novelties.

Real possibility, the possibility for worldmaking in the catastrophic remnants of this world, demands renewal now of lost capacities for pluralistic design. There is a sort of practical wisdom that starts by rummaging in the discard bins of culture, where our origins are.

We can find good friction for a run at humanizing, I'm suggesting, in archaisms, ideas or ways of living no longer immediately germane to how a world is organized and yet that have been worldmaking in the past. The archaic is who we are in civilizational resting states, those redoubts to which peoples and communities fall back when relentless and supposedly "forward" motion can no longer be sustained. Archaisms are originating practices, concrete elements of how our own worlds have been made. The quickest of glances at human history indicates clearly, though, that not all archaisms are created equally.

Indeed, "archaic" is often a bit of a slur word, and for good reason. "We" have been (and are) a lot of pretty lousy things, civilizationally, When the horizon of the future shimmers and fades, people don't necessarily turn to the best of the past. Especially for those who won't remain long enough with panic to arrive at wonder and novel social forms, the most immediately appealing archaisms can be very rigid.

Before getting into archaisms that may help in humanizing, then, it's worth spending a little time with a *dehumanizing* archaism that's gained disturbing popularity as CaCaCo has begun crumbling.

One of many politically concerning trends in recent years has been the spilling of a "Traditionalist Catholic" or tradcath movement beyond the bounds of intra-Catholic doctrinal disputes.[79] In its especially online iterations it goes hand-in-hand with a "tradwife" movement of women rejecting gender equality,[80] and both bleed quickly into the extremely vigorous anti-abortion and anti-queer/trans politics that infuse a frighteningly large number of people's political calculations today.

Tradcaths or Traditionalist Catholics are in the most anodyne sense a group of people who very strongly prefer Catholicism's old (pre-1960s) Latin Mass, or who believe that *only* that Tridentine Mass is properly Catholic.[81] As a political tendency and individual mindset spinning out from that preference or belief, they offer an example of how easily turns to the archaic can go badly.

On its face, of course, there's nothing wrong with a group of religionists rejecting dominant trends in their religion's official self-understanding. Just such moments, whether Jesuitical or Sufi or Lubavitcher, are simply one of the things religionists habitually do and long have done.[82] Turning back to some earlier, "more correct" set of ceremonies or doctrines is a pretty common move in the history of religions (and pretty much every other durably organized body of thought and practices).

We do today need archaisms that foster fluid and open-ended invention, and some of these may be religious. But there's a more comforting, false but easier promise in the siren call to recreate lost worlds instead. In the case of Traditionalist Catholics, a turn to the archaic ends up driving newly dehumanizing efforts. There's plenty of panic in it, but this is definitely not a practical wisdom that could help in becoming peoples of Gaia or global humanity. Instead, longing for the lost past sponsors rigid projects of archaic restoration.[83]

The cautionary example offered by tradcaths comes in the way their claim to have the exclusive truth of the past—and concomitant claim that an archaic way of living constitutes the exclusive truth for all time—sponsors dehumanizing attitudes as guides to an uncertain future. For Traditionalist Catholics in a strong sense, it's not simply that the 1962-1965 "updating" of the religion (in the Second Ecumenical Council of the Vatican, or Vatican II) was unfortunate or misguided. Rather, the modernizing impulse was wrong across the board, and wrong particularly in its emphasis on tolerance. The Vatican Council never should have made a whole host of decisions that accord broad human dignity to people outside the old fold. Allowing the Catholic sacrament of Mass to be said in vernacular languages was capstone to a pantheon of ills that, together, have been at the root of panickable social breakdown for decades.[84] Traditionalist Catholicism promises to turn back the clock.

The Tridentine Mass is an archaism, but in that not intrinsically bad or good. Holding fast to explicitly repudiated "old ways" (in this case, the Traditional Latin Mass promulgated in 1570 and replaced by Vatican II), offers a strategy for constituting community under religious and social conditions felt to be unviable. If that were all there were to it, we could leave the Catholics to their squabbles (and they leave the rest of us to ours). But, of course, that's not all there is to it.

Traditionalist Catholic online communities today foreground a real danger for anyone who would valorize the archaic. Reaching back to the distant past is often anti-pluralist, a retrenchment or reflexive grasping for old hierarchies rather than a source of invention and novel worldmaking.

In one fairly typical tradcath forum, user (and forum administrator) Voxxkowalski explains a supposed decline of American masculinity as having followed from "giving women the right to vote..big mistake."[85] The same user elsewhere explains the purpose of the forum itself:

"to allow Traditionalist Catholics a place of discussion free from the distractions and errors of the world. We are committed to defending Catholic doctrine and principles, and are faithful to the 2,000 years of Catholic Magisterium. As such, we recognize the undeniable existence of an unprecedented crisis in the Church, wrought by the Modernist revolution known as the Second Vatican Council."[86]

The two positions are interwoven. For this style of thought, the counter-Reformation Council of Trent and 1570 promulgation of the Tridentine ("of Trent," by that city's Latin name) Mass represented the high point of Catholic identity, its most authentic version. "Good" gender roles and models of political participation are those of the (thinly understood) sixteenth century. It can surprise no one that many tradcaths are also fervent monarchists, even more dubious than Voxxkowalski about the entire institution of voting.

To be human, here, is to belong in a Great Chain of Being. Some belong a good deal more than others.[87] Clean lines arcing from fidelity to an old ceremony toward dehumanizing tendencies in the present highlight the danger lurking in turns to archaisms. Elsewhere in tradcath forums, anti-vaccine sentiment commingles with antisemitism and simmering white resentment and pro-monarchy attitudes. Here and there, such communities also leak into the face-to-face, 3-dimensional world.

It is a short step from historical claims like those of popular Canadian tradcath Youtuber Brian Holdsworth—that the Crusades were basically reasonable, for instance—to instructions for Catholic Traditionalists to avoid all civic pluralism (Christians should avoid making friends with "wicked" non-Christians, for example).[88]

Of course, there may be only a few hundred thousand or so tradcaths out there on the world wide web, earnestly extolling the virtues of monarchy, patriarchy, and homogeny as correlatives of the Traditional Latin Mass.

My point isn't that they represent a significant material danger (though of course they may to some); I'm also not especially concerned about what "real" Catholicism does or doesn't entail. Rather, it's that their style of thought is one to which *we all* may far too easily be disposed. Tradcaths find anchoring for community in restorative nostalgia. Their turn to archaism warrants exclusion and refusal of the very possibility of pluralistically designing new futures.

It's easy to look at this from outside and see something risible and obviously bad. But does being able to so look place us beyond reach of our own versions of tradcaths' organizing conceptual error, inoculating us against comforting promises to install some preferred past in place of the dispiriting present? I suspect not.

In embracing the archaisms that speak to each of us, we do well to reflect on the (often spurious, frequently dehumanizing of at least *somebody*) quest for authenticity that can accompany such embraces. Wanting to get back to the "real thing" or "who we really are" can be a powerful motivation. But in a world where origins are always at least partially invented, trying to remake this world in the image of some lost one is fraught: more novel than archaic, as an actual political practice, but incompatible with novel social forms that might accommodate all Gaia's peoples.[89]

Though worrying for all of us with not much place in the world thus imagined,[90] tradcaths' efforts to derive contemporary morality and politics from key points of archaic "correctness" are understandable. Everyone and every community needs anchoring-points. We need them all the more when we encounter the end of a world (even a world as lousy as CaCaCo substantively is). A challenge for any turn to archaism is to discover past possibilities that are not merely comfort objects, but that bid fair to address our real and present polycrisis—by helping us to become peoples of Gaia, prepared to resist coming barbarisms and design alternative next worlds.

Authoritarianism, Catholic or otherwise, appeals to some as a bulwark against social disintegration, chaos, despair. But those are coming for us all. On the other side of panic, opened up by it, is not more holding-at-bay or attempts to rescue lost pasts. Rather, feeling our way through panic empowers us together to seek out archaic worldmaking practices that speak to the material character of our present catastrophes. There's risk in it but remaining as we are and recreating the past are both impossible and bad.

There's no going back to the lifeways that anchored archaisms, so the specific practices we draw from the archaic matter quite a lot. What have some of us, we humans, once done that, should we begin doing it again today, will help us to live better together under conditions of difficulty? Are there archaisms that can maybe even help to avert the worst?

More than nearly anything, especially where the sixth mass extinction we are brutally prosecuting is concerned, we need to find our way back to older relations with the more-than-human world. But can we?

It is mostly just *some* of our species' fault that Gaia is doing so badly,[91] but it is some of *most* of our species' fault that all our nonhuman kin are suffering and dying. The distribution of culpability varies, but its general tilt is clear. Of all the mammals living on the earth today, just 6% are estimated to be wild—that drops to under 2% for land-based mammals. All the rest are human (36%) or human-domesticated livestock (58%).[92] It was not always thus.

When we speak of a human-caused sixth mass extinction, we are taking a clear-eyed look at the impact of humans (especially CaCaCo humans) on planetary life. It's not just that wildlife (and its *many*, basally sustaining "ecosystem services") has disappeared a bit. It's that there's a death-chain underway; we caused and continue to cause and to accelerate every day a great dying-out. It's that, given current trends, life in general within the ambit of Gaia is being radically reduced for millennia to come. Our non-human kin are not simply "biodiversity" "disappearing." They are living someones starving, suffering, displaced, and dying. A great many of them are sensate, feeling beings. We are killing most of the other participants in Gaia's ongoing coming into being.

What archaisms might help us to feel this reality differently, to know it differently enough to make something altogether new with care and love? How can we become the peoples of *this* Gaia we have so cancerously impinged on from within?

If we want to do anything but numb out the pain of others, if we want to be *able* to mourn the Anthropocene and pursue new practices of caring,[93] we have to learn to regard not just the earth itself as a living entity, a biosphere, but all those who share it as our relations. We need ourselves to become very different sorts of people.

An archaism we can turn to here is ceremony.[94] For most of us, perhaps not the Traditional Latin Mass (not that there's anything *wrong* with that). So, then, what ceremonies?

A lot of discourse, especially for climate and biodiversity preservation, has turned to indigenous stewardship practices (both archaic and current) for help finding our way into relation.[95] Given that CaCaCo was predicated on stamping out indigenous lifeways to the fullest extent possible, and given that many (though of course not all) peoples prior to European colonialism had far more kin-based land and nonhuman animal relations than nearly anybody (*except* a subset of indigenous peoples) still has today, it's both practically and theoretically one good place to start.[96]

But perhaps we can hope to understand, in a way that our well-meaning, wildly white predecessors of the 1960s and '70s did not when they donned ceremonial-replica feathered headdresses as they played at finding/founding a state of nature by turning on, tuning in, and dropping out, that appropriating indigenous ceremonies ain't it.

Which means, here we are—we CaCaCo humans from all swathes—stuck killing off everyone else on earth. And we need ways of making sense of this reality that can help us design whatever comes after the awful civilizational assemblage we've turned out to be. And it does seem like indigenous archaisms offer some guidance for that. But, for most of us, *they're not ours.* You can't just pick up other people's ceremonies and expect them to work for you.

We have to become peoples of Gaia. For that, we need new ceremonies. But for newness that wouldn't just be more CaCaCo expropriation, excavation, exclusion, and extirpation, we need also something old. But most of the practical dimensions of origination that made *this* world are either lost from view or, like the Tridentine Mass and also most indigenous ceremonies, not exactly for everyone.

Perhaps, then, some basis for ceremony that's older still?

One archaism that might offer an axiom for humanity-designing ceremonies in the ruins of CaCaCo to come can be found scrawled on the sides of buildings around the world. It is ubiquitous on the Diné/Navajo Nation reservation restlessly circumscribed by state highway 89 to the west and Interstate 40 to the south, spilling across the map-lines defining Arizona, Utah, Colorado, and New Mexico in the Four Corners area near to where I live: "Water is Life."

Water is life not only for humans, but for all the nonhuman kin we are murdering as well. We share this basic principle, an axiomatic truth of what it is like to be somebody.

The slogan resonates powerfully, too, with one of the oldest meanings of the Greek *archē*, the root from which we have "archaic" and "archaism" both.[97] The pre-Socratic philosopher Thales of Miletus regarded water as the "first principle" or "material principle" organizing all that exists. The archē of everything, on this view, literally was water.[98]

Whether first principle or not, water is life. Water is one basis for any organization of life. But this is very generally true. What can it mean to know this truth in particular terms, specific terms, local terms? What can it look like to make new ceremonies from that knowing?

As Nick Estes (Lower Brule Lakota Sioux) writes in *Our History Is the Future*, "Concepts such as Mni Wiconi (water is life) may be new to some, but like the nation of people the concept belongs to, Mni Wiconi predates and continues to exist in spite of white supremacist empires like the United States."[99] The concept of Mni Wiconi is and is not the concept "water is life." More than merely generally true, it is true in particular for the Oceti Sakowin (Dakota-, Nakota-, and Lakota-speaking Siouxan peoples). It is theirs, even as something like it is available to anyone. For the Oceti Sakowin, Mni Wiconi defines particular relations of place: "Mni Sose, the Missouri River, is one such nonhuman relative who is alive, and who is also of the Mni Oyate, the Water Nation."[100]

Water is not only life for humans and our nonhuman kin but is also life in and for itself. Like anyone else's, water's life is always contingently organized, partial to one or another place and so to the peoples of that place. Still, even if we cannot quite know or hold the concept Mni Wiconi itself, humanizing in the midst of the sixth extinction we are causing will require ever more of us to apprehend something like the archē *water is life*.

And indeed, it is not only the Oceti Sakowin who know this, know that "nothing owns [Mni Sose or any other river], and therefore she cannot be sold or alienated like a piece of property."[101] Similar understandings emerge in Aotearoa, for instance, where Māori peoples long fought for decolonizing recognition of rivers' personhood. Such recognition includes but extends beyond mere legal rights within a CaCaCo order.

The foundation for a growing legal movement to recognize the rights of rivers uneasily pairs two very different ways of experiencing the world.

In one, consistent with the CaCaCo legal system generally, rivers must be protected because they provide ecosystem services. Like corporations, they aren't *really* persons, but it's a convenient fiction to treat them as such. Doing so allows states to pursue environmental protection strategies that they could not otherwise, in much the same way the fictional personhood of corporations allows for risk-distribution that eases the friction of capital's flow into speculative new endeavors.[102] The other way is to apprehend rivers—pathways of water, and so too the rest of the more-than-human world—as living beings, constituent-persons of the peoples of Gaia. This isn't make-believe. It's taking the archē *water is life* seriously.

In Aotearoa, the Whanganui River is somebody. She has always been somebody, and the Whanganui Iwi Māori's efforts to secure legal recognition of this somebodiness comprise one dimension of longstanding work on decolonization.[103]

Whanganui (like Mni Sose) is not simply a currently extant physical stretch of water between two banks, but all that water's tributaries and deltas as well. And, too, all its relations braiding out across past and future, and its spiritual or metaphysical existence as well. In sum: Te Awa Tupua.[104] Recognizing the River's life means extending our understanding beyond its banks. Like any other person, a river is a network of relations woven into the fabric of innumerable lives, visions, and experiences. Humanizing means becoming human persons who know themselves within and as such networks.

"Water is life" is a concept at once both proprietary and general. To apprehend it is immediately to reorder CaCaCo social relations; and at the same time the concept belongs to some peoples and not to others. What do those to whom the concepts Mni Wiconi, Te Awa Tupua, and their correlates belong share in common? What else but knowing and being in relation with the waters.

The challenge for the rest of us, here in this dying CaCaCo world, is to come ourselves into such relation. By what ceremonies, if any, might we accomplish this?

To recognize that water is life is to understand something of the motivation of the Standing Rock Water Protectors, Oceti Sakowin and others. CaCaCo property rights guarantee harm to water's life, choking black oil stealing the vivacity of the river from below and above. The *something* a person knows in knowing this is shared not only from Standing Rock to the Navajo rez but with Thales of Miletus and the Whanganui Iwi and with all our kin being extirpated by CaCaCo logics as well. It is that "if the water, a relative, is not protected, then the river is not free, and neither are its people."[105]

This originary, worldmaking knowledge is the sort of archaism from which political movements spring.[106] It is the sort of archaism that establishes beyond question our human interconnection with the rest of this living world we are currently killing. There's no lost world to be restored here, only new ones to be made. The old has flowed on.

Water is not only human life or even nonhuman animal life. It is life itself. But it is *definitely* and at the very least a material principle of human life. As Giulio Boccaletti puts that point in *Water: A Biography*, this primordial or superordinate principle shapes at the deepest level our sense of what it is like to live as vulnerable participants in a larger, also living world. "Ever since the first communities wrestled with water as it streamed down from retreating glaciers—ever since people began telling stories about it—water has been the dominant agent in people's relationship with the environment.[107]

We do not know how to make sense of land, to tell the stories of who we and many animal relations alongside us are, without starting from water.

All too often, though, and all too easily, we think of water (never mind that water is constantly flowing, gives life, remains ever in motion) as somehow inanimate. With Estes and the Water Protectors at Standing Rock, we have instead to ask, "What does water want from us? What does the earth want from us?"[108]

We become peoples who *can* ask these questions, peoples of Gaia, through new-old ceremonies and rituals. It is not enough to simply say "I am different now." We need ways of practicing relation differently, becoming other to ourselves in the places where we each and collectively are now CaCaCo's people. May I not thank the wash that flows, now a trickle now a flood, for sustaining so much beauty in the place where I, too, live?

Learning to mourn our necrotic Anthropocene takes not only action and reflection, but also ceremonies that draw on the archaic. Not to wish or wash away the sins of the fathers, which are our own as well, but to become newly the peoples of Gaia in the places where we find ourselves.

What the tradcath movement offers its adherents is anchoring. It is a deadly anchoring, unhappily. But that's not because there's anything wrong with religion in general or Catholicism in particular. I don't share that increasingly-for-now popular view. Rather, it's because the archaisms tradcaths turn toward are precisely those that have driven the worst, most rigid and exclusionary, most world-destroying aspects of CaCaCo. They want to restore a bygone world, but do not turn all the way back to a dimension of origination. And so they end up excising from the bounds of community just those whose voices a pluralistic design demands.

It isn't like the CaCaCo world primes the rest of us for responsivity to rich communal life beyond small slivers of humanity either, though.

What *can* it look like to make anchoring ceremonies that would place us in different relations with this wounded and touchy world we have both made and not made, ceremonies to align us with Gaia? Thanking the waters near to you, asking them what they want, is one way to start.

When you start asking that question, expect some people to look at you funny. In *God Is Red*, a kind of philosophical-religious codex to the twentieth century U.S.'s American Indian Movement, Vine Deloria, Jr. observes,

"A belief in the sacredness of lands [and personhood of rivers] in the non-Indian context may become the preferred belief of an individual or group of people based on their experiences or on an intensive study of pre-selected evidence. But this belief becomes the subject of intense criticism and does not, except under unusual circumstances, become an operative principle in the life and behavior of the non-Indian group."[109]

It may seem a little woo-y—indeed, out of nowhere for those who don't feel it yet—to claim that rivers and lands are sacred living persons. More-over, today (after decades of real and appropriate concern about white set-tler appropriation of indigenous cultures), some readers will be skeptical of the very idea that non-indigenous people can or should pursue radically different relationships to the more-than-human world.

But, of course, "water is life" in its most general form precedes us all. Nor, even as particular forms like Mni Wiconi or the Diné/Navajo "Tó Éí Iiná At'é" are not for everyone,[110] is the idea ungeneralizable. To the con-trary, it's an idea available to anyone. The question is what we—you and I, where we are—can do with it, what particular forms of relation it sponsors.

I live alongside a year-round creek (currently) called Pumphouse Wash. In spring snowmelt and late summer monsoons the wash is full, rushing over driveways and cutting new channels as water moves around the de-caying branches that construct obstacles behind stable rocks. Some in my neighborhood have "water rights" that allow them to draw directly from it without other humans exercising violence against them, and long insulated pipes snake up steep hillsides to houses above me. Others' water rights are more seasonal but no less real: the geese who nest in tall grass alongside the wash, coming repeatedly to the same places (until they don't), the elk who migrate up for summer's heat from the winter warmth they found below the Mogollon Rim, tracing backward the path of water that drains down to Oak Creek's sharp canyon cut beneath us.

What does Pumphouse Wash want from me, or Oak Creek below it, or the Verde River still lower? What does the great Colorado River want as it drains down to the Sea of Cortez? How can I live best in concert with all those persons, human and nonhuman, who share in the networks of these rivers who are persons themselves?

This isn't first and foremost a technical question. It's that, too, and one we can only answer by listening to others—from water "managers" and biologists to elk and the occasional murmurations of swallows who live from this place in passing, too. Before that, though, it's a spiritual question, a question about who we are in relation with all these nonhuman others. Where ceremony comes in is to help us become people who *can* be in relation with all these nonhuman others.

There's no returning to before CaCaCo. But in the space of collapse, where carbon-burning and capitalism fall away, the legal and political lega-cies of colonialism will also fall into disarray. One answer to what comes next, and it's an answer we do well to develop in vibrant heterogeneity today, is to develop ceremonies based in archaisms like *water is life*.

Robin Kimmerer's (Citizen Potawatomi) *Braiding Sweetgrass* develops a sense of what it can look like to treat *water is life* as the basis for new-old ceremonies.[111] Beginning with the Anishinabekwe story of Skywoman's fall to earth (like rain), Kimmerer notes that, "Like any good guest, Sky-woman had not come empty-handed." She brought life with her when she "toppled from the hole in the Skyworld."[112] But this is not my story to tell, not even to retell.

You should read Skywoman's story in *Braiding Sweetgrass*, or else ask someone who knows. The point to take *here* is about how Kimmerer's book names, again and again, the rich, living fullness of this world Gaia we Ca-CaCo humans are doing our damndest to destroy. And not only names, but offers stories of as gifts for all—twined together from her own overlapping ways of knowing, as biologist and self-conscious bearer of indigenous tales alike.

Kimmerer is to her readers a visitor. Every author is. Part of what she shares with any reader who receives her is a sense of what it means to make ceremonies in a living, ever-renewed world.

Subverting a reader's expectations, one ceremony that appears early on in *Braiding Sweetgrass*—in which Kimmerer's father pours a little coffee on the ground each morning when their family canoe camps in the Adiron-dacks, thanking the relations of the place as he does so—is not ancient, but new, invented almost by happenstance.

We first encounter the ceremony itself: "I can picture my father, in his red-checked wool shirt, standing atop the rocks above the lake. When he lifts the coffeepot from the stove the morning bustle stops; we know without being told that it's time to pay attention."[113] The setting is bucolic, even stylized, but the act itself mundane. "He stands at the edge of camp with the coffeepot in his hands, holding the top in place with a folded pot holder. He pours coffee out in the ground in a thick brown stream."[114] As he pours, Kimmerer's father recites each time the same words: "Here's to the gods of Tahawus."[115]

But the gods of Tahawus are not Kimmerer's family's concepts. "It was a secondhand ceremony. Somewhere there were people who knew the right ceremony, who knew the lost language and spoke the true names, including my own."[116] To find oneself, it seemed to the young Kimmerer, one needed the right ceremony, the true names. This is an urge she describes at once proudly and with sorrow as carrying along her later studies as a biologist, a student of Ojibwe language, and at length an Indigenous ecologist.

Because the right ceremonies, the true names, are not only carried across the past as oral traditions among communities. Equally, they remain to be invented, understood, known.

For Kimmerer, the necessary work of invention belongs most of all to the nations, the peoples, indigenous to Turtle Island. It is a work of new fashioning, a work of making "a new people . . . with a sacred purpose" in a time when "the young would turn back to the elders for teachings and find that many had nothing to give."[117] In this time of the Seventh Fire, our own era of polycrisis, the archaism of a prophecy foretelling different suturings of new and old sustains the possibility of making different ceremonies.

So much is secondhand now, at best. What's lost to humans, though, isn't lost to everyone. Kimmerer writes, "So much has been forgotten, but it is not lost as long as the land endures and we cultivate people who have the ability to listen and learn." For "the people are not alone. All along the path, nonhuman people help. What knowledge the people have forgotten is remembered by the land. The others want to live, too."[118]

Those of us who do not trace lines of communal belonging to the first peoples of our respective places, who are or who descend from settlers in those places, we too may want to live. We too "can reclaim our membership in the cultures of gratitude that formed our old relationships with the living earth."[119] We can fashion new ceremonies that do not ape those of peoples to whom we do not belong, but that learn from them as they, too, seek to become renewed peoples.

Kimmerer comes to feel that, in fact, her father's invented ceremony "was not secondhand, it was ours."[120] Even as he explains the practical origin of the ceremony—to clear the coffeepot's spout of grounds—he marks its growth beyond that origin. It became over time a way of saying thanks, of sharing back to the earth a little of self because that is all there is to share.[121]

What is ceremony, here? It is "a vehicle for belonging—to a family, to a people, and to the land."[122] Many of us feel we belong nowhere, have no people, are claimed by no land. One way to begin making ceremonies that can help us become peoples of Gaia, feel fully enough our relations to mourn this necrotic Anthropocene we are making and so begin to practice care, is to ask and listen.

What does the river want? What do the frogs, full-throated all the way up to the infinite night sky, know or need or want? What are they saying, asking us in turn?

We can learn to listen.

It's a matter, as Jenny Odell says, of starting to do nothing. In listening I hear not just the creek and frogs. I thank the deer when we pass by in the forest, we stop a moment: tired-out Willa and indefatigable Zada and me on my bike but worn anyhow. What do they tell us? They have shared quietly these glowing late afternoon aspens and impossibly green tufts of knee-high grass, let's drive real slow on the way home. I keen quietly when I drive by a carcass roadside. That was someone. They were here. So many moments have ceremony in them, even for those of us who lack the words.

Because ceremony's more about listening than saying, anyhow. Something is happening; it's time to pay attention. Who might we yet become?

For eras obsessed with novelty, the archaic is a curiosity at best, more often nothing at all. When we set out looking for good archaisms, it's easy to treat what we find as talismans. We hold to markers of past moments that suffuse our necrotic present with otherworldly meaning. At worst, we try to restore something lost, as though you could paint the past over the present.

That includes "getting back to normal" after a pandemic that never really ended just as much as it does clinging to the Tridentine Mass as truest ceremony of Catholic community.

In CaCaCo's time of polycrisis, characterized above all else by the speed that has come to shape collective life's refashioning toward death,[123] archaisms mark the possibility of stability, of balance, of slower ways of being together. They do so, paradoxically, by sponsoring novel-to-us social forms, new-old ways of relating.

We are not just the incredibly capable consumer species that has in a short century quadrupled itself to choke out most other life on the planet. We are *also* the versions of ourselves we have been across millennia past, versions of human species-self ground out in genocides and lost to CaCaCo's consuming rage for novelty, but not lost altogether. We are peoples in relation with other peoples.

It is a point at once philosophical or spiritual and intensely practical.

There is no "noble savage," as killer colonists and the scholars who carried on their legacy once supposed (and went to some pains to persuade themselves) there must be.[124] But there are predecessors. Lots of predecessors, doing lots of different things. A great many of those predecessors are our nonhuman kin, animals and rivers and all else that lives.

Our predecessors, their archaisms. These register threads of possibility bound into the making of CaCaCo from the start, and that yet exist as gestures beyond it. The future-gobbling consumptive appetites of global north denizens (and increasingly many in the thereby "developing" global south) are incompatible with a habitable future for humanity and the rest of most species we have not yet snuffed out. The parade of chemicals, stretching to the horizon, with which CaCaCo's version of "global humanity"—with its billion Black anthropocenes and its necropolitics—has been fashioned promise futures of ever more mutation, deformation, lives sustained by rapid, deathly change at all levels of existence.

The balled totality of a global humanity that is some of our faults far more than others surges toward its own destruction, toward the destruction of all that might be held holy about the living world. What remains?

Archaisms, philosophically speaking, are minor or largely disused dimensions of collective being today that call back to earlier moments of worldmaking. Practically speaking, such practices reinvigorate dimensions of origination once supposed dead.

Just as through prodigious efforts of linguistic recovery and pedagogical commitment many native nations have breathed new life into moribund or dying tongues, so too a great many living archaisms remain to be plucked out from the deathly fabric of CaCaCo. They are threads that might be disentangled as the whole skein unravels, turned toward other ends than maximizing consumption. Ours is to discover these lines of origination woven badly into CaCaCo's necrotic tapestry.

This means tracing figures of possibility for new worlds on the basis of worlds that have come before. We have to listen to all the peoples we share CaCaCo's world with if we are to invent next worlds in the ruins alongside them. What and whom we become able to love, to risk novel social forms together with now, determines everything about what we will be able to make then.

To remember our lost kin in that future moment, to sense them, feel them, seek to revive them then, we have to hear their burbling lives beside us now.

Water is life. What ceremonies can help me listen better to the wash, offer her something of myself, and so perhaps help make a home for us all?

HUMANIZING

In apprehending with love the beauty of a current world we lay groundwork, should we prove exceptionally lucky, for humanizing. That starts with panic about how CaCaCo's collapse is going, and about how it will proceed as this world fails to account for the deferred costs that made it possible in the first place. It plays out in a renewed sense of possibility.

We cannot salvage this world. But we *can* become more truly human in the worlds we design next.

Our chances of humanizing get a lot better if we practice dispositions that open us to richer, more heartful relations in this dying world we inhabit now.

Humans are a species, whatever exactly that means (it's a lot more fluid than one might suppose).[125] But we are, no less than a biotic entity occupying an ever-broader ecological niche, maximizing our metabolization of ever more resources, an as-yet unrealized idea. That idea doesn't *have to* be "the animal that consumed itself and everybody else to death."

The idea of humans can be something a lot more beautiful than CaCaCo's catabolic consumption has made it. But only if we panic in time about who we have been and are becoming now. This chapter's been given over to the bet that we can panic wisely, and that doing so will lead us toward humanizing.

With "humanizing," I implicitly suggest a distinction between "being human" and "becoming *truly* human." The late scholar and father and partner and son and my old friend Sol Neely (Cherokee), from whom I continue to learn, helps clarify that distinction. He mediates a commencement speech given by Tlingít student Crystal Rogers at University of Alaska Southeast in 2012 like this: "She noted, in particular, that the word 'Lingít' means 'human being,' and she announced that she wanted to talk about *Lingít tundataani* (Tlingít thinking)."[126] *Lingít tundataani* offers a sense of how becoming truly human happens.

This thinking is characterized by the presence of the archaic, by something older than even elders: "the 'ancient ones,' whose lives, she noted, 'were more difficult than we can imagine, but figured out how to survive in the world because they figured out how to rely on each other, how to be responsible for each other.'"[127] Alongside these *Tlagu ḵwáanx' i yán* is a certain heaviness of language, a phrase—*Wooch yax yadáal*—that registers "recognition of all the things, all the circumstances, that make words heavy."[128] This relational, recursive heaviness of language and thought, Crystal and Sol suggest, is at the heart of really humanizing.

We are all inheritors of a world made by people, human and nonhuman alike, who figured out how to be responsible for each other. The weight of this world hangs heavy already in everything we have yet to say.

Neely explains, "It is these qualities of 'Tlingít thinking' (*Lingít tundataani*), Crystal told us, that mark the difference between simply 'being human'—which is automatic—and being 'truly human,' or *Kunáx Lingít haa wustee* (which translates as, 'We really have become human beings')."[129]

Humanizing, on this view, happens at a place where we find relations and gravity alike, a depth of obligation and being-with that exceeds the merely automatic and traces back through our relations in and with a world.

Ultimately, humanizing in the sense I have from Sol and, through Sol, from Crystal Rogers, "means to take up our responsibility inspired by the voices of ancestry made legible through the language and the sounds of nature."[130] As suggested by Sol Neely's mediation of Crystal Rogers, echoing Robin Kimmerer's description of the Seventh Fire, sometimes the voices of ancestry we become able to hear are those not of elders but of youth. Always, they speak from and on behalf of Gaia, whose peoples we can become now, as CaCaCo is falling apart.

A few years before he published that article, Sol and I walked far out on the Matanuska glacier. Amid disconcerting creaks and groans and the hissing of an ice-river melting all around us but none too close, Sol joked, following the old tv show M*A*S*H (itself channeling a still-older Allan Sherman song, "Turn Back the Clock"), "Ladies and Gentlemen, take my advice: pull down your pants and slide on the ice." I'm probably not the first person to get a glacial ass-burn from that show. A few footfalls later, Sol placed a boot on white snow that fell away into the abyss below, pivoted on the nothingness, and faced me, smiling. His father George called right then, and he took the call.

Isn't just such a heavy combination of living and dying in a web of relations that includes the frozen, living water what we'd mean by humanizing, becoming truly human? Isn't it something about the impossible fullness of our relations all together?

It's easy enough to look at our necrotic Anthropocene and despair, to suppose that this is what the human idea in its fullest materiality is. But, after all, "Anthropocene" was just a few of us naming an age after all of us. And even if nearly all of us have been caught up in the swirling CaCaCo hurricane that made this planetary era catastrophic, only a very few of us have ever rested easy, traveling along in the eye of that storm.

What a true global humanity might mean, as a heavy network of relations among humans and with more-than-human kin, remains yet to be invented.

What it probably *won't* be is a League of Nations on the CaCaCo model, with a G7 or G8 or G20 setting the agenda for all of life on earth. That's still our dominant model on the world stage, but humanizing begins at home. In thinking beyond the deadly version of "global humanity" that CaCaCo's disposed us to be, I want to turn back to an early articulation of who "we" are in the most general sense and tarry with it. In making "home" differently, we need to take what matters from CaCaCo's own formative moments.

Immanuel Kant's *Perpetual Peace* is a quintessential tract of European Enlightenment thought and a precursor to CaCaCo's most dramatic expansions in the nineteenth and twentieth centuries. Here, the great Prussian philosopher announces the possibility of a global humanity.[131] The world is comprised of nations, each of which is "a society of men [*sic*] whom no one other than the nation itself can command or dispose of."[132] Because it is, per Kant, in the nature of humans to exist in and as nations, a fully developed global humanity can only be achieved in the context of peace— which is to say, perpetual and ongoing peace—among all the nations of the world. But figuring out how to rely on each other, be responsible for each other, does not come easy.

Kant's perpetual peace is to be forged against the backdrop of perpetual war. The latter is "a sad necessity in the state of nature (where no tribunal empowered to make judgments supported by the power of law exists), one that maintains the rights of a nation by mere might."[133] Over the course of the tract, it becomes clear that Kant's vision of a universal league of peace, which is the template for today's United Nations (and the early twentieth century League of Nations before it), is unachievable. Starting from European nations, Kant imagines expansion toward a peaceful global humanity, but at every stage both throws up new codicils and confirms the justness of existing (colonial) relations of inequity.

There's a beauty in this vision of peace. Every nation of the world will eventually "give up their savage (lawless) freedom, just as individual persons do, and, by accommodating themselves to the constraints of common law, establish a *nation of peoples* (*civitas gentium*) that (continually growing) will finally include all the people of the earth."[134] It's motivated an awful lot of well-meaning political projects over the last couple hundred-and-change years, including for instance the IPCC itself (whose remit is to establish core empirical realities about climate that might serve as the basis for global common law). But, and that "savage" really gives it away here, Kant's schema rapidly proved an ugly justification for colonialism.

Kant's global humanity is ordered hierarchically from most human to least. That is to say, ordered from those nations with sufficient reason to accommodate themselves to common law down to those "savages" who, supposedly, are hardly nations at all.

Naturalizing along the way a very particular idea of what a "nation" is, *Perpetual Peace* offers a template for CaCaCo's ongoing global organization. The essay at once suggests a universally equal *global humanity* as goal or endpoint for human development and foresees incremental movement toward that goal, in which Europeans—global north colonizers and settlers—will at any given moment be the most reasonable nations in the world, and so (naturally!) the most powerful. It's a neat trick.

Kant publishes the tract in 1795. Around that time, enslaved Haitians are setting out on the project of emancipating themselves from their French overlords and a small cabal of formerly English landholders are affirming the moral validity of their genocide against indigenous peoples through ratification of the United States Constitution.[135] Kant is a fan of the latter, not so much the former.[136] One of those nations today anchors the G7, as it has done for most of a century. The other is currently in its worst period of collapse since founding. Again.

There's a lot *not* to mourn about the fact that CaCaCo is cracking up. And yet, there really is something to the basic idea of *Perpetual Peace*. We might not want to ditch too readily the notion that humanizing is a process requiring our whole species to be in relation. We might need to accept that this could only proceed incrementally in some way. *Who* is "most human" right now and *what* the "increments" ought to look like cannot merely remain open questions, though. Rather, they demand radically different answers than CaCaCo gave them. Designing next worlds from within this one's failing horizons, we should keep a keen eye out for dimensions of CaCaCo humanity that are especially worth being shaped by.

An anticipatory global humanity is a basically good idea. The uses CaCaCo put it to derive not from the idea but from the relations of ownership and wastage in which it flowered.

Happily, Kant is hardly the only source for imagining a disposition toward humanizing. Jamaican philosopher Sylvia Wynter offers a similar, more timely and in many ways more compelling, vision of humanizing as ongoing global praxis: inventive practice oriented by theory and contributing to it in turn.

If we don't have some theory of what humanizing might entail, there's little basis for consistency in political struggle. We will continue to flounder within the limits of CaCaCo's richly impoverished vision of "global humanity," reform a little here or there, try on some justice. But we will not becomes peoples of Gaia.

Indeed, there's a reason most justice-oriented efforts today seem so ad hoc, come in the end to so little. Today, the cause célèbre is X. Tomorrow, it will be Y. Without a panicful sense of the polycrisis, we'll keep meandering from one GoFundMe to the next, one news cycle to the next, one most important election ever to the next, one astounding technological innovation to the next, one revolutionary daydream to the next, and so on. Practice without theory in a dying and badly ordered world is little more than rearranging deck chairs, increasingly frantically, on the Titanic. At the same time, though, any theory worth its salt—and who knows how precious salt may yet become again?—has (like Cooperation Jackson) constantly to learn from practice. And theory that does not know panic is theory that has not learned the lessons of the polycrisis.

In conversation with Katherine McKittrick, Wynter foregrounds the role of storytelling, and the storytelling character of humans, in humanizing praxis. She calls us *homo narrans*, storytelling man.[137] And if storytelling, then also mythmaking. We can make myths to guide solidaristic peace of a very different sort than the "global humanity" process that's produced us as CaCaCo's monstrous and all-consuming Cronos-anthropos so far. But what myths could be adequate to imagining us all as, and helping us to practice becoming, peoples of Gaia? How can we undertake processes of humanizing when a world is ending around us?

Wynter frames this in terms of accountability for our stories. We practice humanizing by accounting for our myths in real time, taking responsibility for their weightiness in ever-widening networks of relation with others. Becoming human starts with recognizing "the defining characteristic of our hybrid human origin [and so destination]: the *fully completed co-evolution, with the human brain, of the faculties of language and of storytelling*."[138] That's where *we* started. At the very same time, we've got work to do if "we" really want to get there.

Humanizing in Wynter's sense is accomplished not by fidelity to a dead past (though that matters, too), but by broadening the sorts of relations each new moment of mythmaking enables.

We need to account for global humanity as a species-process of long standing. In so doing, "nations" start to look different. People have been agentially engaged in humanizing mythmaking all the way back, at least, to the early human nations making themselves as myths in Blombos Cave (in contemporary South Africa). Telling stories of humanness that take stock of the storytelling humans have been doing all along is what makes it "possible for the peoples of contemporary post-Mandela South Africa, as well as our also Western and Westernized global selves, to now collectively give humanness a different future."[139] Accounting for ourselves opens up, again and again, rich new possibilities for becoming, in ever-wider webs of relation, a global humanity.[140]

This book is only one such effort at accounting. Many are needed.

As CaCaCo staggers into increasingly painful, frightening, and withal devastating episodes of catastrophe and collapse, owing something to Gaia, to one another, and to the living waters we come from—and naming that owing—maintains spaces of possibility for designing next worlds. We humans *"cannot/do not preexist our cosmogonies*, our representations of our origins," because humanness is itself both biological and mythological.[141] We are biological beings, but within our biology is story. And through storytelling, especially through stories about where we come from (and so where we are going), we are never wholly constrained by the physical facts of who we have been thus far (except the fact of storytelling itself).

As chapter two's brief discussion of intelligence suggested, I doubt humans are entirely alone in this. Other biocultural creatures are, like us, symbolic animals. And any symbolic animal of sufficient social cohesion and complexity probably performs a certain amount of more or less intentional collective self-making. A characteristic of human collective self-making, which may or may not be unique, is the depth with which we *believe* in our origin stories. A crucial dimension of becoming human and a reason that reflective praxis is so important, for Wynter, is that "even though it is we ourselves who invent those cosmogonies and then retroactively project them onto a past,"[142] we can't stop believing we are the people we have said we are.

Humanizing in the sense I have in mind involves stories that retroject for us dense webs of originary, human and more-than-human relations. Such stories allow us to hold close the heaviness of all our relations and our symbols.

Humanizing's challenge is to go beyond merely believing we are the peoples we have said we are, and in fact to become them. This is hard. It's going to be even harder. At stake is an ever-growing efflorescence of *"genres of becoming human"* that open us, as meaning-making recipients of symbols, to ever-more forms and processes of personhood.[143]

The wager of this book is that, in practicing solidarities, sustaining disruptions, inventing novel social forms, and turning with love and care to archaisms, we can become the humanizing peoples of Gaia.

Who will that make us?

Chapter Five

WHO WILL WE BE?

On the opposite shores of panic, as we undertake the grand and threatening adventure of—at long last—humanizing (even as the CaCaCo world falls down around us), who will we become?

"Global humanity" is a grand aspiration in theory, but what can this mean in practice? If we *do* manage to panic in time, if we muster the right combination of solidarities, disruptions, novelties, and archaisms to undertake humanizing as a project on the global scale, who will we be on the other side of the carbon-capitalism-colonialism assemblage? The reality is, there's no knowing.

We won't save CaCaCo, but that's no cause for despair. The kinds of worlds it becomes possible to make in the coming ruins will be substantively disposed by the forms of political struggle we pursue today. We enjoy now greater social stability and widespread access to metabolic resources than we will in days ahead. This is a time for designing worlds, and living toward them, prefiguring them.

The scope of our polycrisis demands wholesale remaking of human experience. If most of our species is to survive, still less thrive, in coming decades, it will take nothing less than transformation of our collective ways of being in the world.

Happily, this isn't our first time.

Aligning with Wynter's story of *homo narrans*, David Graeber and David Wengrow detail the ways groups of humans have been remaking their worlds—and themselves—for, well, pretty much all of human history. Indeed, "human beings, through most of our history, have moved back and forth fluidly between different social arrangements, assembling and dismantling hierarchies on a regular basis."[1] Humans at most times have done lots of "humanizing," in the sense offered here in chapter four.

Graeber and Wengrow's exhaustive survey of human history finds that, "Without permanent kings, bureaucrats, or standing armies," small communities throughout all discernible eras and locations have "formed civilizations in that true sense of extended moral communities."[2] Human peoples have *become truly human* in the way highlighted by Rogers and Neely, reaching for ways of engaging symbols that can carry the depth and heaviness of broad networks of relation. Along the way, it's been not kings and rulers and scribes that made culture possible, but all these versions of *we, ourselves*. With minimal stable hierarchy and maximal openness to possibility, "In some regions they pioneered metallurgy, the cultivation of olives, vines and date palms, or the invention of leavened bread and wheat beer; in others they domesticated maize and learned to extract poisons, medicines, and mind-altering substances from plants . . . [or] developed the major textile technologies applied to fabrics and basketry, the potter's wheel, stone industries and beadwork, the sail and maritime navigation, and so on."[3] We're really no slouches.

The point, though, is that inventive activity, shared and developed in symbols, is something we humans are pretty good at. We may not know how to save CaCaCo (we don't), but we do know how to invent culture (in general, at least).

The stakes for such invention are today higher than ever before. Not just for ourselves, but for the rest of our nonhuman relations as well. Around the world, we nearly *all* have to change, and have to do so pretty quickly. And we're also (contra the rosy optimism of the hope peddlers) not yet sure how to accomplish that. Heck, this book hasn't even focused on all the relevant crises.

We won't invent new "we"s fast enough to pay what CaCaCo owes, but if we panic wisely we may very well be able to leave good artifacts lying around. Those artifacts can help people design better worlds in the ruins of this one.

Another framework for thinking about polycrisis is that of planetary boundaries.[4] As Will Steffen and colleagues suggested in 2015,[5] updating a famous paper on this topic by Rockström *et al.*,[6] of seven planetary boundaries delimiting an earth system within which humans can generally thrive, at least four have already been surpassed. Between climate change, biodiversity loss (the sixth mass extinction), massive disruption of biochemical flows (the nitrogen and phosphorus cycles), and land system change, humans have already moved into a risk zone on the wrong side of planetary boundaries that made human evolution and the contemporary organization of society possible. In the nearly a decade since that 2015 publication, matters have only worsened (and even Steffen *et al.*'s estimate, worried some researchers at the time,[7] probably undershot the mark). See also chapters one and two of this book.

The bottom line is that we're *not* going to change (in time to save Ca-CaCo). And that's going to leave many humans to pursue worldmaking under far more difficult conditions, at least from a metabolic resource perspective, than the present. Hence all the panic.

Still, as CaCaCo falls into disarray, new possibilities for collective self-fashioning are emerging. These will arise in many different, locally discrete moments of a broad and general collapse. Staggered collapse does not demand an apocalyptic imaginary, in which some grand event ushers in the end of time. Rather, we're soberly sitting down to the fact of staggered collapse, reckoning realistically with piecemeal processes of falling apart that vary from one place to another. The bet is that we thereby create better tools for those who come next.

Structures that have barely held together already (social ties, labor relations, infrastructures) will tend piece by piece, place by place, toward disintegration. Sometimes that will happen quickly, all at once, like Haiti's recent slide into lawlessness. Other times it will seem indiscernible altogether (for global north people above a particular wealth line), as when New Yorkers forget the looming threat of a hurricane in quiet years. Eventually, a collapse that's already ongoing and that can only proceed—because Ca-CaCo cannot pay the debts, either internal to its constituents or external to Gaia, that define it—will come for everyone. That "eventually," in which global humanity finds new opportunities for collective worldmaking in CaCaCo's ruins, is a lot *less* likely to arrive in 2100 than 2050. Or even sooner. And it's, above all else, likely to be extremely fucking difficult.

The question is, who will "we" be then? Answers depend to a great extent on what we do now, what dispositions we practice in becoming peoples of Gaia. Left to their own devices, CaCaCo's biggest beneficiaries—even "good" billionaires like Bill Gates, who certainly don't mean to[8]—place us on the road to walled borders, new fascisms, armed lifeboats. The sooner a great many of us can panic, the better our odds of replacing business-as-usual futures with some others we've an honest hand in making

No matter how great our attunements and sense of wonder, though, we should expect at least a few hard constraints to prevail in any future contiguous with the present. Whoever we might yet become in the hotter, darker, weirder future, it's no good pretending we can simply escape who we are now. Humanizing is a narrative and symbolic biopoetics, an embodied set of mythmaking practices. As such and like any other meaning-making project it cannot realistically promise, for instance, a world without hierarchy.

THE SAME

At any given moment, most of us are going to be awfully much like we were in the minute before. That's true for individuals and species alike. It's mostly true for societies, but sometimes it's hardly at all the case.

What's at stake in our long polycrisis, an emergency unfurling at once slowly (relative to individual lifespans) and with extraordinary rapidity (relative to the geologic timescale of past changes in the earth system, in Gaia), is radically transformative civilizational change.[9] On the unlikely chance (but what fool bets against their own species?) that we prove up to the task, there's a lot that will look very familiar about our future after CaCaCo.

Who "we" will be, though it's tempting to imagine otherwise, is along most axes a lot like who we've been so far. The good news is that humans have built all sorts of wildly different societies over the millennia of being more or less a single species. Who we've been so far is mostly *not* the people of CaCaCo. That particular stuckness is a pretty recent innovation, and not even hard-coded in the histories of CaCaCo's own biggest winners. Graeber and Wengrow detail, for instance, an alternative to our common imaginings of classical Greece in the Minoans of Crete.

On this largest and southernmost island in the Aegean, "Pretty much all the available evidence . . . suggests a system of female political rule—effectively a theocracy of some sort, governed by a college of priestesses."[10] From that system, which produced its share of the usual frescoes and pottery shards and palaces, there remains little evidence of participation in the perpetual wars spidered across the rest of the (patriarchal) Greek and Mediterranean worlds. It's unclear if Cretan society was organized in terms of dominance at all. I'm not trying to inject a little second-wave feminism and make claims for the essential pacificness of female rule here (video footage of Hillary Clinton's glee at devastating portions of the Middle East is as chilling as any of her male counterparts'). But, it's useful to register that literal violent competition for power—even at archaic Greek sites of origin for the "western" global north—is simply not a static feature of human social organization.

The bad news, however, is that few human societies have been as fluidly egalitarian or harmonious or Gaia-aligned as in our fondest, salvific imaginings.[11]

It's invigorating to suppose a world without hierarchy, to focus on one dimension of frequently preferred human-imagining, but there's little evidence that any complex social animal inhabits such a world.

Something like hierarchy comes along with the territory of being a symbolic animal. If narrating and listening, then privileging some stories over others. To use symbols is to hold focus *here* and not *there*.[12] To do so with any real consistency at all is to advantage whichever of us are most associated with *here* and not *there*. To tell stories that advantage some of us over time is to construct (at least moderately stable) hierarchies. There's no way out of that, besides perhaps the Mel-Gibson-in-a-muscle-car nihilism of George Miller's 1979 *Mad Max*. Social animals produce hierarchies. Symbolic animals stabilize those hierarchies, give them duration, and tie them to resource metabolization.

So, even if we do manage to panic wisely and well, we'll still almost unquestionably wind up producing and reproducing forms of organization that privilege some lives over others.

Indeed, even at its ultra-relational best, a fully realized global humanity would still be a *humanity*, privileging human life in general over many other forms of life. Easy to say it doesn't have to, harder to pursue the consequences of that saying in a thoroughgoing and serious way.

What would be the immediate consequences of refusing all species particularism? One can imagine a billionaire supervillain (but I repeat myself) persuaded they have discovered the only way to save complex life on planet Earth, calling themselves "posthumanist" and declaiming against anthropocentrism, setting loose viruses to kill off 80% or so of the 8 billion humans currently occupying the globe and offering a vaccine (perhaps as a subscription service) only to those who pledge their lives to ecological remediation and rewilding.

It's an absurd thought experiment, but the absurdity should be telling. Surely, if we set each human life equal in value to the lives of every other living thing, a person who recognizes the immeasurable crime of an Anthropocene that takes trillions of nonhuman lives and who has the means to accelerate humanity's near-total extinction would be hard-pressed to avoid wiping out most of anthropos. It would, after all, accomplish an extremely uncertain thing: clawing back a planetary future for most living creatures and their progeny. To dismiss such a vision—and before anyone starts worrying about me, let me be clear that I do—is, whether outright or only implicitly, to place a *particular value on current human life*.

At our best, we may want to be part of a global humanity that recognizes nonhuman lives as also dignified, also meaningful, also worthwhile. As relations. (This is my own imperfect practice.) But there's no denying that we have some special species-affinity.

And from special species-affinity, hierarchy.

The challenge of humanizing is to navigate the correctness of panic at how badly we humans have organized the metabolic possibilities of a world all animals and rivers and other living entities share. One way to take up the challenge is to grapple directly with some of our own species limitations.

The way we habitually (but not always) do hierarchy is definitely a problem. As suggested in chapter four, our necrotic Anthropocene was not written in the stars of our prehistoric ancestors, but CaCaCo does seem to have cashed out some of humanity's worst species-traits. If we want to become different enough to design ways of living well together and with other life on earth, it's worth keeping close tabs on some ways we're nearly sure to remain the same.

Take symbolicity itself as a representative anecdote for how we'll remain the same. After all, you're a human reading symbols written by another human.[13] And with symbols come hierarchy and much else that's unlovely.

Perhaps surprisingly, better attunement to our helpless symbolicity brings into focus what newness really may be possible, should we panic wisely enough to humanize.

Twentieth-century rhetorical theorist Kenneth Burke describes the pathologies of symbolicity at once trenchantly and amusingly in books like *Language as Symbolic Action*, *A Rhetoric of Motives*, and *A Grammar of Motives*.[15] The core of his decidedly uncelebratory view of human animals is that, in language (and symbol systems more broadly), we find tendencies toward hierarchizing, moralizing, and massive, constant overextension. While perhaps not one hundred percent dispositive, it's a useful guide to how future versions of us are liable to remain the same—for the worse.

In an essay on the "Definition of Man [*sic*],"[16] Burke arrives at a powerful assessment:

[The human] is
the symbol using (symbol making, symbol misusing) animal
inventor of the negative (or moralized by the negative)
separated from [their] natural conditions by instruments
    of [their] own making
goaded by the spirit of hierarchy (or moved by the sense of order)
and rotten with perfection.[17]

We don't need to take Burke at his human exceptionalist word, since by his own argument these traits would seem to obtain for any symbolic animal.[18] And we can say with some certainty that humans are not the *only* symbolic animal.[19]

What's important here is the sense that symbolic structures impose value structures, require value hierarchies, and impose a kind of overgraspingness.

To live together in language and other sorts of symbolicity is to differentiate between, and value differently, different elements of the world. Every symbol, every word or gesture or painting or dance or piece of architecture or sculpture, *is not* whatever it points to. And every arrangement of symbols brings some things to mind and *not* others. And every symbolic exchange tends to beget more exchanges like it. Over time, any culture-group exchanging symbols (regardless of whether those symbols are made by humans, machines, or nonhuman animals)—and this describes every group of people that ever have been and, short of a singularity, ever will be—tends to produce ways of living that value some bits of the world over others.

Moreover, in valuing some bits of the world over others, we end up pulling for those bits of world. That is, we affiliate with the things we've made repeatedly come to mind. Even if we don't like them (as, say, Democrats with Donald Trump), we also kind of want to see more of them, almost *need* to. We recognize any world at all through the bits of world we've most frequently foregrounded.[20] In doing so, we privilege some bits of world—and with them, some people most affiliated with them—over others. They literally sit atop a structure of principles, a hierarchy, in our minds. And not only in our minds. In the worlds we narrate and, so, act into being as well.

In no remotely plausible reorganization of the world (none, at least, that can be written and then read) are humans going to stop being symbolic animals.[14] Symbolic animals with all of the pathologies thereto appertaining.

But that doesn't mean we need to stay stuck as the *sort* of symbolic animals assumed by CaCaCo. At our very best, on that old rendering, we can do little more than to lurch from war to war in search of peace, presupposing all the way that a particularly powerful chunk of us are the *real* humans, praying in vain for markets to save us from our own catabolic appetites. Accepting symbolicity and hierarchy as hard constraints doesn't oblige us to all that, thankfully.

That there is no way around hierarchizing is not an excuse for any and every existing hierarchy. Emphatically not! If we are doomed to hierarchy, moved by the sense of order and rotten with perfection, we are all the *more* responsible for choosing very carefully what sorts of hierarchy to value and what sorts to reject.

Digging into ways we may be condemned to hierarchy by the mere fact of symbols helps to temper hopes and expectations. Humbly meditating upon the depth of our susceptibility to damaging organizations of world, we can better grasp how CaCaCo's current order assures pathologies far greater than necessitated by our basic character as symbolic and so hier-archical animals. This helps deepen panic.

Panicking in a somewhat timely fashion opens the door for new attune-ments to the world around us and, with those attunements, new forms of collectivity that proceed through wonder into action that might help us approach hierarchy differently.

If panic is a good affective starting-point, a solid approach to honestly admitting that we do not know what to do and can no longer bear the suf-fering of our current trajectory, it nonetheless is only one step on a jour-ney. Ultimately, humanizing has to be our destination. I've offered a few ways of cashing out progress toward that horizon (new solidarities, ways of sustaining disruption, participatory novelties, and regenerative archa-isms), but of course there are thousands more. The tools for humanizing offered here merely gesture toward what you, the reader, may yet invent.

So, how might we yet be different, after all that?

DIFFERENT

There may be nothing new under the sun, but, equally, there's no end to difference. Part of where panic comes from is the sudden understanding of *how incredibly different* a near future is likely to be.

Who will we be in that future? Who can we be? Notwithstanding unreal-istic framing (the authors suppose more flexibility from existing political and social structures than has been apparent for many decades), books like Rebecca Solnit and Thelma Young Lutunatabua's *Not Too Late* gesture at real possibilities for who we might yet become,[21] as do anthropological excavations like Graeber and Wengrow's *Dawn of Everything*. Such texts offer visions of human coexistence—with one another and the world be-yond us—that are radically different from what we have come to think of as normal or even necessary.

As Graeber and Wengrow emphasize, the "normal" of CaCaCo isn't even all that old. Sure, "we've" made the world incredibly different from how it was just a short few hundred years ago, but this wasn't transcen-dentally necessary. Even now, though it's not possible to stop CaCaCo's bankruptcy process or most of its consequences, it may be possible to opt in some sense out of CaCaCo itself—to live together toward whatever comes next instead.

It's happened before.

For two or three hundred years starting around 1050, a city we call Cahokia sprang up in the area that now is East St. Louis. With fifteen

WHO WILL WE BE?

thousand inhabitants and another twenty-five thousand in satellite communities, Cahokian culture was influential throughout a large geographic area before the city collapsed over the course of seventy-five years or so in the thirteenth century.[22] With growth likely driven by ritual significance for religious pilgrims and enabled by favorable soil conditions,[23] Cahokia drew migrants from throughout the Mississippi River Valley and beyond, urbanizing rapidly (perhaps in response to some religious revelation). It developed an elite and a priestly class, well-defined haves and have-nots. It seems to have been an all-encompassing place. As Graeber and Wengrow put it in their survey of the archaeological literature, "For those who fell within its orbit, there was nothing much left between domestic life—lived under constant surveillance from above—and the awesome spectacle of the city itself," replete with not just "games and feasts" but "mass executions and burials, carried out in public," as well.[24] This was not just a city, but a total world.

When it "abruptly dissolved," whatever exactly Cahokia had been in its heyday, its collapse came because "it seems to have ended up being overwhelmingly and resoundingly rejected by the vast majority of its people."[25] Where once it stood, by the time Europeans came on the scene "the descendants of Cahokia's subjects and neighbors appear to have reorganized themselves into *polis*-sized tribal republics, in careful ecological balance with their natural environment."[26] In its context and for a time (around 1200 CE, say), the monumental Cahokian culture must have seemed central, perhaps even inevitable or necessary, to life in the region—all the life most inhabitants knew.

And then it ended.

Cahokians scattered to the winds and were no more. They left behind a vast fertile terrain that none would settle for generations, referred to by archaeologists and anthropologists as "The Vacant Quarter." A world ended, for the most part voluntarily it seems, but not without some great wrenching dislocation. Indeed, "Among descendants of Cahokian subjects, migration is often framed as implying the restructuring of an entire social order."[27] Cahokians refused, for whatever reasons exactly, the world that had made them. And yet, the artifacts and religious practices of this mound city in its moment would factor into the culture-making of next-worlders occupying adjacent spaces for centuries to come.[28] But not only that: Subsequent cultures in the area seem to have been formed explicitly in rejection of the particular forms of hierarchy associated with Cahokia.

No culture-group is necessary, including our own. The question is how we might walk away from a social world that is, uniquely in human history, pretty much *the whole world*. In moving from panic to dispositions that may help us humanize (solidarities, disruptions, novelties, and archaisms), we find ways of "walking away" from CaCaCo even as we yet remain within it.

The necrotic Anthropocene we inhabit now wasn't intrinsic to the human species. Rather, this deadly Anthropocene is the deferred costs of CaCaCo falling due, the "externalities" of a form of life that became globally dominant over a few short centuries turning out to be "internal" to Gaia after all. On the other side of panic, there are new ways of life to make.

With Jenny Odell, let us begin by simply *stopping doing so much*. We can become less frenetic. Odell closes *How to Do Nothing* with a beautiful meditation on how different a nonextractive relationship with the world around us can look:

"Now the pelicans were flying plentifully past me, so close that I could see their faces, greeting me one at a time with their joyous six-foot-wide wingspans. . . . Standing perpendicular to the earth, not pitching forward, not falling back, I asked how I could possibly express my gratitude for the unlikely spectacle of the pelicans. The answer was nothing. Just watch."[29]

Nothing. Just watch. Just be present to Gaia's unfolding, within which we are and can be humanizing. Start there. More often than it feels like, there's *nothing we need to be doing*. The peoples of Gaia need not be the hyperactive, hyper-consumptive global humanity of CaCaCo.

As a species that doesn't need to do as much as we think, who might we be when realizing the project of a global humanity in a new way? On the other side of wise and timely panic, *we* might look incredibly different, to one another and to the machines we make, and to the nonhuman world as well.

Think of it again in terms of hierarchy.

To recall the dour start of this book: Things are going badly, terribly even. They're not going badly in some random and unforeseen or unforeseeable way, though. The polycrisis just now forcing itself into the consciousness of people around the world is, in essence, a mixture of deferred costs coming due and new costs, both social and resource metabolization costs, being imposed. Those latter, as in the case of AI-based profit-maximization for shareholders (who constitute, in terms of shares owned, a miniscule minority of any potential global humanity), still appear to many people in the guise of opportunity. As chapter two made clear, however, the AI revolution's costs are organized in much the same way as the various humanmade "natural" catastrophes that comprise the rest of the Anthropocene.

We are very badly stuck in this CaCaCo world that cannot pay its debts.

And the hierarchy by which CaCaCo is organized means that most of us will be forced to shoulder those long-deferred costs earlier and far more painfully than a very few of us.

In the latter moments of *The Dawn of Everything*, that exhaustive study of human culture groups across time and space, Graeber and Wengrow remind us that it didn't—and perhaps still doesn't—have to be this way. They explain,

"Nowadays, most of us find it increasingly difficult even to picture what an alternative economic or social order would be like. Our distant ancestors seem, by contrast, to have moved regularly back and forth between them. If something did go terribly wrong in human history—and given the current state of the world, it's hard to deny something did—then perhaps it began to go wrong precisely when people started losing that freedom to imagine and enact other forms of social existence, to such a degree that some now feel this type of freedom hardly even existed, or was barely exercised, for the greater part of human history."[30]

It is easy to suppose that hierarchy naturally stabilizes as oligarchy, with the rule of a wealthy few oppressing an impoverished many. That is, after all, what history looks like from the vantagepoint of *both* triumphant and chastened modernity.[31] But as Graeber and Wengrow clarify throughout, that supposition is a sort of intellectual malady, a pathology of the imagination that comes from being ourselves so badly (and atypically, relative to species-history) stuck.

Oligarchy and overshoot is what human history looks like, in other words, when we suppose the world *had to* end up looking more or less as it does today. In order to conceive of and act toward becoming global humanity, we have to see that the contemporary order of the world is as particular, contingent, and ultimately still malleable as any other. Indeed, the contemporary order of the world is already falling away.

A staggered collapse of many orders is underway. For U.S. American and other global north readers, as CaCaCo breaks down likely failure points will include the Westphalian order of nation-states,[32] the post-WWII order of American global hegemony,[33] the economic order of world trade anchored in the USD as global reserve currency and oil as core energy source,[34] the infrastructural order of road systems and stable energy delivery,[35] the social order of neighborly consideration and hospitality,[36] and the political order of modestly participatory decision-making on issues with third-party consequences.[37] (As already noted, who exactly benefited from each of these dimensions of CaCaCo varied quite a bit; it was certainly never "global humanity," but it may well have been you, reader, as it was me.)

The end of the world means that any "we" to come will, and *can*, be very different from whatever "we" we have been. We needn't to try to stop that.

Where thinkers of megathreats and polycrisis—represented in chapter two by Roubini and Janzwood and Homer-Dixon—still see a great deal of uncertainty about core infrastructural continuity, I do not. In effect, this book has set out from the notion that the world organized by CaCaCo for the last several hundred years *just is* breaking down now. There will be a lot of misery and distress in the end of this world, but also a lot of novelty and possibility. If we do nothing to prevent CaCaCo from collapsing, this does not mean we do nothing at all. New attunements open new possibilities for humanizing.

These latter, even if not possibilities for "us" in the way "we" have been accustomed to, entail responsibility. Rhetorician Sarah Allen lays out the stakes nicely in *Kairotic Inspiration*: "Ultimately, life as we know it is over and ... the only thing that matters now is making sure that other beings survive."[38] Ours is not the end of all worlds, surely (probably?), but it is the end of one world. What can we (inventive receivers and producers of symbols, all of us!) do, here in the earlyish moments of polycrisis still, to foster more life for other beings?

Each new world thus far has been built on the ruins of some other. But worlds don't end all at once. They fail in bits and pieces. Where the old falls away, the new struggles to be born. That's where *we* come in.

A part of our work, as Joshua Trey Barnett argues, is the reflective and relational work of mourning. We have to practice "attending to some of the ways in which humans express their own ecological grief and induce it in others" in order to open up to "other ways of dwelling on earth" in the midst of a catastrophe that is our own.[39] From panic can come attunement to loss, to the unavoidability of further loss, and to the possibility of new ways of caring or being responsible for one another—human and nonhuman alike. Mourning well, inventing space for our nonhuman kin and human relations alike, is only possible when we see not just the present but also something of a future that refuses meaning to much of the present. This starts with Pan's *phobos*.

How we panic now will determine to a large extent not simply an individual capacity to survive or thrive, as Roubini and the Davos set emphasize, but what worlds we will find ourselves able to make a little down the road of staggered collapse—and so what worlds may be possible still further along, even worlds without us in them. We can value a world that might not have us in it, and so practice deep and inessential solidarities in even this necrotic present.

Sarah Allen writes, "If we do manage to survive, human life will look totally unrecognizable to those of us living today, but if part of that un-recognizability is due to the fact that we have stretched to understand and care for other beings and concepts, by becoming-with, perhaps in ways that make us look monstrous to ourselves now, then we will have gained a soul."[40] This book's bet is that our collective capacities for becoming-with, our pluralistic design of better *nexts* in the hotter, darker dispersal of worlds to come, will have begun in this world we yet occupy with panic at realizing we are well and truly *stuck*. We are destroying ourselves and everyone else via CaCaCo infrastructures we cannot readily escape or effectively disavow.

To humanize in response to this is to refuse the false absolution of despair and the distraction of last-ditch, still-more-catabolically-consumptive hedonisms.

Throughout this book, I have tried to invite readers who may not have words yet for their well-warranted sense of panic into a way of naming it and a few ways of negotiating it. But really, we'll need a lot more ways than I've written down here.

Panic's question is what to do at the end of the road, where a sinkhole opens to swallow the boulevard entire. The world implied by a burgeoning polycrisis disperses into a plurality of worlds, shatters into barely inter-secting audiences, and at the same time becomes ever more one sort of a thing, becomes specifically a world that is ending, a vector that in its very disintegration encounters the place where all horizons shimmer, where futures blink in and out of existence.

What hierarchies—more fluid, more loving, more self-correcting, more attuned—can we hope to find on the other side of this world's horizons?

Probably not the ones we usually imagine. Probably not even the sorts a leftist like me would usually hope for. It's all very well to say, with the Italian Marxist Antonio Gramsci upon the ascendance of fascism in 20th-century Italy, that "the old is dying and the new cannot be born," and thereby to acknowledge that "in this interregnum a great variety of morbid symptoms appear.[41]" But this still presumes a future contiguous enough with the past to offer clear horizons over which to fight.

For Gramsci, the old world's dying represents a "crisis of authority" that in fact bodes well for the construction of new ideologies.[42] At stake is a "death of the old ideologies that takes the form of skepticism with regard to all theories," and in that skepticism emerges "the possibility and necessity of creating a new culture."[43] The problem and solution Gramsci details is ideational, discursive. The material, infrastructural order upon which culture may be re-constructed is vexed, but remains relatively stable.

Gramsci's crisis of authority opens a way for everyday people to think differently. If they think differently, they can act differently. And if they act differently, they can remake their world for the better.

Writing of still-newly fascist Italy, from old Europe, within a Westphalian order, in the Holocene geologic era, Gramsci imagines (wrongly as it happened, but plausibly) new authority for historical materialism. He hopes for a communist reorganization of Italy. This is to be (although in the end it would not be) remaking of an old world along new lines.

By contrast, what's dying in our necrotic Anthropocene is not only a discursive realm of authority, but the complex chains of material infrastructure that make our world—any world—a world at all.

What's struggling newly to be born may not have a name yet. Or maybe it's about humanizing, finally. Or maybe its names are more archaic still. Maybe the different worlds catastrophe opens onto are ones where we practice solidarities and sustain disruptions as peoples of Gaia. That could look a lot different from anything we've ever imagined.[44]

How fast will the CaCaCo world die, exactly? When will the weight of its deferred costs, falling due with punishing interest, become so great that the spring can take it no longer and bursts its housing? Who's to say? A world can stagger around for a good while before falling to the ground.

Take Lebanon, for example. I had the good fortune to live a few years by the sea in this beautiful, long-collapsing country (between 2014 and 2017).

After a devastating and inconclusive civil war (1975–1989 or –1991, depending how you count), Lebanon had been substantially rebuilt by the mid-2000s. Wide swathes of the country's infrastructure were again obliterated, this time by Israeli bombs, in 2006. Sporadic fighting between different militias both preceded and followed the civil war, which had never been fully resolved, and also followed 2006's July War with Israel.

During the three years I lived in Beirut, basic governance failed in all sorts of ways. Crises both political (difficulty finding and keeping president and prime minister, the spillover of a million-and-change refugees from neighboring Syria, and more) and ecological (some of the world's highest cancer rates from dumping/burning carcinogens, multiple trash removal stoppages, ongoing deforestation of Lebanon's iconic cedars, and more) threatened national integrity and interrupted day-to-day life. But those were fairly quiet years, on the whole. One ate a mana'eesh in peace, the Lebanese lira's peg to the dollar remained stable at 1500 LBP / 1 USD, and anyone who liked could buy a yellow AK-adorned Hezbollah t-shirt from a friendly vendor while visiting the famed Roman ruins at Baalbek.

In the few years before my arrival, there had been militia skirmishes in the heart of both Beirut and Lebanon's second city, Tripoli. After my departure, there was the meltdown of the central bank and the beginning of something like hyperinflation as the LBP lost its longtime dollar peg— hitting 100,000 LBP / 1 USD on the informal market even as the Banque du Liban eventually established official rates of not even an eighth that and semi-official rates fluctuated to still other rhythms. Lebanese and foreigners alike could not access funds held in dollar-denominated bank accounts. Protests swelled to a *thawra*, a revolution, though this in turn gave way to more of the old sectarian political system. The Beirut port explosion of 2020, which killed over 200 people and injured thousands of others, was one of the most powerful accidental explosions in human history. Prime ministers and cabinets resigned, and powerful political parties sat out elections.

And yet, Lebanon muddled on. "That's Lebanon!" friends would respond with cheerful resignation when I complained in the relatively peaceful years I spent there about some annoyance. Lebanon, arguably, has been collapsing for the entirety of its modern existence.

That's not a dig at Lebanon. Far from it! The whole CaCaCo world is collapsing. The shit company's failing. But a world can stagger through collapse, crumble in bits and pieces, for a pretty long time without being succeeded by some next world.

The polycrisis that names how CaCaCo is falling down goes well beyond the four dimensions I've explored here. And it could be going on for a while. But, unlike the case of Lebanon—this small country overwritten by others' desires at a dense node of geopolitics, whose people suffer the world and each other with grace and humor and violence by turns—the CaCaCo world is the *whole world*. It's the broad sum of how global humanity, such as it is thus far, gets organized. And its crises are mounting increasingly quickly.

There's every reason to think the climate crisis's effects will shatter supply chains as ever-higher seas roil with more energy each passing year and drought drains rivers. And that's even if, somehow, decarbonization emerges as a real possibility in ways it hasn't yet.

There's no reason to think the AI revolution will leave existing work relations, and the political economies built around them, intact. Nor should we hope it will not be mobilized against large populations by economically powerful small groups and entities. To say nothing of what it will or does or should mean to be human.

The loss of what's finest in our humanity, and perhaps also of our ability to grow food through natural pollination, will continue to follow our extirpation of our nonhuman kin. And there's no telling which of the hundreds of thousands of novel entities we've loosed on the world, with more pumped out each day and week and month, will turn out to change everything for the worse in ways yet unforeseen.

Will the world as we know it today exist in 2040? For some, those sheltered a bit longer by wealth from the ravages of the polycrisis, maybe? Sort of? Can we call it the "same world" if, as Italy was despite Gramsci's fond hopes, it has been reorganized entirely by fascism, by the brutality of armed lifeboats from which ever more of the ever larger and ever more desperate global population of the poor are repelled with deadly and dehumanizing force? What world, at length, is that?

But other worlds are possible, though in the ashes of this one. When we get honest enough to panic, they start coming into view. The end of this world is not tomorrow or next year, but already today. Our challenge is remaining present to its endings, to be here and to become new sorts of people in the partial ruins growing already like flowers on a blighted landscape.

As CaCaCo staggers through its extended collapse, it's worth recalling that the (Nazi) philosopher Heidegger was still giving seminars at Freiburg in 1943—two years after Germans' systematic mass murder of Europe's Jewry had begun and well toward the Axis powers' loss of WWII and so their world. As Hitler's willing executioners unspooled the machinery to accomplish a "final solution to the Jewish question," Heidegger lectured roomfuls of budding young (Aryan) philosophers.

For those who want and can afford it, there will be plenty of business-as-usual in our worsening world to come, plenty of banally evil "normalcy."

Or, you can look to the worlds you hope to begin laying foundations for. There are plenty of alternative futures to start building as this world crumbles.

One needn't wait for the end of the CaCaCo world to build new solidarities, on behalf of liberation to forge new identifications with people one is not supposed to relate to. There will be disruptions. How we sustain them, the habits of love and alignment to Gaia we bring to them, will determine who we become as they unfold. Nor must one wait to try out new forms of life, from egalitarian anarchic community to household waste management. And it's never too soon to return to what's archaic, to find something wild and free—and/or something rich with meaning, ceremony, and even discipline—in the worlds before CaCaCo whose inheritors we all are.

There's much to do right now, in *this* collapsing world, to determine what global humanity might yet mean. How we metabolize resources now, in this time of comparative abundance, has everything to do with what ideas will be lying around for worldbuilders in futures marked by scarcity and loss.

CaCaCo was not born, Athena-like, full-formed from Zeus's forehead. It came patchily to be the hegemonic logic of a thus-global humanity, with great violence and promise alike. Likewise, the end of this world is not event but process. We cannot save our world. We can regain a relatively recently lost capacity for imagining and designing its successors. We can act so as to leave some better ideas lying around in the ruins to come.

What other worlds might next be born? Who might we be in them? This depends almost entirely on who we decide to be now.

Acknowledgments

I wrote this book in something of a frenzy. Though I haven't taken drugs in twenty-odd years, the focused intensity of writing *Panic Now?* was like Nietzsche's *Rausch*, a creative madness. I'm usually a slower writer—but these words wanted out. The work's finer qualities, then, are due enormously to the generous reading of others and to many conversations over the years adding up to it.

I am profoundly grateful to and for that first intimate and critical and sustaining and—yes—liberating, readership.

This book would not exist at all without Robin Bedenbaugh's invitation to write it, critical support for it at every step, and thoughtful camaraderie about logistics and ideas alike. I have other projects underway and paused them all in order to write something that, I hope, can be of service in meeting the urgency of our polycrisis. Thank you, Robin, for seeing the need for the book and helping me see how to write it. One could not ask for a better editor.

The University of Tennessee Press has been magnificent start to finish. From initial encouragement by outgoing director Scot Danforth and swift follow-through by Stephanie Thompson, Jon Boggs, and the production team to the brilliant cover and interior design of Kelly Gray (with Robin's handwriting) and savvy and committed marketing vision of Walt Evans, it's been a gift to work with the whole UT Press team. Thank you.

For opportunities to present and converse about the germs that grew into this book, I am especially thankful to Robert Terrill and the Indiana University Department of English's invitation to give a Distinguished Rhetoric Alumni Lecture in Fall 2021; to Jeremy Engels and the Paterno

Fellows Contemporary Issues Forum at Pennsylvania State University in Fall 2022; and to Jason Barrett-Fox and the Composition Conversations series at Weber State University in Spring 2023; as well as to audiences who on each occasion pushed me to think better.

Readers whose comments on drafts or elements of this book shaped it, without exception, for the better (and some a great deal), include Saul Allen, Eyal Bar, Jason Barrett-Fox, Chris Basgier, Iuri Bauler Pereira, Andrew Bisto, Crystal Colombini, Jeremy Engels, Luis Fernandez, Danielle Hodges, Mark A. Johnson, Lauren Lefty, Laura Noll, Davide Panagia, Sean Parson, Joe Rhodes, Emily Schneider, KT Thompson, Pamela VanHaitsmaa, Lydia Wilkes, and Kurt Zemlicka. My deep thanks to you all, especially Professors Engels, Panagia, and Johnson as readers for the press and Saul, Sean, Lydia, Chris, and Jason for exceptionally intensive engagement with full drafts. What is good and useful in this book owes much to you, both individually and collectively (and the collocation CaCaCo is due to Saul, who in offering it advised me, "Nobody wants to read *carbon-capitalism-colonialism assemblage* over and over for 200 pages"). Thank you all.

Entire worlds go into any book, perhaps this one especially. To even begin thanking the communities who helped me find useful clarity here would need a new book—my hope is that this one enacts that thanks.

At home, Laura Noll has listened for hours she did not have to spare as I read moments from the book aloud. She is my closest interlocutor and I would be poor in world without her. The book would be a lot worse, too. Thank you, Laura. And though they're not big readers, thank you no less to Zada, Willa, and little Ali, by whose sides and shared warmth and light *Panic Now?* was written. I know the best way to thank you is getting out into the woods together.

Hope we all can.

Notes

Introduction

1. Mathieu, Edourd, *et al.* 2023. "Coronavirus (COVID-19) Deaths." *Our World in Data*, Accessed 6 May 2023. Web.

2. In the U.S., despair can be measured in terms of ever-increasing overdose deaths, declining workforce participation, and intensifications of social violence such as mass shootings. For a centrist/mainstream perspective on the durability of this reality (i.e., that it is not simply a short-term reaction to the coronavirus pandemic or other "one-shot" causal factors), see Graham. Carol. 2021. "America's Crisis of Despair: A Federal Task Force for Economic Recovery and Societal Wellbeing." *Brookings Blueprints for American Renewal and Prosperity*, 10 February 2021. Web. Look too, in China, at the "lie flat" movement (cf. Davidovich, Ivana. 2022. "'Lying Flat': Why Some Chinese are Put-ting Work Second." *BBC*, 16 February 2022. Web.) and, tellingly, at the worried tones of much Western reportage thereon. For a richer snapshot of the U.S. case, see Baker, Erik. 2023. "The Age of the Crisis of Work." *Harper's*, May 2023. More prosaically, see Witters, Dan. 2023. "U.S. Depression Rates Reach New Highs." *Gallup*, 17 May 2023. Web.

3. At the cost of hours that might have been spent doing something with my life, I have read both Pinker and MacAskill. Pinker's cherrypicked and badly framed *The Better Angels of Our Nature* has been around long enough to receive many thorough debunk-ings, so I encourage anyone curious about either to start with Jon Shaffer's review of MacAskill's *What We Owe the Future*: "Longtermism, or How to Get-Out-of-Caring While Feeling Moral and Smart." *Peste Mag*, 10 October 2022. Web.

4. "For a large share of humanity," Achille Mbembe observes, "the end of the world has already occurred. The question is no longer to know how to live life while awaiting it; instead it is to know how living will be possible the day after the end, that is to say, how to live with loss, with separation" (29). Mbembe, Achille. 2019. *Necropolitics*. Durham: Duke UP.

5. For two thoughtful discussions of masses and crowds, see Dean, Jodi. 2018. *Crowds and Party*. London: Verso. and Toscano, Alberto. 2017. *Fanaticism: On the Uses of an Idea*.

London: Verso. On social movements as vital to democratic possibility, even and especially where democratic possibility itself is diminished, see Woodly, Deva. 2021. *Reckoning: Black Lives Matter and the Democratic Necessity of Social Movements*. Oxford: Oxford UP and Thimsen, Freya. 2022. *The Democratic Ethos: Authenticity and Instrumentalism in US Movement Rhetoric After Occupy*. Columbia: South Carolina UP.

6. Or perhaps a much shorter period, as a collapsing Atlantic Meridional Overturning Circulation (AMOC) threatens to throw the climate zones on which social stability relies into wild disarray. One good proxy for such disarray in the near term—even *without* AMOC collapse—is breadbasket failure. On climate risks to the food system, see Coughlan de Perez, Erin, *et al.* 2023. "Potential for Surprising Heat and Drought Events in Wheat-Producing Regions of US and China." *npj Climate and Atmospheric Science* vol. 6, art. no. 56. Web. On the possibility that the AMOC may change phase far sooner than commonly supposed, see Ditlevsen, Peter, and Susan Ditlevsen. 2023. "Warning of a Forthcoming Collapse of the Atlantic Meridional Overturning Circulation." *Nature Communications*, vol. 14, art. no. 4254. Web.

Chapter 1

1. Faulkner, William. 2011 [1951]. *Requiem for a Nun*. New York: Vintage, 73.

2. For several fine instances, see Fraser, Nancy. 2022. *Cannibal Capitalism: How Our System Is Devouring Democracy, Care, and the Planet—and What We Can Do About It*. London: Verso; Copley, Jack. 2021. *Governing Financialization: The Tangled Politics of Financial Liberalization in Britain*. Oxford: Oxford University Press; and Brown, Wendy. 2015. *Undoing the Demos: Neoliberalism's Stealth Revolution*. Princeton: Princeton University Press.

3. For important work on the climate crisis's villains, for instance, see Oreskes, Naomi, and Erik M. Conway. 2019 [2010]. *Merchants of Doubt: How a Handful of Scientists Obscured the Truth on Issues from Tobacco Smoke to Climate Change*. New York, Bloomsbury; Speth, Gustave. 2021. *They Knew: The US Government's Fifty-Year Role in Causing the Climate Crisis*. Cambridge: MIT Press.

4. Cf. Allen, Ira. 2022. "A Non-Defensive Gun: Violence, Climate Catastrophe, and Rhetorical Education," in *Rhetoric and Guns*. Eds. Lydia Wilkes, Nate Kreuter, and Ryan Skinnell. Logan: Utah State University Press: 218-235.

5. Though hardly a global force for justice, the Pentagon's take on what this might look like is instructive. Klare, Michael T. 2019. *All Hell Breaking Loose: The Pentagon's Perspective on Climate Change*. New York: Picador.

6. Throughout, I refer to CaCaCo as a relatively recent historical development: just a couple or few hundred years old. This story foregrounds carbon-burning and industrialism. An alternate, equally reasonable, genealogy would trace our planetary woes to the emergence of whiteness, colonialism, capitalism, and chattel slavery in the 16th century. See the excellent Horne, Gerald. 2020. *The Dawning of the Apocalypse: The Roots of Slavery, White Supremacy, Settler Colonialism, and Capitalism in the Long Sixteenth Century*. New York: Monthly Review Press.

7. The locus classicus is Catton, William. 1980. *Overshoot: The Ecological Basis of Revolutionary Change*. Urbana: U Illinois P. For a good instance of current work on how we are overshooting the capacities of the human ecological niche to sustain our resource consumption, see Fanning, Andrew L., *et al.* 2022. "The Social Shortfall and Ecological Overshoot of Nations." *Nature Sustainability*, vol. 5: 26-36.

8. Pontzer, Herman, *et al.* 2016. "Metabolic Acceleration and the Evolution of Human Brain Size and Life History." *Nature*, vol. 553: 390-392.

9. For thoughtful discussion of the inadequacy of "ecosystem services" and "natural capital" for understanding the hybrid nature of work in human history, see Battistoni, Alyssa. 2017. "Bringing in the Work of Nature: From Natural Capital to Hybrid Labor." *Political Theory*, vol. 45, no. 1: 5-31.

10. Cf. Zorrilla-Revilla, Guillermo, Jesús Rodriguez, and Ana Mateos. 2021. "Gathering Is Not Only for Girls: No Influence of Energy Expenditure on the Onset of Sexual Division of Labor." *Human Nature*, vol. 32: 582-602; Ocobock, Cara. 2020. "Human Energy Expenditure in Anthropology and Beyond." *American Anthropologist*, vol. 122, no. 2: 236-249.

11. See Smil, Vaclav. 2017. *Energy and Civilization: A History*. Cambridge: MIT Press. For another view, imagining what it might look like to reconfigure human civilizations *away* from a corresponding investment in power, perhaps especially for those to come after CaCaCo finishes breaking down, see Heinberg, Richard. 2021. *Power: Limits and Prospects for Human Survival*. Gabriola Island, BC: New Society Publishers.

12. It is a default ideological position of CaCaCo's proponents that this arrangement of the world has "lifted" unprecedented numbers people out of poverty. That, quite the contrary, extreme poverty is largely an *effect* of compressing everyone into a CaCaCo world, which has only fairly recently begun ameliorating that effect, is compellingly demonstrated in Sullivan, Dylan, and Jason Hickel. 2023. "Capitalism and Extreme Poverty: A Global Analysis of Real Wages, Human Height, and Mortality Since the Long 16th Century." *World Development*, vol. 151, art. no. 106026. Web.

13. Radical differences in access to fossil fuel energy and to the work-energy enabled by electricity remain distributed almost perfectly along lines associated with colonialist violence. Cf. Malm, Andreas, and Alf Hornborg. 2014. "The Geology of Mankind: A Critique of the Anthropocene Narrative." *The Anthropocene Review*, vol. 1, no. 1: 62-69; Lewis, Simon L., and Mark A. Maslin. 2015. "Defining the Anthropocene." *Nature*, vol. 519: 171-180. Web. For visualizations of contemporary energy sources and uses, see Hannah Ritchie, Max Roser, and Pablo Rosado. 2022. "Energy." *Our World In Data*. Web.

14. Moore, Jason W. (Ed.). 2016. *Anthropocene of Capitalocene? Nature, History, and the Crisis of Capitalism*. Oakland: PM Press. See also Grove, Jairus Victor. 2019. *Savage Ecology: War and Geopolitics at the End of the World*. Durham: Duke UP, especially chapter three, "From Exhaustion to Annihilation: A Martial Ecology of the Eurocene."

15. Waldman, John. 2009. "With Temperatures Rising, Here Comes 'Global Weirding.'" *Yale Environment 360*, 19 March 2009. Web. Although the globe is on the whole heating dramatically, a limited subset of regions are not and others are heating far faster than average. Meanwhile, animal behavior and species phenology are shifting before our eyes, with dramatic consequences for ecological webs. Regardless of local variation, once-predictable patterns are becoming unpredictable and extremely intense almost everywhere, becoming *weird*.

16. On the emergence of fossil capitalism, i.e., the onset of CaCaCo, see Malm, Andreas. 2013. "The Origins of Fossil Capital: From Water to Steam in the British Cotton Industry." *Historical Materialism*, vol. 21: 15-68. For an intriguing treatment of how an emerging ideology of liberal individualism not only navigated but was dependent upon the massively illiberal forces of CaCaCo, see Ince, Onur Ulas. *Colonial Capitalism and the Dilemmas of Liberalism*. 2018. Oxford: Oxford University Press.

17. For much richer discussion, see Mau, Søren. 2023. *Mute Compulsion: A Marxist Theory of the Economic Power of Capital*. London: Verso. For an economics textbook that gives a useful window into how U.S. understandings of capital consolidated in the post-Soviet era, see Shaffer, Harry G. 1999. *American Capitalism and the Changing Role of Government*. Westport: Praeger.

18. Rosa Luxemburg's classic description in *The Accumulation of Capital* remains a useful grounding: "The regular repetition of production is the general precondition and foundation of regular consumption, and is thus a prerequisite of human civilization in each of its historical forms. . . . Production cannot be resumed—there can be no reproduction—unless certain preconditions are fulfilled: tools, raw materials, and labor-power must be available as the result of the preceding period of production" (7). Capital institutions are the social and material frameworks within which capitalism ensures some version of this continuity, frameworks the ownership of which allows such owners (i.e., capitalists) to profit. The rub, though, is that it's not profitable simply to reproduce society as is, a fact that results in both gluts and shortages: "As can be observed, in certain periods all the necessary material means of production and labor-power are available, and yet the consumption needs of society are not met, reproduction being either completely interrupted, or occurring only on a much reduced scale. . . . In this case it is profit, as an end in itself and as the determining moment, that regulates not only production but also reproduction—i.e., it does not merely determine how the labor process is configured, what labor is carried out, and how the products are to be distributed; it also decides the question of whether, on what scale, and in which direction the labor process is to be resumed after the conclusion of a period of labor" (9). Capital institutions are distinct from other frameworks for maintaining the continuity of a given society's resource metabolization, production, and reproduction in being directed by small groups of people—capitalists, those who own majority shares in these institutions—for their own enrichment, irrespective of whether this enrichment serves the general good. Luxemburg, Rosa. 2016 [1913]. "The Accumulation of Capital: A Contribution to the Economic Theory of Imperialism," in *The Complete Works of Rosa Luxemburg, Vol. II: Economic Writings 2* Eds. Peter Hudis and Paul Le Blanc, Trans. Nicholas Gray and George Shriver. New York: Verso.

19. A good proxy for the majority shareholder class's ownership of capital assets, which is both legitimately difficult to track and intentionally obscured, is wealth distribution. Those with the most wealth have holdings vastly over and above what's required to sustain even a very lavish personal life, and those holdings—circulating as invested capital and so not immediately accessible as cash—beget ever more wealth, giving rise to the somewhat odd term "net worth" as a kind of middle ground between money and capital. In 2022, 1% of people in the world owned 45.6% of global wealth (Shorrocks, Anthony, James Davies, and Rodrigo Lluberas. Credit Suisse Research Institute. *Global Wealth Report 2022*. 1 September 2022. Web.). That global 1%, moreover, is concentrated primarily in the old imperial core, the places most advantaged by colonialism. We may treat the distribution of net worth as roughly equivalent to the distribution of capital assets. Most people have little, nothing, or less than nothing. For a thrilling exposé of how the majority shareholder class obscures its ownership of assets in order to better maintain exclusive control over them, see Obermaier, Frederik, and Bastian Obermayer. 2017. *The Panama Papers: Breaking the Story of How the Rich and Powerful Hide Their Money*. New

York: Simon and Schuster. Though its authors won a Pulitzer for their reporting, the story receded from public consciousness faster than you can say Scrooge McDuck. On the majority shareholder class's disenchantment with what we like to call democracy as a political structure for maintaining this state of economic affairs, see Slobodian, Quinn. 2023. *Crack-Up Capitalism: Market Radicals and the Dream of a World Without Democracy.* New York: Metropolitan Books.

20. Especially with regard to the colonial and (thus) financial centers of London and New York, see the highly illuminating Pistor, Katharina. 2019. *The Code of Capital: How the Law Creates Wealth and Inequality.* Princeton: Princeton UP.

21. Cf. Mignolo, Walter. 2011. *The Darker Side of Western Modernity: Global Futures, Decolonial Options.* Durham: Duke University Press; Bhandar, Brenna. 2018. *Colonial Lives of Property: Law, Land, and Racial Regimes of Ownership.* Durham: Duke University Press.

22. Allowing, of course, for periodic "resets" via economic depressions (which are definitionally temporary and intermittent) and, more frighteningly, vast populations reductions accomplished by famine, plague, and war.

23. I am sensitive to a distinction between Land as relations exceeding the colonialism that grasps them badly and land as ownership in the sense enforced by colonialism, which Max Liboiron (Métis/Michif) details powerfully. Liboiron, Max. 2021. *Pollution is Colonialism.* Durham: Duke University Press. I've written this book, accompanied no less by birdsong and the bouquet of skunks than by the grinding of heavy equipment building houses nearby, mostly from within the internal edges of a great ponderosa forest that spans the southern squiggle of the Colorado Plateau, on Land that was sometimes home to the Wiipukepaya/Wipukepa (Oak Creek band of the Yavapai) and Tonto Apache peoples before settlers like me got here, and to Pueblan people before them. Also noteworthy is that the very idea of "resources," which I follow common practice in using throughout this book as if it were simple and self-evident, is contested. See Curley, Andrew. 2022. "Resources Is Just Another Word for Colonialism." *The Routledge Handbook of Critical Resource Geography.* Matthew Himley, Elizabeth Havice, and Gabriela Valdivia (Eds.). New York: Routledge: 79-90.

24. And equally again in Nicholas V's *Romanus Pontifex* bull of 1455 (also for Alfonso V). For an accessible treatment of colonialism in terms of religious restrictions on who could count as a person, see Tembo, Josias. 2022. "Unveiling the Entanglements of Western Christianity and Racialisation in Africa. *Social Dynamics* vol. 48, no. 3: 407-427. I quote *Dum Diversas* here from Jennings, Willie James. 2010. *The Christian Imagination: Theology and the Origins of Race.* New Haven: Yale UP, 29-30.

25. Liboiron, *op. cit.*, 9, citing Coulthard, Glen. 2014. *Red Skin, White Masks: Rejecting the Colonial Politics of Recognition.* Minneapolis: U Minnesota P, 7.

26. Chattel slavery was only possible, as a multigenerational political economic technology, through the globalizing patterns of colonialism. European nation-states sponsored military expeditions that simultaneously remapped the world and codified its (mostly!) non-European inhabitants along a spectrum of personhood descending from the nominal full humanity of Europeans. Cf. Mamdani, Mahmood. 2015. "Settler Colonialism: Then and Now." *Critical Inquiry*, vol. 41, no. 3: 596-614. W.E.B. Du Bois' *Black Reconstruction in America: Toward a History of the Part Which Black Folk Played in the Attempt to Reconstruct Democracy in America, 1860-1880* (New Brunswick: Transaction, 2013 [1935]) remains, unhappily, as relevant in this connection as nearly a century ago.

27. Historian Roxanne Dunbar-Ortiz provides compelling arguments in *An Indigenous Peoples' History of the United States* (Boston: Beacon Press, 2014) and *Loaded: A Disarming History of the Second Amendment* (San Francisco: City Lights Books, 2018). See also Ostler, Jeffrey. 2015. "Genocide and American History." *Oxford Research Encyclopedia of American History*, 2 March 2015. Web.

28. Rodney, Walter. 2018 [1972]. *How Europe Underdeveloped Africa*. London: Verso; Denoon, Donald. 1983. *Settler Capitalism: The Dynamics of Dependent Development in the Southern Hemisphere*. New York: Oxford UP. The idea of a "global humanity," arising in this context as it did, was simultaneously risible justification for injustice and seed of future correctives that would emerge around the thus-transformed world. On the way colonialism organizes even reformist impulses in settler nations like Australia and the United States, however, see Lake, Marilyn. 2019. *Progressive New World: How Settler Colonialism and Transpacific Exchange Shaped American Reform*. Cambridge: Harvard UP. The social relations thereby codified in law and practice were also gendered and tended to uphold rigid sexual hierarchies and exclusions. See Glenn, Evelyn Nakano. 2015. "Settler Colonialism as Structure: A Framework for Comparative Studies of U.S. Race and Gender Formation." *Sociology of Race and Ethnicity*, vol. 1, no. 1: 52-72. In fact, "colonialism" means something different for every dispossessed people the world over. To dislocate Tolstoy's *bon mot*, every settler-colony is the same, but every dispossessed people is unhappy in its own way.

29. For just one instance of the durability of colonialism's ordering force not only between nations but also within them, see Rothstein, Richard. 2018. *The Color of Law: A Forgotten History of How Our Government Segregated America*. New York: Liveright/Norton.

30. For a useful insider-economist treatment of the colonial organization of globalizing institutions created in the WWII-era Bretton Woods Agreement (though not in so many words), see Stiglitz, Joseph. 2002. "Globalization and the Logic of Collective International Action: Re-Examining the Bretton Woods Institutions." *Governing Globalization: Issues and Institutions*. Deepak Nayyar (Ed.). New York: Oxford UP: 238-253. Bretton Woods organized a post-war global economic order, with a tightly regulated system of currency exchange organized around the gold-backed U.S. dollar. The Bretton Woods Institutions (International Bank for Reconstruction and Development [now the World Bank] and International Monetary Fund) were treaty-designated by WWII's allied forces. By contrast, the G7 emerged as an informal summit beginning with the economic shocks of 1973-1975, triggered especially by OPEC's fossil carbon production cuts and U.S. President Nixon's decoupling of the USD from a gold standard.

31. On the extent to which decolonization continues not to have occurred for many dispossessed peoples (and continues not to be much aided by academic claims to "decolonize" this, that, or the other), see Tuck, Eve, and K. Wayne Yang. 2012. "Decolonization Is Not a Metaphor." *Decolonization: Indigeneity, Education, and Society*, vol. 1, no. 1: 1-40.

32. For a highly accessible history of the G7's origins and operations, on which I draw liberally here, see Hajnal, Peter N. 2018 [1999]. *The G7/G8 System: Evolution, Role, and Documentation*. London: Routledge.

33. The myriad domains where the G7 serves as quasi-formal agenda-setting body for world politics beggars description. For a celebration of this, see Morin, Jean-Frédéric, *et al.* 2019. "How Informality Can Address Emerging Issues: Making the Most of the G7." *Global Policy*, vol. 10, no. 2: 267-273. For *Time*, Sanya Mansoor offers a typical popular

framing: "On the agenda at the June 26-28 event are Russia's invasion of Ukraine, the global economic crises exacerbated by the war, vaccine equity, and the climate emergency." Mansoor, Sanya. 2022. "What to Know About the 2022 G7 Summit." *Time*, 24 June 2022. Web.

34. G7 members held 53.46% of global wealth in 2020, with 30.2% of that being held by entities within the United States economy alone. U.S. dominance was challenged in this regard only by China, which held 17.9% of global wealth in 2020—astronomically up from merely 3.14% at the end of 2000. At odds with this wildly disproportionate share of benefit in the spoils of capitalism is the relatively small population of G7 countries, which accounts for merely 11.56% of the world's adult population. Compare with British-colonized India, which despite having won independence midway through the twentieth century and comprising 17.21% of the globe's adult population held only 3.07% of its wealth in 2020. In comparing India's and China's trajectories, it is noteworthy that though subjected to a variety of colonial impositions, the latter was never effectively conquered by foreign powers across the majority of its vast land mass. Shorrocks, Anthony, James Davies, and Rodrigo Lluberas. 2021. *Global Wealth Databook 2021*. Credit Suisse Research Institute, June 2021. Web.

35. Wolfe, Patrick. 2016. *Traces of History: Elementary Structures of Race*. London: Verso. Complicating this picture somewhat, though, see Kelley, Robin D.G. 2017. "The Rest of Us: Rethinking Settler and Native." *American Quarterly*, vol. 69, no. 2: 267-276.

36. For the U.S. case, see Dunbar-Ortiz, Roxanne. 2021. *Not "A Nation of Immigrants": Settler Colonialism, White Supremacy, and a History of Erasure and Exclusion*. Boston: Beacon. But against a too-easy equation of the logics of slavery and genocide under the penumbra of colonialism, of which my reductive sketch here is guilty, see Jodi Byrd's (Chickasaw) carrying forward of her longstanding project in Byrd, Jodi A. 2019. "Weather with You: Settler Colonialism, Antiblackness, and the Grounded Relationalities of Resistance." *Critical Ethnic Studies*, vol. 5, no. 1-2: 207-214.

37. Levander, Caroline, and Walter Mignolo. "Introduction: The Global South and World Dis/Order." 2011. *The Global South*, vol. 5, no. 1: 1-11.

38. Cf. Benson, Eleanor, *et al.* 2023. "Mapping the Spatial Politics of Australian Settler Colonialism." *Political Geography*, vol. 102: 1-11; Hunt, Dallas, and Shaun A. Stevenson. 2017. "Decolonizing Geographies of Power: Indigenous Digital Counter-Mapping Practices on Turtle Island." *Settler Colonial Studies*, vol. 7, no. 3: 372-392.

39. In *How to Hide an Empire: A History of the Greater United States* (New York: Farrar, Straus and Giroux, 2019), Daniel Immerwahr shows that in the contemporary era, where capitalist organization of economic life through the "energy efficiencies" of fossil carbon-burning has partially replaced the direct violence of older colonialisms, and yet where colonialism's international legal order remains fully in place, the 20th- and 21st-century United States is well understood as imperial.

40. But recall Sullivan and Hickel, *op. cit.*

41. The sense of crisis as entailing uncertainty and grave threat, but also possibility, is nicely detailed in Colombini, Crystal Broch. [Forthcoming]. "Pandora's *Krisis* as *Phantastic* New Parable of Judgment." *Journal for the History of Rhetoric*, forthcoming.

42. For useful discussion of this tendency, see Klein, Naomi. 2008. *The Shock Doctrine: The Rise of Disaster Capitalism*. New York: Picador.

43. Solnit, Rebecca, and Thelma Young Lutunatabua (Eds.). 2023. *Not Too Late:*

Changing the Climate Story from Despair to Possibility. Chicago: Haymarket. Solnit, Rebecca, and Thelma Young Lutunatabua. "FAQ." *Not Too Late Climate*, https://www .nottoolateclimate.com/faq.

44. *Ibid*.

45. For empirical data on the near-total ineffectiveness of ordinary people's policy preferences in the United States, see Bartels, Larry. 2016. *Unequal Democracy: The Political Economy of the New Gilded Age, 2nd Ed*. Princeton: Princeton UP. For a rich theoretical view of the democratic inefficacy of many decades of mass action, see Kyong-Min, Son. 2020. *The Eclipse of the Demos: The Cold War and the Crisis of Democracy Before Neoliberalism*. Lawrence: UP of Kansas. On a longer tradition of American political disappointment, as the mechanisms of CaCaCo crush hopeful visions of mass politics, see Marcus, Sara. 2023. *Political Disappointment: A Cultural History from Reconstruction to the AIDS Crisis*. Cambridge: Harvard UP. Rosier pictures typically rely on the study of moments in presumptively long-term processes of incremental change. They thus contrast sharply with the rapid and radically transformative change Solnit and Lutunatabua cheerfully announce is within reach, and that would be necessary to "save" CaCaCo.

46. For one of hundreds of looks at the complexity of even determining what to count as equitable adaptation, see Singh, Chandni, *et al*. 2022. "Interrogating 'Effectiveness' in Climate Change Adaptation: 11 Guiding Principles for Adaptation Research and Practice." *Climate and Development*, vol. 14, no. 7: 650-664. Given that CaCaCo is predicated on a global hierarchy of nations, and that the dispossessed of this system understandably want to burn fossil carbon to increase their share of the economic pie, and that everyone must more or less immediately stop burning carbon, it's clear that anyone in the global north who hopes to continue consuming at roughly their current rate is assuming forced "underconsumption" by most of the global south to offset that. This surely includes most of Solnit and Lutunatabua's audience—alongside many readers of this book as well. As an instance of how much "green growth" talk bakes in CaCaCo assumptions about who can have and do what, see Holechek, Jerry L., Hatim M.E. Geli, Mohammed M. Sawalhah, and Raul Valdez. 2022. "A Global Assessment: Can Renewable Energy Replace Fossil Fuels by 2050?" *Sustainability*, vol. 14, no. 8: 4792. The authors assume nearly four times the per capita energy use for global north residents that they propose for global south residents, in an "equitable" pathway to decarbonization by 2050.

47. This and the next claim are extensively warranted in Smil, Vaclav. 2022. *How the World Really Works: The Science Behind How We Got Here and Where We're Going*. New York: Viking.

48. For an excellent discussion of how much of a strain eight billion humans put on the world, which manages to avoid falling into the unsavory legacy of racist eugenics that haunts overpopulation discussions, see Oreskes, Naomi. "Eight Billion People in the World Is a Crisis, Not an Achievement." *Scientific American*, 1 March 2023. Web. For a profoundly confused response to Oreskes, which falls into a long tradition of business-as-usual CaCaCo denialism misunderstanding itself as virtue, see Ramachandran, Vijaya, and Alex Trembath. "The Malthusians Are Back." *The Atlantic*, 22 March 2023. Web. Perhaps most notable about the latter is that its authors occupy full-time leadership at the ultracapitalist Breakthrough Institute, a think tank/lobbying group dedicated to persuading as many people as possible that CaCaCo will somehow fix itself.

49. To put into perspective how badly things are going, and how quickly they are going badly, consider that across 2023 a staggering 345.2 million people worldwide were

expected to be food insecure, with more than 800 million—10% of the global population—unsure where their next meal was coming from and nearly a million struggling to survive in famine or famine-like conditions. That's compared, respectively, with 2020's 200 million food insecure and 2018's 90,000 in famine. I take this description near-verbatim from WFP. "A Global Food Crisis." World Food Programme. Web. Note, too, the IMF's vaguely blameful description of those who suffer most disproportionately: "Low-income countries with weak growth prospects, large fiscal and external deficits, and elevated debt levels will likely continue to suffer the most." Left unspoken is that these are the hallmarks of colonial dispossession. Rother, Bjorn, *et al.* 2023. "Global Food Crisis Update: Recent Developments, Outlook, and IMF Engagement." *IMF Notes*, 12 April 2023. Web, 7. For a powerful vision of famine's unfolding in conditions of relative "privilege," see Brand, Tylor. 2023. *Famine Worlds: Life at the Edge of Suffering in Lebanon's Great War*. Stanford: Stanford University Press.

50. In a monumental report for Finland, already one of the most renewable-powered global north countries and aiming for decarbonization more seriously than most, geologist Simon Michaux arrives at the stark conclusion that "replacing the existing fossil fuel powered system (oil, gas, and coal), using renewable technologies, such as solar panels and wind turbines, will not be possible for the entire global human population." Michaux's recommendation? "What might be required, therefore, is a significant reduction of societal demand for all resources, of all kinds. This implies a very different social contract and a radically different system of governance to what is in place today." Michaux, Simon P. 2021. "Assessment of the Extra Capacity Required of Alternative Energy Electrical Power Systems to Completely Replace Fossil Fuels." Geological Survey of Finland / GTK Open File Work Report 42/2021, 20 August 2021.

51. SEI, Climate Analytics, E3G, IISD, and UNEP. 2023. *The Production Gap: Phasing Down or Phasing Up? Top Fossil Fuel Producers Plan Even More Extraction Despite Climate Promises.* Stockholm Environment Institute, Climate Analytics, E3G, International Institute for Sustainable Development and United Nations Environment Programme, November 2023.

52. That's coming from a research team led by the scientist who first put greenhouse gases on the global legislative agenda in his 1988 testimony to the U.S. Congress. Hansen, James E., *et al.* 2022. "Global Warming in the Pipeline." *Arxiv.org*, 12 December 2022: arXiv:2212:04474 (physics.ao-ph).

53. This is central to the visions being pursued by various strands of degrowth economics—but there's no way to get there without giving up on CaCaCo continuity. On degrowth, see esp. Timothée Parrique's tireless curation at timotheeparrique.com, and the still-only French-language book that came out of his exceptional dissertation. Parrique, Timothée. 2022. *Ralentir ou périr: L'économie de la décroissance*. Paris: Seuil.

54. Even as real markers of human wellbeing—life expectancy, infant mortality, nutritional variety and sufficiency, economic mobility, and some forms of social equality—have dramatically improved in some places over the several hundred years in which CaCaCo dominated global life, there can be no denying that these goods have been bought on genocidal terms, destroying lifeways, land relations, and countless millions of individual lives from Appalachia to the Sahel, Amazonia to Siberia.

55. Yusoff, Kathryn. 2018. *A Billion Black Anthropocenes or None*. Minneapolis: University of Minnesota Press. Mbembe, Achille. 2019. *Necropolitics*. Durham: Duke University Press.

56. Gross, Terry. "How 'Modern-Day Slavery' in the Congo Powers the Rechargeable Battery Economy." *NPR: Goats and Soda*, 1 February 2023. Web; Radwin, Maxwell. "Five Pressing Questions for the Future of Lithium Mining in Bolivia." *Mongabay*, 12 December 2022. Web.

57. Yusoff, *op. cit.*, 104.

58. Returning from a trip to Pakistan in the wake of megaflooding, Guterres said, "I looked through a window into the future. A future of permanent and ubiquitous climate chaos on an unimaginable scale." His clearly sincere, and desperately ineffective given the organization of CaCaCo, plea was an urgent one: Given that "the world's most vulnerable—who did nothing to cause this crisis—are paying a horrific price for decades of intransigence by big emitters," their adaptation to an only-worsening climate crisis must be financially prioritized. Does one even need to bother saying that it would not be? Guterres, António. "Press Conference by Secretary-General António Guterres at United Nations Headquarters." *United Nations Meeting Coverage and Press Relations*, 14 September 2022. Web.

Chapter 2

1. *Polycrisis* shows up first in French theorists Edgar Morin and Anne Brigitte Kern's prescient 1993 book *Homeland Earth*, but has been bandied about by the Davos set since EU Commission President Jean-Claude Juncker used it in a 2016 speech to Greek business association the Hellenic Federation of Enterprises. For Morin and Kern, polycrisis is the "complex intersolidarity of problems, antagonisms, crises, uncontrollable processes, and the general crisis of the planet." Morin, Edgar, and Anne-Brigitte Kern. 1999 [1993]. *Homeland Earth: A New Manifesto for A New Millennium*. Trans. Sean M. Kelly and Roger LaPointe. Cresskill, NJ: Hampton Press, 74. The term is also with frequency misattributed to the (thoughtful user of it) historian Adam Tooze.

2. Janzwood, Scott, and Thomas Homer-Dixon. 2022. "What Is a Global Polycrisis?" Discussion Paper 2022–4. Cascade Institute, 27 April 2022. Web, 1.

3. Roubini, Nouriel. 2022. *Megathreats: Ten Dangerous Trends That Imperil Our Future, and How to Survive Them*. New York: Little, Brown, and Co.

4. *Ibid.*, 7

5. Cf. Serhan, Yasmin. 2023. "Why 'Polycrisis' Was the Buzzword of Day 1 in Davos." *Time*, 17 January 2023. Web.

6. A cottage industry devoted to collapse has, appropriately enough, emerged in recent years (taking some older texts as touchstones). A good introduction to that would include at least Servigne, Pablo, and Raphaël Stevens. 2020 [2015]. *How Everything Can Collapse: A Manual for Our Times*. Trans. Andrew Brown. Medford: Polity; Bardi, Ugo. *Before the Collapse: A Guide to the Other Side of Growth*. Cham, Switzerland: Springer Nature; and various works by Anne and Paul Ehrlich, such as Ehrlich, Paul R., and Anne H. Ehrlich. "Can a Collapse of Global Civilization Be Avoided?" *Transactions of the Royal Society B*, vol. 280, no. 1754: 20122845. Many go back to the dated, but still informative, touchstones of Catton, *op. cit.*, and Tainter, Joseph A. 1988. *The Collapse of Complex Societies*. Cambridge. Cambridge UP. The resources and conversations of the subreddit r/collapse also comprise a carefully moderated, habitually (though, such being the nature of anonymous digital conversation, not always) thoughtful entry-point. Anon [Collective]. 2023. "reddit.com/r/collapse." *Reddit.com*. Web.

7. In *The Black Box Society: The Secret Algorithms that Control Money and Information*

(Cambridge: Harvard University Press, 2015), Frank Pasquale lays bare the extent to which we have yet to learn what and how machines in fact are "learning," even when their outputs control our lives. For attention to this same fact with an emphasis on data architectures' carrying forward of the biases of physical architectures, see Chun, Wendy Hui Kyong. 2021. *Discriminating Data: Correlation, Neighborhoods, and the New Politics of Recognition*. Cambridge: MIT Press.

8. On the need for a very different paradigm than that presently prevailing if such aims are to become even plausible, much less possible, see Newfield, Christopher. 2023. "How to Make 'AI' Intelligent; or, The Question of Epistemic Equality." *Critical AI*, vol. 1, nos. 1-2. Web.

9. Goldberg, Natalie Rose. 2023. "'AI Exposure' Is the New Buzz Term to Soften Talk about Job Losses. Here's What It Means." *CNBC*, 27 October 2023. Web.

10. For a useful summary of deep learning back through the neural networks of the 1980s, published toward the outset of the current revolution, see Sarker, Iqbal H. "Deep Learning: A Comprehensive Overview on Techniques, Taxonomy, Applications, and Research Directions." *SN Computer Science*, vol. 2: 240. Many sources on AI's underlying technologies offer better overviews than the present text. As with each crisis here, I flag some of those fuller overviews, but my chief concern is not to explain recent developments in AI—which will already have been surpassed by your time of reading—but rather to highlight ways in which an AI revolution is bound up with the structure of cost deferral that maintains CaCaCo and is its downfall.

11. For a complementary, more strenuously articulated view (I suspect both unduly hopeful and a little short of the mark, as forecasts go), see Lanier, Jaron. 2023. "There Is No A.I." *New Yorker*, 20 April 2023. Web.

12. Policy, in the United States as in most of the colonized world (and to a lesser extent in the EU and China), notoriously lags far behind practical applications and implementations of technological capacities. This is hardly specific to AI, but may be uniquely dangerous there. See, for instance, the misleadingly titled but good reportage of Papachristou, Lucy, and Jillian Deutsch. "ChatGPT Advances Are Moving So Quickly Regulators Can't Keep Up." *Bloomberg Businessweek*, 17 March 2023. Web. In late October 2023, U.S. President Biden signed an executive order packed to the brim with intentions to "create guidance and benchmarks," "establish appropriate guidelines," and the like for private AI companies and government alike. The EO contains plenty of good aspirations, little that is binding. It may be an excellent start or, by the time you read these words, may have served little purpose beyond perhaps regulating competition a little and managing AI's integration into the security establishment. Biden, Joseph R. 2023. "Executive Order on the Safe, Secure, and Trustworthy Development and Use of Artificial Intelligence." Executive Order 14110, 30 October 2023. United States of America. On the general inadequacy of current policy approaches to organize AI development for widespread flourishing, see Ulnicane, Inga, *et al.* 2021. "Framing Governance for a Contested Emerging Technology: Insights from AI Policy." *Policy and Society*, vol. 40, no. 2: 158-77.

13. See, for instance, Deacon, Terrence W. 1997. *The Symbolic Species: The Co-Evolution of Language and the Brain*. New York: Norton; Kitcher, Philip. 2011. *The Ethical Project*. Cambridge: Harvard UP; Taylor, Charles. 2016. *The Language Animal: The Full Shape of the Human Linguistic Capacity*. Cambridge: Harvard UP.

14. Altman was eventually and with great drama fired from OpenAI, and immediately secured a role directly at Microsoft. Days later and following mass employee threats

of resignation, he was reinstated as CEO of OAI. His removal appears to have involved
movement toward developing AGI. Tong, Anna, Jeffrey Dastin, and Krystal Hu. 2023.
"Exclusive: OpenAI Researchers Warned Board of AGI Breakthrough Ahead of CEO
Ouster, Sources Say." *Reuters*, 22 November 2023. Web. In a much earlier ABC interview
about his company's GPT models, then-OpenAI CEO Sam Altman claims that "people
should be happy that we are a little bit scared of this," while also calling AI "the greatest
technology humanity has yet developed" and promising that AI will function as a "co-
pilot" in individual lives, such that "we can also have new things we can't even imagine
today." Cited in Ordonez, Victor, Taylor Dunn, and Eric Noll. 2023. "OpenAI CEO Sam
Altman Says AI Will Reshape Society, Acknowledges Risks: 'A Little Bit Scared of This.'"
ABC News, 16 March 2023. Web. Altman is hardly alone in this fear-excitement framing.
Competitor company Anthropic, founded by ex-OpenAI employees with a massive fund-
ing push from disgraced crypto bro Sam Bankman-Fried, long billed itself as fundamentally an "AI safety" company. The company's leaders "founded Anthropic because we
believe the impact of AI might be comparable to that of the industrial and scientific revolutions, but we aren't confident it will go well" because "so far, no one knows how to train
very powerful AI systems to be robustly helpful, honest, and harmless." Anthropic. 2023.
"Core Views on AI Safety: When, Why, What and How." *Anthropic.com*, 8 March 2023.
Web. Highlighting that it's not *humanity* that developed this technology, but rather a very
specific subset with a historically poor track record of concern for human wellbeing and
safety, before long, Anthropic became tech giant Amazon's primary AI investment.

15. A third, infinitely less powerful—but still, not without agency—group was working people themselves. At my time of writing, data on how much utility working people
found in AI as a timesaver that had not yet been converted into profitability at their
expense was slim to nonexistent. Anecdotally, some white-collar workers with particularly fluid work conditions and low oversight incorporated AI for some tasks. Most early
implementation of AI, however, would come from above, some through explicit shifts in
company work allocations and even more through platform-level integration of AI tools.

16. Ford, Brody. 2023. "IBM to Pause Hiring for Jobs that AI Could Do." *Bloomberg*, 1
May 2023. Web.

17. For a lightning overview of the stakes, see Zhou, Cisssy. "Signal President Warns
of Risks from U.S.-China AI Race." *Nikkei Asia*, 6 April 2023. Web. For a fuller discussion of the material imbrications of AI with CaCaCo at literally every level, one of the
best books around (and one on which I draw extensively for background), is Crawford,
Kate. 2021. *Atlas of AI*. New Haven: Yale UP. On the extractive character of surveillance,
see the essays of a special issue of *Screen Bodies* beginning with Allen, Ira. "Negotiating
Ubiquitous Surveillance." *Screen Bodies*, vol. 4, no. 2: 23-38. See also the excellent Whit-
taker, Meredith. 2023. "Origin Stories: Plantations, Computers, and Industrial Control."
Logic(s), no. 19. May 2023. Web.

18. Alternately and far more optimistically, perhaps by the time you read these words
AI development will have been supercharged by relatively small, localizable and hard-
to-own projects like AutoGPT—drawing on finetuned "small" language models that
have themselves been cribbed from leaked or stolen LLMs. In this rosy future, artificial
general intelligence (AGI) emerges as a kind of distributed machine consciousness that
reflects—and so is self-limited via—the conflicting wills and impulses of as much of
global humanity as has access to a smartphone. Alignment problems are not resolved

but effectively deferred, and the oligarchic pressure of unequal access to intellection production moderated dramatically. Such a future strikes me as wholly unlikely, given the current landscape in April 2023 (and again as I revise this manuscript in November 2023), but a gal can dream. For one reasonable articulation of what it means for a more-or-less democratic society to "contain" its crises, see Przeworski, Adam. 2019. *Crises of Democracy*. Cambridge: Harvard UP.

19. GPT stands for Generative Pretrained Transformer. This particular sort of AI model is a natural language processing tool, meaning that it generates new discourse (early on, just text) on the basis of a human-language prompt. Though swiftly proceeding on toward machine-generated "natural language" prompts, and replacing text inputs with massively multimodal input and output options alike, early publicly accessible versions of AI (including several well before OpenAI's ChatGPT) mostly relied upon the human input of text as a prompt. The question of what outputs can be produced by what inputs—entered by whom or what, on whose behalf—is central to the human meaning of AI.

20. The signal instance was surely Herman, Daniel. 2022. "The End of High-School English." *The Atlantic*, 9 December 2022. Web.

21. For the signal higher ed instance, coming in slightly ahead of Herman, see Marche, Stephen. 2022. "The College Essay Is Dead." *The Atlantic*, 6 December 2022. Web.

22. Kennedy, Susan. 2023. "A Moral Panic: ChatGPT and the Gamification of Education." *Markkula Center for Applied Ethics at Santa Clara University*, 6 February 2023. Web. Those pushing unconcern might benefit from taking stock of how concretely inaccurate past dismissals of AI concerns as moral panic have been. See, for instance, the dismissals in Blue, Violet. 2016. "Hacking and AI: Moral Panic vs. Real Problems." *Endgadget*, 19 August 2023. (Notably, the "real problems" of that essay *also* remain for the most part unfixed.)

23. Higdon, Nolan, and Allison Butler. "Who's Afraid of ChatGPT? In the Real World, Teachers Have Little to Fear." *Salon.com*, 11 March 2023. Web. Indeed, a good portion of public discourse about AI is—and for years has been—devoted to telling people not to panic. See, for instance, Browne, John. "Don't Panic about AI." 2019. *Scientific American*, 10 December 2019. Web. Call me old-fashioned, but when the cultural apparatus of Ca-CaCo spills gallons of ink telling me both *to* and *not to* panic, I start thinking there may be something to this panic business.

24. Belton, Pádraig. 2021. "The Computer Chip Industry Has a Dirty Climate Secret." *Guardian*, 18 September 2021. Web.

25. Qtd. in Bowman, Emma. "A College Student Created an App that Can Tell Whether AI Wrote an Essay." *NPR Technology*, 9 January 2023. Web.

26. Kirchner, Jan Hendrik, Lama Ahmad, Scott Aaronson, Jan Leike. 2023. "New AI Classifier for Indicating AI-Written Text." *OpenAI Blog*, 31 January 2023. Web.

27. One early study, made either more or less trustworthy by its first author's OpenAI affiliation, predicted that 80% of the US workforce would see at least 10% of their work affected by AI, and that nearly 20% would have half of their tasks impacted by LLMs. Eloundou, Tyna, Pamela Mishkin, and Daniel Rock. 2023. "GPTs are GPTS: An Early Look at the Labor Market Impact Potential of Large Language Models." *Arxiv.org*, 27 March 2023: arXiv:2303.10130 (econ.gn). Although the self-submission scholarship repository *arxiv.org* is filled to bursting with interesting-at-a-glance papers, anyone operating outside their home discipline should cite only with care. ArXiv papers have not yet been validated by their disciplinary communities via peer review.

28. Frankly, no one can keep adequate track of developments. As an example of how more-than-humanly graspable the pace of change has been, especially for scholars not directly embedded in Big Tech firms, see Togelius, Julian, and Georgios N. Yannakakis. 2023. "Choose Your Weapon: Survival Strategies for Depressed AI Academics." *Arxiv.org*, 31 March 2023: arXiv:2304.06035 (cs). It is perhaps ironic that just this sort of socially significant, rapid development is a prime candidate for automated event-tracking, synthesis, and summary.

29. See Dustin Tran's blog for one pretty staggering snapshot of that moment. Tran, Dustin. 2023. "Major AI Advances This Month." *Dustintran.com*, 23 March 2023. Web.

30. OpenAI. 2023. "ChatGPT Plug-Ins." *OpenAI Blog*, 23 March 2023. Web.

31. In one interview, Altman observed, "I think the bad case—and I think this is important to say—is, like, lights out for all of us." Qtd. in Jackson, Sarah. "The CEO of the Company Behind AI Chatbot ChatGPT Says the Worst-Case Scenario for Artificial Intelligence Is 'Lights Out for All of Us.'" *Business Insider*, 25 January 2023. Web. Whether sincere or Altman's particular form of hype or both, no one can now doubt such concerns have real grounding.

32. The technical details are a little more complicated that that—and as with most tech novelties, were dramatically overhyped at first. Since those details have been long since superseded by the time you read these words, I haven't bothered with them. What's most important to understand is that the open-source software for AutoGPT and BabyAGI interfaced, in both instances, with OpenAI's proprietary LLM through a user's API keys (generated for users with an account, who were then charged for new discourse generation by OpenAI). This quickly raised the possibility that the future of AI might not be quite so locked down by tech giants as most had previously assumed. See viz. Kahn, Jeremy. 2023. "BabyAGI Is Taking Silicon Valley by Storm. Should We Be Scared?" *Fortune*, 15 April 2023. Web. Could the same results be accomplished without OpenAI's, Google/Alphabet's, Facebook/Meta's, etc. LLMs, i.e., with open-sourced or collaboratively created *new* natural language processing engines? The possibility of democracy itself hinges on how this question ends up being answered.

33. I don't mean to imply that the education conversation focused exclusively on plagiarism, though. There was also a great deal of very thoughtful and rich discussion of pedagogy more broadly. For one of the finer instances, see Mills, Anna R. 2023. "ChatGPT Just Got Better. What Does that Mean for Our Writing Assignments?" *Chronicle of Higher Education*, 23 March 2023. Web. Mills has been one of the most consistently capacious higher ed negotiators of what AI means for our collective work.

34. A long tradition of discourse on AGI includes much produced by tech hype men but also much that is scholarly. The question of machine personhood implied by AGI is fascinating, and may well have imposed itself dramatically even before this book reaches your hands. I'm interested here, however, less in the meaning of machine personhood than in the more mundane—and yet, still revolutionary—question of machinic intellection in a still-human world, the automated production of a vast range of symbolic artifacts that historically have been characteristic of human worldmaking or culture. For a fictional treatment that opens the AGI question in particularly interesting ways, see Newitz, Annalee. 2018. *Autonomous: A Novel*. New York: Tor/Tom Doherty Associates.

35. Between my writing and your reading, those positions have been argued out quite a bit more, by many more people. A summary with my current time stamp seems pointless. The bottom line of existential risk arguments is that AI alignment to human well-

being is not only difficult, maybe impossible as a general proposition, but in fact misses the most important fear of all: that any sufficiently powerful AGI will be self-advancing (in its ratiocinative powers) beyond the human capacity to manage and eventually will either decide to end all human life or do so somewhat accidentally. To be clear, though I don't align ideologically at all with Yudkowsky and the longtermist/effective altruism groups with which he is most closely associated, his arguments are anything but stupid or readily dismissible, and the same is true of many in his cluster. There are far worse ways to spend a few hours than in browsing the blog/platform/forum Yudkowsky maintains at https://www.lesswrong.com. If you're a human reader of this book, it's likely that the worst fears about AGI have not come to pass (yet).

36. I've thought this through a bit in the discussions of "symbolicity" animating *The Ethical Fantasy of Rhetorical Theory* (Pittsburgh: U Pittsburgh P, 2018).

37. Refusal to learn from nonhuman cultures, as indigenous peoples have known for longer than pretty much anybody, was one of colonialism's many violences in the sphere of epistemology.

38. Taylor, Alex H. "Corvid Cognition." 2014. *WIREs Cognitive Science*, vol 5, no. 3: 361-372; Pika, Simone, *et al.* 2020. "Ravens Parallel Great Apes in Physical and Social Cognitive Skills." *Nature Scientific Reports*, vol. 10: 20617.

39. Alami, Ilias, Jack Copley, and Alexis Maraitis. 2023. "The 'Wicked Trinity' of Late Capitalism: Governing in an Era of Stagnation, Surplus Humanity, and Environmental Breakdown." *Geoforum*, in press 16 February 2023, corrected proof. Web.

40. The real depth of risk is highlighted in the *Economist*'s highly atypical call for a governing international agency to manage that risk. Marcus, Gary, and Anka Reuel. 2023. "The World Needs an International Agency for Artificial Intelligence, Say Two AI Experts." *Economist*, 18 April 2023. Web. To my knowledge, the best place to get a rich sense of how a variety of people are thinking through these risks from multiple different angles in real time remains https://www.alignmentforum.org. A core, somewhat deflationary statement of alignment risks (with the added benefit of treating the material infrastructure of AI as part of the alignment problem) may be found in Bender, Emily, Timnit Gebru, Angelina McMillan-Major, and Margaret Mitchell. 2021. "On the Dangers of Stochastic Parrots: Can Language Models Be Too Big?" *FAccT'21*, 3-10 March 2021, Virtual Event, Canada: 610-623. Alignment is a tricky word because it leaves open the question of *whose interests and values* AI should align with. Alignment to genocidal Belgian King Leopold colonizing the Congo is clearly at odds with alignment to something like general humanity—even if the former may well "solve" alignment problems at the user level, it is clearly at odds with alignment of the latter sort. Both these are different again from aligning with a user's efforts to create deepfake pornography videos or an individual corporation's profit imperative, and those are in turn far different from alignment to a strong local culture of egalitarianism and democracy. On top of that, there is the problem of individual humans' opacity or non-identity to our own selves, a problem we sometimes think of in terms of unconscious motivations. There is no natural endpoint to alignment questions, since there is no overarching stance shared by humanity at large, nor even a clearly unified will residing within any individual human.

41. The essays of *Augmented Education in the Global Age* are instructive here, especially Brynjolfsson, Erik. 2023. "The Turing Trap: The Promise & Peril of Human-Like Artificial Intelligence," in *Augmented Education in the Global Age: Artificial Intelligence and the Future of Learning and Work*. Eds. Daniel Araya and Peter Marber. New York: Routledge:

103-116. See also Benanav, Aaron. 2022. *Automation and the Future of Work*. London: Verso. For a useful history of the cost of technological progress in units of social stability, see Frey, Carl Benedikt. 2019. *The Technology Trap: Capital, Labor, and Power in the Age of Automation*. Princeton: Princeton UP. It should not need saying that the polities of Ca-CaCo in these, its early moments of collapse, don't have a lot of social stability to spare.

42. Two of the most important essays on the algorithmic disposition of life precede the more stunning phases of the generative AI revolution. Focusing on algorithmic power as exercised through platform capitalism, state apparatuses, and data harvesting, but most of all on the algorithmic organization of life as a distinct form of power, they characterize well the socially dispositive force of generative AI. Cf. Panagia, Davide. 2019. "On the Political Ontology of the *Dispositif*." *Critical Inquiry*, vol. 45, no. 3: 714-746; Panagia, Davide. 2020. "On the Possibilities of a Political Theory of Algorithms." *Political Theory*, vol. 49, no. 1: 109-133.

43. This conversation has been richest with regard to the racializing algorithm dispositif. See, for instance, Noble, Safiya Umoja. 2018. *Algorithms of Oppression: How Search Engines Reinforce Racism*. New York. New York UP; Brown, Simone. 2015. *Dark Matters: On the Surveillance of Blackness*. Durham: Duke UP.

44. I discuss this in some depth in chapter five of Allen, Ira. 2018. *The Ethical Fantasy of Rhetorical Theory*. Pittsburgh: U Pittsburgh P. But that is not to say that humans are the *only* symbolic animal. We are just, unavoidably, our own clearest instance of what it means to be such a creature. On other symbolic animals, see the essays of Bjørkdahl, Kristian, and Alex C. Parrish (eds.). 2018. *Rhetorical Animals: Boundaries of the Human in the Study of Persuasion*. Lanham: Lexington Books.

45. This insight is central to virtually all rhetorical scholarship. For one (among many) engaging tracings of it, see Battaglia, Deborah (Ed.). 1995. *Rhetorics of Self-Making*. Berkeley: U California P. For my thinking of it in the context of pedagogy, see Allen, Ira. "Composition Is the Ethical Negotiation of Fantastical Selves." 2018. *College Composition and Communication*, vol. 70, no. 2: 169-194.

46. Cf. Crable, Bryan. "Rhetoric, Anxiety, and Character Armor: Burke's Interactional Rhetoric of Identity." 2006. *Western Journal of Communication*, vol. 70, no. 1: 1-22; Davis, Diane. 2008. "Identification: Burke and Freud on Who You Are." 2008. *Rhetoric Society Quarterly*, vol. 38, no. 2: 123-147.

47. Cf. Hwang, Tim. 2020. *Subprime Attention Crisis: Advertising and the Time Bomb at the Heart of the Internet*. New York: Farrar, Straus, & Giroux.

48. Butler, Judith. 1990. *Gender Trouble: Feminism and the Subversion of Identity*. New York: Routledge.

49. Anderson, Benedict. 2006. *Imagined Communities: Reflections on the Origin and Spread of Nationalism*. London: Verso.

50. "Free-range rhetorician" Rosa Eberly has been thinking about doxa for many years. In one particularly evocative formulation, she describes it as "shared values, shared pasts, a shared sense of causality, and shared hopes for a shared future." Eberly, Rosa A. 2003. "Deliver Ourselves from 'Evil.'" *Rhetoric & Public Affairs*, vol. 6, no. 3: 551-53, 553. For an overview of some more ways rhetoric scholars have thought about doxa and invention, see chapter 3 of Allen, *The Ethical Fantasy*.

51. Panagia, Davide. "On the Political Ontology," 715.

52. Cf. Ruckenstein, Minna, and Julia Granroth. 2020. "Algorithms, Advertising, and the Intimacy of Surveillance." *Journal of Cultural Economy*, vol. 13, no. 1: 12-24; Park, Yong

Jin. 2021. *The Future of Digital Surveillance: Why Digital Monitoring Will Never Lose Its Appeal in a World of Algorithm-Driven AI*. Ann Arbor: U Michigan P.

53. On the one hand, "fake news" is an intellection product of longstanding—its perils in the digital age bear temporizing, and its production serves many purposes. See, for instance, the helpful work of Skinnell, Ryan. 2021. "Teaching Writing in the (New) Era of Fake News." *College Composition and Communication*, vol. 72, no. 4: 546-569. On the other hand, misinformation isn't always *for* something beyond the capture of eyeballs for advertisements. On the profitable meaninglessness of much fake news, see Graham, Rosie. 2017. "Google and Advertising: Digital Capitalism in the Context of Post-Fordism, the Reification of Language, and the Rise of Fake News." *Palgrave Communications*, vol. 3, art. no. 45. Web.

54. See, for an early instance, Hao, Karen, and Amy Webb. "Why AI Is a Threat to Democracy—And What We Can Do to Stop It." *MIT Technology Review*, 26 February 2019. Web. As generative AI's capacities exploded, the warnings grew more panicked. One typical example is Wong, Matteo. 2023. "Conspiracy Theories Have a New Best Friend." *Atlantic*, 2 March 2023. Web.

55. Panagia, Davide. "On the Political Ontology," 721.

56. For a related view of the dangers inherent in human disposition by algorithms, see the exceptional Pfister, Damien Smith, and Misti Yang. 2018. "Five Theses on Technoliberalism and the Networked Public Sphere." *Communication and the Public*, vol. 3, no. 3: 247-262.

57. Alami, Copley, and Maraitis, *op. cit.*

58. A 2017 report by consulting behemoth and habitual CIA partner McKinsey suggested that at least 800 million jobs worldwide might be automated by 2030. Manyika, James, *et al.* 2017. *Jobs Lost, Jobs Gained: Workforce Transitions in a Time of Automation*. McKinsey Global Institute, December 2017. Web.

59. Citton, Yves. 2020. "Collapsology as the Horizon." *Electra*, no. 9: 87-104, hal-04011103. Web, 3.

60. Crutzen, Paul, and Eugene F. Stoermer. "The 'Anthropocene.'" 2000. *Global Change Newsletter*, vol. 41. May 2000: 17-18. For thoughtful discussion of the uses and abuses implicit in the term, see Haraway, Donna, *et al.* 2016. "Anthropologists Are Talking—About the Anthropocene." *Ethnos*, vol. 81, no. 3: 535-564. For a compelling argument that we should have ended up with Capitalocene instead, see Moore, Jason. 2017. "The Capitalocene, Part I: On the Nature and Origins of Our Ecological Crisis." *Journal of Peasant Studies*, vol. 44, no. 3: 594-630; and Moore, Jason. 2018. "The Capitalocene, Part II: Accumulation by Appropriation and the Centrality of Unpaid Work/Energy." *Journal of Peasant Studies*, vol. 45, no. 2: 237-279.

61. So inescapable that, in the surest sign of a term's dominance, it has spawned hundreds if not thousands of think pieces, scholarly essays, and even books assailing it and proposing alternate terms. Crutzen and Stoermer's point, of course, was to secure adherence to the notion that the Holocene is over and that ours is a new geologic era.

62. For a genial—totally inadequate to end the crisis but still genuinely valuable—set of actions regular people can both take and urge, see the excellent Grover, Sami. 2021. *We're All Climate Hypocrites Now: How Embracing Our Limitations Can Unlock the Power of a Movement*. Gabriola Island: New Society Publishers.

63. Rice, Doyle. "'We Have Already Lost' in 2 Key Climate Change Signals, According to UN Report." *USA Today*, 21 April 2023. Web.

64. Sengupta, Somini. "Climate Change Comes for Rich Countries." *New York Times*, 21 July 2021. Web.

65. On the mispricing of coastal real estate relative to flooding and hurricane risk (with dramatic consequences for local government tax bases), for example, see Gourevitch, Jesse D., *et al.* 2023. "Unpriced Climate Risk and the Potential Consequences of Overvaluation in US Housing Markets." *Nature Climate Change*. 16 February 2023. Web. As one instance of the racial inequality of climate change-induced flood risk distribution within the US (to say nothing of global flood risk distribution, which in many ways tracks the history of colonialism), see Sanders, Brett F., *et al.* "Large and Inequitable Flood Risks in Los Angeles, California." 2022. *Nature Sustainability*, vol. 6: 47-57.

66. Donald Trump's 6 November 2012 tweet reads: "The concept of global warming was created by and for the Chinese in order to make U.S. manufacturing non-competitive." Qtd. in Ohlheiser, Abby. 2016. "Donald Trump Didn't Delete Tweet Calling Global Warming a Chinese Hoax." *Washington Post*, 27 September 2016. Web.

67. On the general case, see Oreskes, Naomi, and Erik M. Conway. 2010. *Merchants of Doubt: How a Handful of Scientists Obscured the Truth on Issues from Tobacco Smoke to Global Warming*. New York: Bloomsbury. For Christians in particular, see Douglas, Christopher. 2018. "Religion and Fake News: Faith-Based Alternative Information Ecosystems in the U.S. and Europe." *Review of Faith & International Affairs*, vol. 16, no. 1: 61-73; Veldman, Robin Globus. 2019. *The Gospel of Climate Skepticism: Why Evangelical Christians Oppose Action on Climate Change*. Oakland: U California P; Marshall, K.L. 2021. "Revisiting the Scopes Trial: Young-Earth Creationism, Creation Science, and the Evangelical Denial of Climate Change." *Religions*, vol. 12. № 2: 133. Web.

68. Americans, regardless of party identification, have come generally to acknowledge—once more, as when G.H.W. Bush was elected in 1988—the reality of climate change. Young people in particular support phasing out fossil fuels. And yet, dismally, even as Democrat-identified Americans have come increasingly to see climate change as a major threat (78% do), Republican-identified Americans remain deeply dubious (only 23% acknowledge the climate crisis as a serious threat). Those numbers compare abominably with, say, France or Germany—where 81% and 73% of all adults, respectively, describe climate change as a major threat. And most Americans, across all affiliations, don't regard climate change as a truly top political priority. Which is a staggering refusal to recognize basic physical reality. We remain a very long way from recovering from the epistemic debility described at the outset of this book. Tyson, Alec, Cary Funk, and Brian Kennedy. "What the Data Says about Americans' Views of Climate Change." *Pew Research Center*, 18 April 2023. Web.

69. But this is not to downplay the power of productive religious responses to the climate crisis. I'm not criticizing religion in general or Christians in particular. For a rich Christian climate realism, see Moo, Jonathan, and Robert White. 2014. *Let Creation Rejoice: Biblical Hope and Ecological Crisis*. InterVarsity Press. See also, notwithstanding some problems in Hayhoe's approach, Von Bergen, Megan, and Bethany Mannon. 2020. "Talking Climate Faith: Katharine Hayhoe and Christian Rhetoric(s) of Climate Change." *Enculturation*, 10 November 2020. Web. Veldman, *op. cit.*, esp. in ch. 1, "The End Time Apathy Hypothesis," details a number of ways in which popular stories about Christian climate denial have been inaccurate or unjust.

70. See the generally low priority accorded climate action in Tyson, Funk, and Ken-

nedy, *op. cit.* More disturbingly still, a 2022 survey of nineteen countries found U.S. residents dramatically out of step in regarding the climate crisis as the least significant threat to their country from a list of five. Poushter, Jacob, Moira Fagan, and Sneha Gubbala. 2022. "Climate Change Remains Top Global Threat Across 19-Country Survey." *Pew Research Center*, 31 August 2022. Web.

71. Veldman, *op. cit.*, 163.

72. Batchelor, Christine L., *et al.* 2023. "Rapid, Buoyancy-Driven Ice Sheet Retreat of Hundreds of Meters Per Day." *Nature*, 5 April 2023. Web.

73. A useful tool for getting a sense of these numbers for many stretches of global coastline may be found at https://sealevel.nasa.gov/ipcc-ar6-sea-level-projection-tool, with the caveat that new modeling over time has consistently found trends worse than projected. See also Michon, Scott. "Understanding Climate: Antarctic Sea Ice Extent." *Climate.gov*, 14 March 2023. Web.

74. Pappas, Stephanie. 2023. "The Surface of the Ocean Is Now So Hot It's Broken Every Record Since Satellite Measurements Began." *Livescience.com*, 14 April 2023. Web.

75. University of Texas [Anon]. 2022. "Greenland's Glaciers Might Be Melting about 100 Times as Fast as Previously Thought." *UT News: Science & Technology*, 15 December 2022. Web.

76. The notion that friend-enemy distinctions are the ultimate basis for all politics, a final reduction where "the political" really emerges, is due to the Nazi jurist Carl Schmitt. It's been taken up by a lot of decidedly un-Nazi political theorists in intervening decades. But anyhow, that's not the point I'm making here. Maybe Schmitt was right and maybe not. Definitely, though, thinking through friend-enemy lenses disposes our thinking. When these lenses are activated with strong "directional" feelings, like hope or scorn or anger, not only how but also what we think follows predictable patterns of schismogenesis. We think *not* whatever the other person thinks.

77. For a political theory that explains this well, see Connolly, William. 2005. "The Evangelical-Capitalist Resonance Machine." *Political Theory*, vol. 33, no. 6: 869-886.

78. Younger, Sally. 2022. "NASA Study: Rising Sea Level Could Exceed Estimates for U.S. Coasts." *NASA Global Climate Change*, 15 November 2022. Web. See also Dangendorf, Sönke, *et al.* 2023. "Acceleration of U.S. Southeast and Gulf Coast Sea Level Rise Amplified by Internal Climate Variability." *Nature Communications*, vol. 14, art. no. 1935, 10 April 2023. Web.

79. Charles Colson, qtd. in Veldman, *op. cit.*, 173.

80. Abramoff was fired from her position at Oak Ridge National Laboratory after staging, with Kalmus (NASA Jet Propulsion Laboratory), a banner-drop at a December 2022 conference of the American Geophysical Union. The two have inspired many by offering examples of how to politically engage as scientists, refusing to sacrifice realism about CaCaCo's hardline commitment to the end of a stable global climate in exchange for access to CaCaCo politicians and prestige media outlets.

81. Hassol, Susan Joy, and Michael E. Mann. 2023. "Enjoy the Weather. Worry about the Climate." *The Hill*, 23 February 2023. This is simply not physically true. On the reality that we do not even have a viable mineral supply for vehicle electrification, itself only one segment of an energy transition, see Zhang, Chunbo, *et al.* 2023. "Trade-off between Critical Metal Requirement and Transportation Decarbonization in Automotive Electrification." *Nature Communications*, vol. 14, art. no. 1. Web. See also Michaux, *op. cit.* And

that's before getting into the political fabulism that ignores the basal incapacity of even extraordinarily mobilized publics to force national governments into action that runs contrary to core CaCaCo interests.

82. Hassol and Mann, *op. cit.*

83. Tienaara, Kyla, *et al.* 2022. "Investor-State Disputes Threaten the Global Green Energy Transition." *Science*, vol. 375, no. 6594: 701-703.

84. Hertsgaard, Mark, Saleemul Huq, and Michael E. Mann. 2022. "How a Little-Discussed Revision of Climate Science Could Help Avert Doom." *Washington Post*, 23 February 2022. Web.

85. Mann, Micheal E. 2021. *The New Climate War: The Fight to Take Back Our Planet.* New York: Public Affairs, [first page of chapter 8].

86. A great example of the—absurdly dishonest—insistence that regular people and scientists alike avoid speaking in dark tones may be found in Becker, William S. "How to Avoid Apocalypse Fatigue." *The Hill*, 9 April 2023. Web. Becker pretends that CaCaCo's rulers' decades-long refusal to take climate action has been caused by too much doom and gloom talk, rather than by the fact that not taking climate action was in the short-term interests of CaCaCo's majority shareholder class. It's the sort of resolutely silly article that gets published a lot, in different variations, in outlets like *The Hill*, while the political class continues the dithering to which it has remained militantly committed since at least 1989 (quite regardless of how ordinary people talk about the climate crisis or pretty nearly anything else)

87. That's not to say hope is bad, of course. Hope is fine. It's even necessary. But nobody with a better product to sell is out there peddling it.

88. Never mind that your recycled yogurt cup probably isn't. Osborne, Margaret. 2022. "At Least 85 Percent of U.S. Plastic Waste Went to Landfills in 2021." *Smithsonian Magazine*, 9 May 2022. Web.

89. Hayhoe, Katharine. 2021. "In the Face of Climate Change, We Must Act So That We Can Feel Hopeful—Not the Other Way Around." *Time*, 12 August 2021. Web. Such injunctions, while perfectly harmless and maybe even of limited utility (though that yogurt cup is most likely being incinerated or buried after you "recycle" it), are farcically out of step with political economic realities. "Call Congress?" If you're a millionaire or better, go for it! If you're anybody else, get real. Pretending that we have working democratic institutions is a terrible way of addressing a real crisis.

90. Qtd. in Moran, Padraig. 2023. "Climate Change Fear Can Be Paralyzing. But You Can Spur Action Through Hope, Says Scientist." *CBC The Current*, 21 March 2023. Web.

91. For a good primer on the difficulty of that aim, and also a vision of its possibility as CaCaCo falls away, see Schmelzer, Matthias, Andrea Vetter, and Aaron Vansintjan. 2022. *The Future Is Degrowth: A Guide to a World Beyond Capitalism.* London: Verso.

92. For a sobering view of this reality, see Larry Bartels' revised edition of *Unequal Democracy*, which extends the empirical insights of the original through the Obama era. Importantly, despite being the most sustained nationwide protests since the civil rights era, much like the anti-Iraq War movement before it, 2011's Occupy movement and the many preferences of ordinary people it agglomerated had effectively no impact on policy. This is the fault of a system, not a movement. Bartels, *op. cit.*.

93. Though the phrase is most associated with George H.W. Bush's turnabout on climate, his refusal to pursue a binding global treaty in 1992, it's no less pertinent to the explosion in fossil fuel exploration and extraction overseen with pride by first Obama

and later Biden. On the longstanding failures of the Democratic Party, not merely to achieve transformative action on the climate crisis, but really even to try to do so, see for instance Gunderson, Ryan. 2022. "Powerless, Stupefied, and Repressed Actors Cannot Challenge Climate Change: Real Helplessness as a Barrier between Environmental Concern and Action." *Journal for the Theory of Social Behavior*, vol. 53, no. 2: 271-95. Web; and Speth, *op. cit.* On the inaccessibility of transformative change through ordinary avenues of protest and civil disobedience in the current moment of CaCaCo, see Fraser, Nancy, *op. cit.* In this connection, it's worth noting too that extraordinary advances in renewable energy generation have thus far added to, rather than replacing, the fossil-fuel anchoring of CaCaCo. For a rather desperate attempt to find a positive spin on this fact, hear the resounding emptiness in Marvel, Kate. 2023. "I'm a Climate Scientist. I'm Not Screaming into a Void Anymore." *New York Times*, 18 November 2023. Web.

94. Cf. Shearman, David. "Wake Up, America: Your Economic Citadel Is Driving You to Oblivion." *The Hill*, 14 February 2023. Web.

95. UNEP. 2023. "Governments Plan to Produce Double the Fossil Fuels in 2030 than the 1.5°C Warming Limit Allows." *United Nations Environment Programme*, 8 November 2023. Web. On the commitment, baked into U.S. President Biden's "biggest climate legislation ever," to continuing to expand fossil fuel investment, see Conley, Julia. 2023. "Biden's Key Climate Law Gives Big Oil a 'Massive Escape Hatch': Analysis." *CommonDreams*, 20 November 2023. Web.

96. Von Schuckmann, Karina, *et al.* 2023. "Heat Stored in the Earth System 1960-2020: Where Does the Energy Go?" *Earth System Science Data*, vol. 15, no. 4: 1675-1709.

97. Cf. Tamburino, Lucia, Philip Cafaro, and Giangiacomo Bravo. 2023. "An Analysis of Three Decades of Increasing Carbon Emissions: The Weight of the P Factor." *Sustainability*, vol. 15, no. 4: 3245, which demonstrates the unavoidability of questions about population for any serious effort at re-producing a widely habitable climate.

98. Guterres, António. 2022. "Secretary-General's Video Message on the Launch of the Third IPCC Report." *United Nations Secretary General*, 4 April 2022. Web.

99. In addition to the useful archive of degrowth material maintained by Parrique, *op. cit.*, the newly established *Degrowth Journal* adds an important component to the tradition of ecological economics.

100. Ritchie, Hannah, and Max Roser. 2021. "Greenhouse Gas Emissions." *Our World in Data*, Accessed 24 April 2023. Web.

101. Most dramatically for 2020, one year of the multi-year covid-19 pandemic. Note that even in recessions greenhouse gas emissions only dropped slightly—back to levels from a couple years earlier—before rising again. Note, too, that absent technology-that-remains-yet-to-be-invented for scrubbing carbon from the air at scale, even after carbon emissions actually do begin dropping—assuming they do before things have fallen apart too much for anyone to keep track at all—that will still mean *adding* carbon to the atmosphere. Adding GHGs to the atmosphere more slowly is less catastrophic than doing so more quickly, but it's a far cry from not doing so.

102. Conley, Julia. 2023. "Ocean Warming Study So Distressing, Some Scientists Didn't Even Want to Talk About It." *Common Dreams*, 25 April 2023. Web.

103. Gallogly, Nell. 2023. "Do You Even Decarbonize, Bro?" *New York Times*, 22 April 2023. Web.

104. McGuire, Bill. 2022. *Hothouse Earth: An Inhabitant's Guide*. London: Icon, 143.

105. McGuire, *op. cit.*, xv.

106. For a stunning, photorealistic fictional forecast of our near futures, see Markley, Stephen. 2023. *The Deluge*. New York: Simon and Schuster.

107. Parenti, Christian. 2011. *Tropic of Chaos: Climate Change and the New Geography of Violence*. New York: Bold Type Books.

108. Cf. Alfred Wegener Institute. 2023. "The Climate Crisis and Biodiversity Crisis Can't Be Approached Separately, Says Study." *Phys.org*, 20 April 2023. Web.

109. For a highly accessible overview of the concept of ecosystem services, see Bennett, Elena M., Garry D. Peterson, and Line J. Gordon. 2009. "Understanding Relationships among Multiple Ecosystem Services." *Ecology Letters*, vol. 12, no. 12: 1394-1404.

110. For a sense of just how crushingly unequally that cashes out in the moment-by-moment unfolding of the polycrisis, see Chancel, Lucas, Philipp Bothe, and Tancrède Voituriez. 2023. *Climate Inequality Report 2023*. World Inequality Lab Study 2023/1.

111. Research on this reality is surveyed at length in Kolbert, Elizabeth. 2014. *The Sixth Extinction: An Unnatural History*. New York: Henry Holt.

112. For a primer with a useful focus on the role of capitalism, see Dawson, Ashley. 2016. *Extinction: A Radical History*. New York: OR Books.

113. The Intergovernmental Science-Policy Platform on Biodiversity and Ecosystem Services (IPBES), established in 2012, offers some of the most definitive episodic surveys of the biodiversity crisis. Like the IPCC, its reports are conservative, aggregating established science. Accordingly, they do not always adequately capture rapidly developing ecosystem changes. Still, these reports are invaluable in determining what can be said for certain about biodiversity loss, an exceptionally complicated thing to study. The most recent IPBES Global Assessment Report on Biodiversity and Ecosystem Services found that most global biodiversity loss thus far was due to a concatenation of (what I've been describing here as) CaCaCo values and social systems, which have driven global human population growth into increasingly invasive land- and sea-use patterns. Balvanera, Patricia, *et al.* 2019. "Chapter 2.1 Status and Trends—Drivers of Change." *Global Assessment Report of the IPBES*. Eds. E.S. Brondízio *et al.* Bonn: IPBES Secretariat, esp. 55-62.

114. "The largest transformations in the last 30 years have been from increases in urban area, expansions of the areas fished, and the transformations of tropical forests (well established)." *Ibid.*, 60.

115. I have been speaking throughout of CaCaCo. For a helpful view of the way suppressing and controlling human labor—directly in line with a culturally specific, non-relational view of nonhuman animal labor power—was involved in the rise of CaCaCo, and concomitantly in driving the biodiversity loss crisis, see Malm, Andreas. 2016. *Fossil Capital: The Rise of Steam Power and the Roots of Global Warming*. London: Verso.

116. For an exceptional historical view of the U.S. context, where "the culture of US settler colonialism is built upon the genius of Indigenous peoples whose forms of agricultural husbandry, land tenure, and geophysical engineering gave rise to the material vitalities that continue to sustain forms of US agricultural capitalism," which itself and in turn consumes all these, see Waterman, Adam. 2022. *The Corpse in the Kitchen: Enclosure, Extraction, and the Afterlives of the Black Hawk War*. New York: Fordham UP, 126.

117. Dicks, Lynn V., *et al.* 2021. "A Global-Scale Expert Assessment of Drivers and Risks Associated with Pollinator Decline." *Nature Ecology & Evolution*, vol. 5: 1453-1461.

118. After false starts spanning decades, Indonesia seems really to be proceeding with plans for a new "forest capitol" city in Borneo, to replace Jakarta—which is sinking to subsidence and beneath rising tides. Construction of the new capitol, Nusantara, in-

tensifies the already well-established work of tearing the rainforest out from underneath critically endangered orangutans. Thiessen, Tamara. "Indonesia's New Forest Capital in Borneo Heightens Fears for Orangutans' Future." *CNN*, 20 February 2022. Web.

119. Phillips, Tom. "China's 'Extinct' Dolphin May Have Returned to Yangtze River, Say Conservationists." *Guardian*, 10 October 2016. Web. Clickbait title notwithstanding, the baiji has been functionally extinct since the early aughts. What hopeful conservationists probably sighted was the finless porpoise, itself also critically endangered.

120. This is made starkly clear in the IPBES Global Assessment Report. Further to the point, though, see the deeply distressing breakdown offered in Chancel, Bothe, and Voituriez, *op. cit.* On the violent imposition of colonial order that made this radically unequal distribution of deferred costs possible, in many cases not even a century ago, and that continues to organize much of life today, see Thomas, Martin. 2012. *Violence and the Colonial Order: Police, Workers, and Protest in the European Colonial Empires, 1918-1940.*

121. Hayes, Kelly, and Mariam Kaba. 2023. *Let This Radicalize You: Organizing and the Revolution of Reciprocal Care.* Chicago: Haymarket Books, 45.

122. *Ibid.*

123. *Ibid.*

124. One of the tragic ironies of rainforest deforestation is that, in addition to driving the sixth extinction, it also robs us humans of one of the fonts of bioaccessible medicinals. At the same time and despite decades of understanding exactly this fact, CaCaCo's logics of work continue to counterpose the needs of humans whose living depends on deforestation to the needs of humans whose needs depend on halting deforestation. Those are often the very same people. Meanwhile, deforestation (after massive extraction of oceanic life) is one of the worst drivers of the sixth extinction. On the Bornean case in particular, see Ocampo-Peñuela, Natalia, *et al.* 2020. "Impacts of Four Decades of Forest Loss on Vertebrate Functional Habitat in Borneo." *Frontiers in Forests and Global Change*, vol. 3. 5 May 2020, Web.

125. Barnett, Joshua Trey. 2022. *Mourning in the Anthropocene: Ecological Grief and Earthly Coexistence.* East Lansing: Michigan State UP. Barnett and others whose work I appreciate throughout this book draw on posthumanism as an interpretive and inventional frame. I've written in various places and registers about why I find that framework wanting, encouraging instead a chastened humanism, and so I leave the framing question to the side here. Cf., though, Allen, Ira. 2018. "Composition Is the Negotiation of Fantastical Selves." *College Composition and Communication*, vol. 70, no. 2: 169-194; Allen, Ira. 2022. "Parable of the Box." *Figment Magazine*, vol. 1: Imber. Web; Allen, Ira. 2023. "Chastened Humanism and/or Necrotic Anthropocene: Transcendence Toward Less," in *The Routledge Handbook of Law and the Anthropocene.* Eds. Peter Burdon and James Martel. New York: Routledge: 80-96. What's most important, in my view, is Barnett's beautiful vision of who and how we can become in taking the Sixth Extinction seriously and staying with the emotional difficulty of that.

126. Barnett, *op. cit.*, xvii.

127. *Ibid.*

128. *Ibid.*, 153.

129. For a complementary vision, focused especially on the stories with which we come to love the world we are destroying, see McHugh, Susan. 2019. *Love in a Time of Slaughters: Human-Animal Stories against Genocide and Extinction.* University Park: Pennsylvania State UP.

130. Kolbert, *op. cit.*, 17.

131. *Ibid.*

132. *Ibid.*, 258.

133. Leakey, Richard, and Roger Lewin. 1996. *The Sixth Extinction: Patterns of Life and the Future of Humankind.* New York: Anchor Books, 233.

134. *Ibid.*

135. For comparison, it took CaCaCo's first 200 years or so of significant development (from 1700 to 1900) to reduce forest and wild grassland cover from 90% to 75% of earth's surface. Even many otherwise very good articulations of human impacts on earth systems run together pre-CaCaCo deforestation with the massively accelerated impacts of the CaCaCo period. Between 1700 and today, "our" civilization has gobbled up an extra 38% of earth's surface area for agriculture and development, and we do so only ever more rapidly—as is to be expected from the growth mindset that underwrites CaCaCo—as the human population balloons. Numbers for human sea use impacts, though of course the oceans comprise a much larger percentage of the globe's surface, show similar trends. Ritchie, Hannah, and Max Roser. 2021. "Forests and Deforestation." *Our World in Data*, Accessed 24 April 2023. Web.

136. Leakey and Lewin, *op. cit.*, 234.

137. FAO. 2020. *Global Forest Resources Assessment 2020: Key Findings.* Rome: Food and Agriculture Organization of the United Nations.

138. Elbein, Saul. 2019. "Tree-Planting Programs Can Do More Harm Than Good." *National Geographic*, 26 April 2019. Web. There have also been calls to broaden our sense of land-use, getting beyond just forest cover (which can be helpful for fixing free-floating carbon) to fostering a wider range of rewilding practices, especially focused on grassland (which, in some contexts, better supports biodiversity). Cf. Wang, Lanhui, Pil Birkefeldt Møller Pederson, and Jens-Christian Svenning. 2023. "Rewilding Abandoned Farmland Has Greater Sustainability Benefits than Afforestation." *njp Biodiversity*, vol. 2, art. 5: 8 February 2023. Given that farmland is often abandoned as soil quality deteriorates, this is very much a case of making lemonade.

139. Wang, Chao, *et al.* 2021 "A Global Meta-Analysis of the Impacts of Tree Plantations on Biodiversity." *Global Ecology and Biogeography*, vol. 31, no. 3: 576-587.

140. See, from my time of writing, Greenfield, Patrick. 2023. "'Don't Fool Yourself': Billions More Needed to Protect Tropical Forests, Warns New Report." *Guardian*, 19 April 2023. Web. As long as the basic coordinates of CaCaCo remain in place, this state of affairs—which has persisted for ever-worsening decades—seems very unlikely to have improved by your time of reading.

141. Current extinction rates could be as much as 1,000 times higher than (geologically) immediately pre-human rates. Given our current range of activities forcing new extinctions, near-future rates are likely to be around 10,000 times higher than "background" extinction rates. (More conservative estimates place the rate—hardly reassuringly—at 100 times "normal.") This is what a sixth extinction looks like. Cf. De Vos, Juriaan M., *et al.* 2014. "Estimating the Normal Background Rate of Species Extinction." *Conservation Biology*, vol. 29, no. 2: 452-462. To be clear, all this doesn't make re- and afforestation projects *bad.* They're probably better than nothing, and far be it from me to tell people laboring at them to quit and do something else. But they're definitely not *working.*

142. Haskell, Lucy, *et al.* 2022. *State of the World's Birds 2022: Insights and Solutions for the Biodiversity Crisis.* Cambridge: BirdLife International.

143. Brooks, Brad. 2023. "Exclusive: Huge Chunk of Plants, Animals in U.S. at Risk of Extinction." *Reuters*, 6 February 2023. Web.

144. In one of those grim ironies that would be a lot funnier if it weren't so heartbreaking, in 2022 the United Nations Biodiversity Conference (COP15) arrived at a "landmark agreement to guide global action on nature through to 2030." UNEP. 2023. "COP15 Ends with Landmark Biodiversity Agreement." *United Nations Environment Programme*, 20 December 2023. Web. The agreement, the Kunming-Montreal Global Diversity Framework, lays out a (modestly) ambitious set of goals for reducing extinction rates, centering the global finance industry. Much like, and here the grim irony, similarly well-meaning frameworks and sustainable development goals produced by the other COP—for the climate crisis—all the way back to 1988 (and especially 1992), the agreement is nonbinding and contains no mechanisms for enforcement. Would that it were otherwise.

145. For an accessible popular summary, see Asher, Claire. 2021. "Novel Chemical Entities: Are We Sleepwalking through a Planetary Boundary?" *Mongabay*, 23 September 2021. Web. Though microplastics—partially biodegraded novel entities in their own right—are a huge part of this crisis, I leave them to the side in this section in order to focus on novel chemical synthesis itself. But, please, let your reading of the rest of this chapter be haunted by the knowledge that microplastics, too, lurk at every level of our biosphere, promising still-unfolding forms of damage and disruption.

146. For the most minimal conscionable statement of the case, see EPA. 2023. "Our Current Understanding of the Human Health and Environmental Risks of PFAS." *United States Environmental Protection Agency*, 16 March 2023. Web. For popular reportage on the scope of the problem (following on both US and EU soil sampling research), see Perkins, Tom. 2023. "PFAS Levels in Ground and Air Could Be Higher than Expected, Research Suggests." *Guardian*, 26 May 2023. Web.

147. Cf. Tarapore, Pheruza, and Bin Ouyang. 2021. "Perfluoroalkyl Chemicals and Male Reproductive Health: Do PFOA and PFOS Increase Risk for Male Infertility?" *International Journal of Environmental Research and Public Health*, vol. 18, no. 7: 3794; Cohen, Nathan J., *et al.* 2023. "Exposure to Perfluoroalkyl Substances and Women's Fertility Outcomes in a Singaporean Population-Based Preconception Cohort." *Science of The Total Environment*, vol. 873: 162267. But it's not just fertility. Companies' financial exposure to liability for cancer from PFAS is absolutely staggering. See, for instance, Mindock, Clare. 2022. "DuPont Loses Challenge over Cancer Victim's $40 Mln Verdict in PFAS Case." *Reuters*, 6 December 2022. Web; Wallender, Andrew. 2022. "Companies Face Billions in Damages as PFAS Lawsuits Flood Courts." *Bloomberg Law*, 23 May 2022. Web.

148. Ferreira, Becky. 2023. "Scientists Destroyed 95% of Toxic 'Forever Chemicals' in Just 45 Minutes, Study Reports." *Vice*, 3 January 2023. Web.

149. Older readers will remember the iconic 2003 image, a couple years into the United States' failed two-decade war on Afghanistan and six weeks into the U.S. invasion of Iraq that quickly developed into its own years-long murderous debacle. President George W. Bush stands on the deck of an aircraft carrier with "Mission Accomplished" emblazoned on a banner above his head. Earlier the same day, Secretary of Defense Donald Rumsfeld made a similar declaration with regard to the U.S. war in Afghanistan. Declaring a mission accomplished, it turns out, is far easier than accomplishing it.

150. For a comprehensive review of research on BPA (bisphenol A) sponsored by the U.S. Food and Drug Administration, see CLARITY-BPA Research Program. 2021. *NTP*

Research Report on the Consortium Linking Academic and Regulatory Insights on Bisphenol A Toxicity: A Compendium of Published Findings. Research Triangle Park: National Toxicology Program. Research Report 18. Though the report's executive summary is generally deflationary of concerns with regard to a core study conducted by all the participating labs, individual labs' summaries of their findings suggest real cause for concern—for one instance, with regard to prenatal exposure to BPA's effects on gene expression in the developing brain. For an accessible overview of the report, see Saffron, Jesse. 2021. "Insight into Endocrine Disruptor Bisphenol A Advanced by NIEHS." *Environmental Factor: NIEHS*, November 2021. Web.

151. Unless perhaps they read about the discovery of half a million barrels of pure DDT leaking out across the ocean floor near Los Angeles, dumped there in the spirit of cost-deferral or -externalization characteristic of CaCaCo. Xia, Rosanna. "Scientists Discover Startling Concentrations of Pure DDT Along Seafloor Off L.A. Coast." *Los Angeles Times*, 23 March 2023. Web.

152. Carson, Rachel. 2002 [1962]. *Silent Spring*. Boston: Mariner Books. Unsurprisingly, Carson's sounding of the alarm on DDT was anything but welcomed by those with a financial interest in the chemical (and in the general practice of synthesizing and sending out into the world novel chemicals of all sorts). For thoughtful discussion of how Carson's anti-CaCaCo radicalism went well beyond concern with pesticides—and this went enough over readers' heads that her detractors had and today still have the odd rhetorical task of demonstrating her to be villainously radical—see Hecht, David K. 2012. "How to Make a Villain: Rachel Carson and the Politics of Anti-Environmentalism." *Endeavour*, vol. 36, no. 4: 149-155.

153. As I write, highly pathogenic H5N1 virus, avian flu—inculcated and spread and mutated in the viciously, even tortuously close quarters of large-scale commercial bird farming—presents a threat of decimation to wild birds. Jennifer Mullinax, co-author of a recent study on H5N1's mutation to wipe out large wild bird populations, observes, "This high pathogenic virus is wiping out everything in numbers that we've never seen before. . . . This paper illustrates how unprecedented it is, and describes what we think is coming. It's really a call to arms saying, we can't afford to address this from our individual silos. Federal agencies, state agencies, the agriculture sector and wildlife management, we are all going to have to deal with this together, because we can't afford not to." Qtd. in Cutlip, Kimbra. 2023. "Why This Bird Flu Is Different." *Maryland Today*, 19 April 2023. Web. In the continental United States and Canada, wild bird populations have declined by 29%, or nearly 3 billion breeding adults, since 1970. That's over a quarter of "wild bird mass" just *gone* in fifty years, a precursor to species extinctions. Cf. Rosenberg, Kenneth V., *et al*. 2019. "Decline of the North American Avifauna." *Science*, vol. 336, no. 6461: 120-124. In this context, the satirical conspiracy movement "Birds Aren't Real," begun in 2017 by Peter McIndoe and surprisingly long-lived, is less amusing.

154. Carson, *op. cit.*, 2.

155. *Ibid.*, 3.

156. *Ibid.*, 7.

157. *Ibid.*, 6.

158. As with the twinned climate and biodiversity crises, and as seems set to happen for the AI revolution (if all goes *well*), CaCaCo's strongest mechanism for managing global mitigation and adaptation to profitably disruptive novelty is the nonbinding international agreement. This is likely to change at least somewhat in our burning near-future, though long after the horse has left the county. CaCaCo's structural inability to

produce fundamentally just, bindingly enforced global compacts is central to this civilization's untenable accumulation of deferred costs and impoverished vision of "global humanity." That's not to blame most of the generally well-meaning people involved, of course. In the case of the novel chemical crisis, the UN's Stockholm Convention on Persistent Organic Pollutants was adopted in 2001 and entered into force in 2004. For a sense of how unenforceable that "force" is, a person needs only to note that, after several years of open-ended ad hoc working groups devoted to compliance, the entire matter of enforcement was set aside—presumably indefinitely. UNEP. 2019. "Compliance." *United Nations Environment Programme–Stockholm Convention*, accessed 30 April 2023. Web.

159. Carson, *op. cit.*, 6.

160. *Ibid.*, 7.

161. *Ibid.*, 15.

162. EPA. 2023. "Statistics for the New Chemicals Review Program under TSCA." *United States Environmental Protection Agency*, 5 April 2023. Web.

163. The EPA is at times itself a force for ill on exactly this score. Nonprofit investigative journalism outfit ProPublica describes, for instance, the chilling efforts of senior EPA policy advisor Karissa Kovner to prevent global action on some of the very same chemicals forbidden for domestic use in the United States. Lerner, Sharon. 2023. "The U.S. Banned Farmers from Using a Brain-Harming Pesticide on Food. Why Has It Slowed a Global Ban?" *ProPublica*, 8 July 2023. Web.

164. Carson, *op. cit.*, 13.

165. EEA. 2017. *Chemicals for a Sustainable Future: Report of the EEA Scientific Committee Seminar, Copenhagen, 17 May 2017*. European Environment Agency. Luxembourg: Publications Office.

166. Wang, Zhanyun, *et al.* 2020. "Toward a Global Understanding of Chemical Pollution: A First Comprehensive Analysis of National and Regional Chemical Inventories." *Environmental Science & Technology*, vol. 54, no. 5: 2575– 2584.

167. For a breakdown of the industries most reliant on chemical production, see UNEP. 2019. *Global Chemicals Outlook II - From Legacies to Innovative Solutions: Implementing the 2030 Agenda for Sustainable Development*. United Nations Environment Programme, 68-77.

168. On plastics in particular, which could as easily have been the focus of this chapter, see Macleod, Matthew, *et al.* 2021. "The Global Threat from Plastic Pollution." *Science*, vol. 373, no. 6550: 61-65; Borrelle, Stephanie B., *et al.* 2020. "Predicted Growth in Plastic Waste Exceeds Efforts to Mitigate Plastic Pollution." *Science*, vol. 369, no. 6510: 1515-1518; and Ostle, Clare, *et al.* 2019. "The Rise in Ocean Plastics Evidenced from a 60-Year Time Series." *Nature Communications*, vol. 10, art. 1622. Web.

169. For a gold-standard instance of this work, see Persson, Linn, *et al.* 2022. "Outside the Safe Operating Space for the Planetary Boundary for Novel Entities." *Environmental Science & Technology*, vol. 56, no. 3: 1510-1521. It is more than a little noteworthy, and a credit to both authors and editors, that so much conversation about the novel chemical crisis appears in the pages of *Environmental Science & Technology*, a premier journal of the American Chemical Society. We are all herded along by CaCaCo's deathly circuits of resource distribution and metabolization, but this does not preclude our exercising intellectual and even physical courage on the way.

170. Cousins, Ian T., *et al.* 2022. "Outside the Safe Operating Space of a New Planetary Boundary for Per- and Polyfluoroalkyl Substances (PFAS)." *Environmental Science & Technology*, vol. 56, no. 16: 11172-11179.

171. In discussing the vitriolic reception Carson often found, Naomi Oreskes and Erik Conway observe, "Accepting that by-products of industrial civilization were irreparably damaging the global environment was to accept the reality of market failure. It was to acknowledge the limits of free market capitalism." Oreskes and Conway, *op. cit.*, 238.

172. Agricultural giant Monsanto, for another recent instance, makes a pesticide—Roundup—that has played a key role in killing off global populations of honeybees and other pollinators (in addition to harming humans directly). In discussing this devastation, news reports often turn to Carson's *Silent Spring* for framing. But Monsanto continues to make and market Roundup. On the power and the insufficiency of Carson's legacy, see Davis, Frederick Rowe. 2014. *Banned: A History of Pesticides and the Science of Toxicology*. New Haven: Yale UP.

173. Wilson, Edward O. 2002. "Afterword." In Carson, *op. cit.*

174. Introducing a reissue of *Silent Spring*, historian Linda Lear celebrates Carson for "set[ting] in motion a course of events that would result in a ban on the domestic production of DDT and the creation of a grass-roots movement demanding protection of the environment through state and federal regulation" (x). A few pages later, though, she laments that "DDT is [still] found in the livers of birds and fish on every oceanic island on the planet and in the breast milk of every mother. In spite of decades of environmental protest and awareness, and in spite of Rachel Carson's apocalyptic call alerting Americans to the problem of toxic chemicals, reduction of the use of pesticides has been one of the major policy failures of the environmental era. Global contamination is a fact of modern life" (xviii). Lear, Linda. 2002. "Introduction." Carson, *op. cit.* Still, for an instance of the ongoing force of Carson's apocalyptic call, see Dodds, Walter K. 2019. "Release of Novel Chemicals into the Environment: Responsibilities of Authors, Reviewers, and Editors." *Environmental Science & Technology*, vol. 53, no. 24: 14095-14096.

175. Cf. Persson *et al.*, *op. cit.*

176. Carson, *op. cit.*, 13.

177. Liboiron, *op. cit.* 111.

178. McGivney, Annette. 2022. "Skiing on a Sacred Mountain: Indigenous Groups Stand Against a Resort's Expansion." *Guardian*, 19 June 2022. Web. Resistance to Snowbowl's colonial approach to Land has a very long local history, especially since the turn of the 21st century.

Chapter 3

1. The harried endnote-reader may be relieved to know that the note apparatus chills out from here on.

2. Adams, Douglas. 1979. *The Hitchhiker's Guide to the Galaxy*. New York: Pocket Books, 27.

3. *Ibid.*, 53.

4. Building on prior inquiry into the politics that emerge from resentment, Jeremy Engels explores this in beautiful fashion in *The Art of Gratitude* (Albany: SUNY P, 2018). Demonstrating that how we think about our affects matters very much, he invites readers to leave behind common understandings of gratitude as "a feeling of obligation and indebtedness toward those who give us a gift or help us out in some way" (2). An artful practice of gratefulness instead opens up our collective world-making capacities. When we can attune to networks of care without imposing the framework of debt, an affect blocked in usual ways of thinking and feeling gratitude becomes a source of abundance rather than restriction.

5. For one lovely instance of this, see Brennan, Teresa. 2004. *The Transmission of Affect*. Ithaca: Cornell UP. But as a caution against becoming too pleased with our own sensitivity to affect's flows, see Schuller, Kyla. 2018. *The Biopolitics of Feeling: Race, Sex, and Science in the Nineteenth Century*. Durham: Duke UP.

6. Nick Estes draws out the colonial implications of this ultra-capitalist's farmland-hoarding, and the carbon-offset implications as well. Estes, Nick. 2021. "Bill Gates Is the Biggest Private Owner of Farmland in the United States. Why?" *Guardian*, 5 April 2021. Web.

7. Gates, Bill. Qtd. in Cooper, Anderson. 2021. "Bill Gates: How the World Can Avoid a Climate Disaster." *CBS: 60 Minutes*, 15 February 2021. Web.

8. Anderson, *op. cit.*

9. Gates, *op. cit.*

10. For a truly exceptional, detail-driven explanation of the impossibility of simply subtracting carbon from CaCaCo while maintaining overall system continuity, see Buller, Adrienne. 2022. *The Value of a Whale: On the Illusions of Green Capitalism*. Manchester: Manchester UP.

11. Anderson, *op. cit.*

12. Gates, *op. cit.*

13. For a brief popular overview, see McAllister, Sean. 2023. "There Could Be 1.2 Billion Climate Refugees by 2050. Here's What You Need to Know." *Zurich*, 13 January 2023. Web. For an exceptional scholarly overview, realistic on anticipated refugee populations and much else glossed over by Anderson and Gates, see Spangenberg, Joachim H., and Rudi Kurz. 2023. "Epochal Turns: Uncomfortable Insights, Uncertain Outlooks." *Sustainable Development*, Early View: 20 February 2023. Web. It's probably worth mentioning that neither Gates nor Cooper strike me as especially *bad* people. They're just forwarding the sort of view that makes it possible for people in their sorts of positions to not feel too much panic while mostly doing the same sorts of things they've been doing for decades. Shuffling along like everyone else, but with more money.

14. Amusingly, not weeks after signing an open letter urging a pause on further AI development on account of the risks posed to humanity (alongside 1,100 or so other tech luminaries), early OpenAI investor Elon Musk announced incorporation of his own AI company. Such afraid. Very hope. Wow.

15. As usual, an almost too on-the-nose example of the phenomenon can by found in the aggressively upbeat Grey Lady: Coaston, Jane. 2022. "Try to Resist the Call of the Doomers." *New York Times*, 23 July 2022. Web. In a similarly obfuscatory vein, WaPo tries to associate panic and grave concern about the polycrisis with inaction and despair. The antidote? Hope, of course! Osaka, Shannon. 2023. "Why Climate 'Doomers' Are Replacing Climate 'Deniers.'" *Washington Post*, 24 March 2023. This is a militantly silly equivalence with almost no empirical bases and that, to be very blunt, no serious person thinking honestly could possibly arrive at.

16. Happily, I'd gotten the fire out fast enough that the truck was still drivable, though I did end up having to replace cracked and arcing spark plug wires a few hundred miles later.

17. My description of panic's etymology and history draws especially on Borgeaud, Philippe. 1979. *Recherches sur le dieu Pan*. Geneva: Institut Suisse de Rome, translated by Kathleen Atlass and James Redfield as *The Cult of Pan in Ancient Greece* (Chicago: U Chicago P, 1988).

18. Cf. the description in Boardman, John. 1997. *The Great God Pan: The Survival of*

an Image. New York: Thames and Hudson, 35. In early Greek iconography Pan begins as nonhuman, a goat upright on hind legs playing a wind instrument. He is only gradually "domesticated" to the human species.

19. Philosopher of rhetoric Steven Mailloux offers a nice characterization of the conditions that call for phronesis, which has been an abiding concern for rhetoricians all the way back to Aristotle: "Every rhetorical situation is new, even if it resembles those of the past. There is no methodical way to completely determine beforehand the best rhetoric to use in a specific time and place." Thus, "*phronēsis* focuses on the practical activity, not simply to bring it to conclusion but in relation to the how of the action and its effect on the actor. *Phronēsis* is a mode of truth-disclosure at the service of praxis." Mailloux, Steven. 2004. "Rhetorical Hermeneutics Still Again: or, On the Track of *Phronēsis*." *A Companion to Rhetoric and Rhetorical Criticism*. Eds. Walter Jost and Wendy Olmsted. Malden: Blackwell, 457-472. We work to develop practical wisdom so that we can respond well to drastically changing circumstances. For most difficult decisions, and especially for the risk, uncertainty, and urgency of crises, there is no absolute certainty to rely on—not even as a guide toward methods for figuring out how to act, and thus who to be. Phronesis names ways of feeling toward truth in the threatening darkness of crisis. Panic itself can be one such way of feeling.

20. Perhaps this is the evolutionary reason why, as Michael Clune writes at the close of a remarkable essay on the clinical experience of the panic attack, "Because a panic attack doesn't feel like a panic attack. It feels like insight." Clune, Michael W. 2023. "The Anatomy of Panic." *Harper's*, May 2023.

21. Stein, Dan, Kate M. Scott, Peter de Jonge, and Ronald C. Kessler. 2017. "Epidemiology of Anxiety Disorders: From Surveys to Nosology and Back." *Dialogues in Clinical Neuroscience*, vol. 19, no. 2: 127-136.

22. APA. 2022. *Diagnostic and Statistical Manual of Mental Disorders, Fifth Ed., Text Rev.* Washington: American Psychiatric Association Publishing, 235-236.

23. Barlow, David H. 2009. "Foreword." *Culture and Panic Disorder*. Eds. Devon E. Hinton and Byron J. Good. Stanford: Stanford UP, xiii.

24. Hagengimana, Athanase, and Devon E. Hinton. 2009. "'Ihahamuka,' a Rwandan Syndrome of Response to Genocide: Blocked Flow, Spirit Assault, and Shortness of Breath." *Culture and Panic Disorder*. Eds. Devon E. Hinton and Byron J. Good. Stanford: Stanford UP: 205-229. The essays of this remarkable volume, more broadly, offer an excellent window into the cultural variability of what panic can be and mean.

25. For an aligned but less reductive view than the one I'm going with here, see Jackie Orr's fascinating exercise in reflexive sociology, where "panic disorder" is at once real and not real, the product of a period in CaCaCo that led to—and this, panic itself apprehends—a "control society" of ubiquitous propaganda and communication that forms without informing. Orr, Jackie. 2006. *Panic Diaries: A Genealogy of Panic Disorder*. Durham: Duke UP.

26. Borgeaud, *op. cit.*, 181.

27. For a brief history of depictions, including full-goat Pans on Athenian vases c. 490 BCE, see Boardman, *op. cit., passim*.

28. Borgeaud, *op. cit.* 175.

29. *Ibid.*, 152.

30. *Ibid.*, 120.

31. *Ibid.*, 113.

32. Herodotus. 1963. *History of the Greek and Persian War*. Trans. George Rawlinson, ed. and abridged W.G. Forrest. New York: Twayne. More recent historians have speculated a thoroughly mundane cause for Pheidippides' vision: hallucinations induced by excessive running, the Athens-to-Sparta trail far outdistancing the more famous (but apocryphal) Marathon run at 156 miles, an ultramarathon *avant la lettre*. Having crewed a few ultras myself, Forehand's hypothesis rings true. Forehand, Walter E. 1985. "Pheidippides and Pan: A Modern Outlook on Pan's Epiphany." *The Classical Outlook*, vol. 63, no. 1: 1-2.

33. Plato. 1997. "Laws." Trans. Trevor J. Saunders. In *Plato: Complete Works*, ed. John M. Cooper. Indianapolis: Hackett: 815c (1482).

34. *Ibid.*

35. Plato, *op. cit.*, 815d (1482).

36. Borgeaud, *op. cit.*, 89.

37. *Ibid.*

38. For a lightning survey of the nearly non-stop wars in which the Greek world was embroiled for pretty much the entirety of Athens' tumultuous and frequently interrupted democracy, see Samons, Loren J. 2004. *What's Wrong With Democracy? From Athenian Practice to American Worship*. Berkeley: U California P, 31-40.

39. On the homologies and interweaving of ancient Greek cults of Pan and various of the nymphs, see Larson, Jennifer. 2001. *Greek Nymphs: Myth, Cult, Lore*. Oxford: Oxford UP, esp. 96-98.

40. Elsewhere, a co-author and I have described the ordering of such sites in terms of "transcendental signifiers." Allen, Ira, and Saul Allen. 2016. "God Terms and Activity Systems: A Definition of Religion for Political Scientists." *Political Research Quarterly*, vol. 69, no. 3: 557-570.

41. Origin stories for the notion of celestial harmonies trace back to Zhuangzi in one tradition and Pythagoras in another. Surely there are many more. Long before encountering the western philosophical lineage in any systematic fashion, I was fortunate as a young person to be shaped by the exceptional graphics and translation of Tsai, Chih-Chung. *Zhuangzi Speaks: The Music of Nature*. Trans. Brian Bruya. Princeton: Princeton UP.

42. Odell, Jenny. 2019. *How to Do Nothing: Resisting the Attention Economy*. Brooklyn: Melville House, 156.

43. *Ibid.*, 157.

44. *Ibid.*, ix.

45. See Linda Lear's "Introduction" in Carson, Rachel. 1998 [1956]. *The Sense of Wonder*. New York: HarperCollins.

46. Carson, *The Sense of Wonder*, 59.

47. *Ibid.*, 56.

48. Carson, *op. cit.*, 38.

49. In my own small way, I have found loving wonder after panic at megafire in "Climate Anxiety and Topophilia, or, Loving with Fire." 2023. *Local Philosophy*, 7 January 2023. Web.

50. The richest description of this is likely that found throughout Lear, Linda. 2009 [1997]. *Rachel Carson: Witness for Nature*. Boston: Mariner Books.

51. Stengers, Isabelle. 2015. *In Catastrophic Times: Resisting the Coming Barbarism*. Lüneberg: Open Humanities Press.

52. As I finished writing this book, warnings about the extinction risk of AGI had

become increasingly mainstream. See, for instance, Metz, Cade. 2023. "'The Godfather of A.I. Leaves Google and Warns of Danger Ahead." *New York Times*, 1 May 2023. Web. In typical *NYT* business-as-usual fashion, the headline badly undersells the radical significance of the story. More interesting, perhaps, is the "Statement on AI Risk" coordinated by the non-profit Center for AI Safety in May 2023 and signed by a wide range of tech luminaries and academics: "Mitigating the risk of extinction from AI should be a global priority alongside other societal-scale risks such as pandemics and nuclear war." www .safe.ai/statement-on-ai-risk

53. Stengers, *op. cit.*, 156.

54. Latour, Bruno. 2017. *Facing Gaia: Eight Lectures on the New Climatic Regime*. Trans. Catherine Porter. Cambridge: Polity. I pluralize Latour's "people" to emphasize that coming global organizations of life are likely to be characterized by loosely connected heterogeneity far more than by the unicity of CaCaCo's logics.

55. Latour, Bruno. 2018. *Down to Earth: Politics in the New Climatic Regime*. Trans. Catherine Porter. Cambridge: Polity, 99.

56. Stengers, *op. cit.*, 153.

57. A good starting point is Anon. 2023. "France in Flames: Macron Attempts to Crush the Movement Against the Pension Reform with Lethal Violence." *Crimethinc*, 30 March 2023. Web.

58. That's not to say one can't learn *something* from CaCaCo news outlets. Obviously, one can—plenty. But it's crucial to remember who is disposing you, and from that to make some educated guesses about how. You're going to have a very hard time allowing yourself to be shaped by French protesters when the *NYT* is framing those protests. In a similar vein, if I want to understand the extraordinary police repression of protesters fighting against the destruction of Atlanta's Weelaunee Forest, the media outlets belonging to the very same people who want that forest destroyed might not be who I want disposing my way of thinking about it. If I want to allow those political struggles to resonate with me, I'll need to look to (English-language) outlets like *Crimethinc, Current Affairs*, or *Truthout*: sources aligned with the goals of those struggles.

59. For examples, see, respectively, Carpenter-Neuhaus, Harrison. 2023. "DSA Kicks off the Green New Deal in New York." *New York City Democratic Socialists*, 3 May 2023. Web; Feldstein, Steven. 2023. "Evaluating Europe's Push to Enact AI Regulations: How Will This Influence Global Norms?" *Democratization*, forthcoming (advance web publication 27 April 2023); MacDowell, Tate. 2016. "Junk in Public: H2o Trash Patrol." *Death Cookie Entertainment*, YouTube.com. 8 December 2016. Web; and AZGFD. 2023. "Volunteers." *Arizona Game & Fish: Region 2 Flagstaff*, Accessed 3 May 2023. Web.

60. Stengers, *op. cit.*, 153.

61. Lovelock, James. 2021. "Beware: Gaia May Destroy Humans Before We Destroy the Earth." *Guardian*, 2 November 2021. Web.

62. The touchy Gaia Stengers describes throughout *In Catastrophic Times* is not just "a nature to be 'protected' from the damage caused by humans," but also and more "a nature capable of threatening our modes of thinking and living for good" (20). One aim of the book before you is to help move us all from the "cold panic" (32) Stengers associates with this fact to a far more sharply felt, actionable *hot panic*.

63. For a brief but excellent discussion of acquiescence—rather than legitimacy or consent—as organizing principle for CaCaCo in our time, see Engels, Jeremy, and Wil-

liam O. Saas. 2013. "On Acquiescence and Ends-Less War: An Inquiry into the New War Rhetoric." *Quarterly Journal of Speech*, vol. 99, no. 2: 225-232.

64. Escobar, Arturo. 2018. *Designs for the Pluriverse: Radical Interdependence, Autonomy, and the Making of Worlds*. Durham: Duke UP, 235.

65. It is at this point that a certain sort of academic text turns to indigenous lifeways as a salvific invocation. I am skeptical of that move, not because there is nothing to learn from CaCaCo's extractees—of course there is!—but because it positions the one who makes it as being on the side of the angels. Let me be clear. I am not on the side of the angels. If you're reading this book, there's a good chance you aren't either. So, let's be honest with ourselves. CaCaCo is not, on the whole, going to reform itself by learning from indigenous lifeways. That doesn't mean you and I shouldn't. I turn in chapter four to some archaic and still-present indigenous ways of knowing and doing and being that have been excluded from design-power by CaCaCo. But, if you're living in Bruges or Baltimore, or Queensland or Rennes or Sandusky, you're not going to be able to parachute other people's practices into your life, and nobody but billionaires is served by pretending that reading creates salvatory relations of identification. Even they won't be, soon enough. I have no idea whether a sufficient mass of us in the global north can start panicking in time to do anything but the very worst. I hope we can, or else I wouldn't have written this book.

66. *Ibid.*, 21.

67. *Ibid.*, 15. Escobar draws on the lessons of the World Social Forum's first meeting, in 2001 in Porto Alegre, Brazil. That inspiring moment in what we sometimes call "globalization from below" occurred just months before the United States suffered a major terrorist attack. US and begrudging allies' reactions to this attack coalesced CaCaCo beneficiary countries' policy around surveillance, militarization, and securitization—with profoundly dampening effects on global political possibility.

68. *Ibid.*, 161.

Chapter 4

1. And hardly the only such strategies, at that. Two books anyone not engaged by the suggestions here might find more up their alley are De Oliveira, Vanessa Machado. 2021. *Hospicing Modernity: Facing Humanity's Wrongs and the Implications for Social Activism*. Berkeley: North Atlantic Books; and Grover, *op. cit.*

2. You won't be surprised to learn that, dispositionally, I'm only much interested in the latter end of that list. Make no mistake, though: For any futures but the very worst, the others will also be necessary.

3. For another view of the necrotic character of CaCaCo's highly social and coordinated force as a machinery for maximizing resource consumption, see Cowen, Deborah. 2014. *The Deadly Life of Logistics: Mapping Violence in Global Trade*. Minneapolis: U Minnesota P. Perhaps there is no greater collectivity in human history than the violently produced and maintained, fragile but durable supply chains that crisscross every inch of the planet on behalf of CaCaCo trade.

4. Arendt, Hannah. 2006 [1964]. *Eichmann in Jerusalem: A Report on the Banality of Evil*. New York: Penguin, 43.

5. Hunt-Hendrix, Leah, and Astra Taylor. 2024. *Solidarity: The Past, Present, and Future of a World-Changing Idea*. New York: Pantheon, xvii, xxi. Hunt-Hendrix and Taylor's

collaboration is itself a powerful instance of imaginative transit across differences. The former has devoted generational wealth from fossil fuel exploitation (and corresponding social capital) to a variety of CaCaCo-reorganizing ventures, while the latter's long resume of radical activism includes projects like Debt Collective, a debtor's union with the aim of freeing ordinary people from the universal indebtedness demanded by CaCaCo.

6. Another fine vision of what solidarity might look like for many people today appears throughout Hayes and Kaba, *op. cit.*

7. Pineda, Erin. 2021. *Seeing Like an Activist: Civil Disobedience and the Civil Rights Movement*. Oxford: Oxford University Press, 19.

8. For a troubling and helpful historiographical perspective on contemporary approaches to solidarity with the U.S. civil rights movement itself, see Houck, Davis. 2022. *Black Bodies in the River: Searching for Freedom Summer*. Jackson: UP Mississippi.

9. Pineda, *op. cit.*, 19.

10. Hunt-Hendrix and Taylor, *op. cit.*, xxxiv.

11. Pineda, *op. cit.*, 88.

12. John Lewis, qtd. in *ibid.*

13. DuFord, Nathan Rochelle. 2022. *Solidarity in Conflict: A Democratic Theory*. Stanford: Stanford UP, 3. For a very different, but consonant, view of solidarity as both the non-erasure of differences and global imaginative transit, see Engels, Jeremy. 2021. *The Ethics of Oneness: Emerson, Whitman, and the Bhagavad Gita*. Chicago: U Chicago P.

14. Indeed, not only is conflict part of what it means to be for real, but sometimes—often, even—solidarity requires us to avow our own ways of being constructed as these cause conflict or run contrary to solidaristic projects. For a beautiful meditation on the practices of an unsettled white settler finding relations in Newe (Northern Shoshoni) country and beyond, see Wilkes. Lydia. n.d. "Becoming Daiboo': Avowing Settlerness to Reduce Settler Harm in Rhetoric, Communication, and Writing." *College Composition and Communication*, forthcoming unpublished manuscript.

15. DuFord, *op. cit.*, 171.

16. The essential vision of the World Social Forum, as an intimation of post-CaCaCo possibilities, has always been that "another world is possible." As Michael Löwy put this in a talk at the first WSF in 2001, "To conclude: a certain neoliberal press, to confuse things, calls us 'anti-globalization.' This is a deliberate attempt at disinformation. This movement, this forum, is not anti-globalization: it is against *this capitalistic, neoliberal world*, unjust and inhumane, and it seeks *another world* of solidarity and fraternity. This new world is perhaps beginning in Porto Alegre in January 2001." Löwy, Michael. 2005 [2001]. "Davos and Porto Alegre, Two Antagonistic Projects." *The World Social Forum: Strategies of Resistance*. Ed. José Corrêa Leite and trans. Traci Romine. Chicago: Haymarket Books, 90. A new world did not, as it happened, begin in Porto Alegre in January 2001. But this does not mean it cannot begin in the ruins of CaCaCo to come, and even be prefigured in the solidarity relations we pursue right now.

17. For decent reportage on writers' concerns, especially with respect to generative AI, see Longeretta, Emily, and Michael Schneider. 2023. "Julie Plec and More WGA Members Detail Writers Strike Negotiations, Demand Streamers to Release Ratings: 'We're Mad.'" *Variety*, 3 June 2023. Web.

18. Greg Iwinski, qtd. *ibid.*

19. Davis, Diane. 2010. *Inessential Solidarity: Rhetoric and Foreigner Relations*. Pittsburgh: U Pittsburgh P; Citton, *op cit.*, 5-6.

20. Davis, *op. cit.*, 126.

21. See Hansen, *op. cit.*

22. On the climate crisis's planetary character as inducement to action, distinguished political scientist William Connolly writes, "Let's give the politics of swarming and cross-country general strikes a try; then, if such an improbable necessity proves impossible to enact, it may be time to move to the next items on the agenda." Connolly, William E. 2017. *Facing the Planetary: Entangled Humanism and the Politics of Swarming.* Durham: Duke UP, 174.

23. As though to underscore the point, the day after writing this sentence I learned that insurance giants State Farm and Allstate had both ceased entirely to insure new homes in California, citing unrecoverable wildfire risk—a move that, in the way CaCaCo do be, might as easily have been a bid to escape consumer insurance protections that are stronger in California than most other U.S. states. Whether commercially necessary response to climate crisis or cynical deployment of climate crisis to gouge Californians, the point is the same: CaCaCo's costs are coming home to roost all over. Kamisher, Eliyahu, Max Reyes, and Biz Carson. 2023. "It's Not Just State Farm. Allstate No Longer Sells New Home Insurance Policies in California." *Los Angeles Times*, 3 June 2023. Web.

24. Cf. Bennett, Brian. 2023. "Biden's Rightward Shift on Immigration Draws Comparisons to Trump." *Time*, 22 May 2023. Web.

25. One recent study finds that by century's end nearly a third of the human population will no longer live in an ecological niche that, historically, has been able to support large-scale settlement. That's billions of people. Today's growing migration crisis surely registers, at least in part, that climate change has already put more than 600 million people—well more than one-and-a-half times as many as presently occupy the United States, the world's third-largest country—outside of humans' evolutionarily adaptive niche. Lenton, Timothy, *et al.* 2023. "Quantifying the Human Cost of Global Warming." *Nature Sustainability*, forthcoming (advance web publication 22 May 2023). See also Wang, Yuwei, *et al.* 2023. "Future Population Exposure to Heatwaves in 83 Global Megacities." *Science of the Total Environment*, vol. 888, art. № 164142. Web.

26. Is there any more at once comprehensive and meticulously sourced overview of human movements and settlements across time than that offered by Davids Graeber and Wengrow? One of a plethora of instances therein: "In about 1500 the Etowah valley fell under the sway of the kingdom of Coosa, by which time most of the original population appears to have left and moved on, leaving behind little more than a museum of earthworks for the Coosa to lord it over." Graeber, David, and David Wengrow. 2021. *The Dawn of Everything: A New History of Humanity.* New York: Farar, Straus and Giroux, 470.

27. Cf. Scott, James C. 2018. *Against the Grain: A Deep History of The Earliest States.* New Haven: Yale UP.

28. The locus classicus is Hirschman, Albert O. 1970. *Exit, Voice, and Loyalty: Responses to Decline in Firms, Organizations, and States.* Cambridge: Harvard UP.

29. UN IOM. 2023. "World Migration Report 2022—Interactive." *United Nations International Organization for Migration*, Accessed 6 May 2023. Web. This is a truly excellent resource for anyone hoping to visualize the flows of people around the world today.

30. Following Hannah Arendt's trenchant formulation, this is often conceived as a problem of "the right to have rights." For an overview of the issues at play in migration vis-à-vis a "global humanity" that has been carved up into nation-state citizenries, see Kesby, Alison. 2012. *The Right to Have Rights: Citizenship, Humanity, and International Law.* Oxford: Oxford UP.

31. Cf. Gulddal, Jesper, and Charlton Payne. 2017. "Passports: On the Politics and

Cultural Impact of Modern Movement Control." *symplokē*, vol. 25, nos. 1-2: 9-23; Torpey, John C. 2018. *The Invention of the Passport: Surveillance, Citizenship, and the State, 2nd ed.* Cambridge: Cambridge UP.

32. See Obermaier and Obermayer, *op. cit.*, for a distressingly empirical picture of how the capacity for movement is bound to the possession of capital in a never-yet-postcolonial global order.

33. Fredrick, James. 2023. "Mexico Allows Tens of Thousands of Migrants to Travel to U.S. Border." *New York Times*, 10 May 2023. Web.

34. Garsd, Jasmine. 2023. "Border Patrol Sending Migrants to Unofficial Camps in California's Southern Desert, Locals Say." *NPR*, 21 November 2023. Web.

35. "The title of this book is an oblique reference to the Great Migration, the largest single migration event in American history. . . . By the end of this century, climate change will displace more people in the United States than [the six million who] moved during the Great Migration, uprooting millions of people in every region of the country." Bittle, Jake. 2023. *The Great Displacement: Climate Change and the Next American Migration.* New York: Simon and Schuster, xvi. If anything, I suspect Bittle badly understates the case by offering an "end of this century" horizon, since climate displacement will ramp up dramatically in just the next couple decades (if insurance markets are any indication, and one supposes that they are).

36. *Ibid.*, 283.

37. See my NAU colleague's unflinching portrayal in Alvarez, Alex. 2021. *Unstable Ground: Climate Change, Conflict, and Genocide, Updated Ed.* New York: Rowman & Littlefield. On the CaCaCo-ness of it all, see Ajuha, Neel. 2021. *Planetary Specters: Race, Migration, and Climate Change in the Twenty-First Century.* Chapel Hill: U North Carolina P.

38. Taussig, Michael. 2020. *Mastery of Non-Mastery in an Age of Meltdown.* Chicago: U Chicago P, 28.

39. Am I not aware that "disruption" is the term for when tech bros do something that might be profitable down the road and will definitely inconvenience and maybe render homeless a bunch of people no matter what? Why am I using this term like it's a good thing?! Yeah, I'm aware. Just not persuaded we need to jettison it altogether because it got used in an unwise fashion for a while.

40. Though there are some very powerful and *uncommon* invocations of resilience that align more with what I mean by sustaining disruption. Many of these are collected at the website and archive of possibility https://www.resilience.org. See also recent work comparing the "resilience profiles" of Norwegian civilians and military veterans: Nordstrand, Andreas Espetvedt, *et al.* 2023. "Differences in Resilience Profiles Between Military Veterans and the General Population: An Exploratory Latent Profile Analysis Using the HUNT-4 Survey." *Stress & Health* (advance web publication 6 November 2023). An important implication of this work is that "resilience" is a term that finds meanings in ways that *are specific to different groups, especially with respect to their values and intentions.* For anyone not wild about the disposition to sustain disruption that I'm developing here, *determining what to count as resilience and why,* especially in small groups and hyperlocal ways, is a great alternative.

41. For a perfectly well-meaning instance of corporate resilience thinking, of the sort one will find in great abundance as the polycrisis blossoms, see Suarez, Fernando F., and Juan S. Montes. 2020. "Building Organizational Resilience." *Harvard Business Review,* November-December 2020. Web.

42. The point is made particularly cogently in Bendell, Jem. 2020 [2018]. "Deep Ad-

aptation: A Map for Navigating Climate Tragedy, Rev. Ed." IFLAS Occasional Paper 2, 27 July 2020. Web. Bendell's come in for a lot of criticism for this exceptionally widely read piece, some of it thoughtful and scientifically clarifying, but much of it denialist and kind of boorishly ad hominem. Though I don't agree with all of Bendell's conclusions, and though some pieces of the underlying science have either been updated or disputed, I want to acknowledge (and think more people like me should do the same) how impactful this essay was for me when I first read it in 2018.

43. Even CaCaCo media outlets have begun navigating this reality. See, for instance, Little, Jane Braxton. 2023. "Looking for Home in an Overheating World: If Emissions Continue, Will We All Be Migrants Someday?" *Salon*, 6 June 2023. Web.

44. Malm, Andreas. 2021. *How to Blow Up a Pipeline: Learning to Fight in a World on Fire*. London: Verso.

45. In the Anglosphere, these range from a series of state-level laws criminalizing blocking traffic and the general police-state logic of the U.S. to explicit legal attacks on climate activism in the U.K. and Australia. For a brief breakdown of the latter, see McNeill, Sophie. 2023. "Australia's Crackdown on Climate Activists." *The Diplomat*, 27 May 2023. Web. Equally, on this same trend in Germany, see McGuiness, Damien, and Paul Kirby. 2023. "German Police Raid Climate Activists Who Blocked Traffic." *BBC*, 24 May 2023. Web.

46. See again Buller, *op. cit.*, for a careful debunking of "green capitalism's" more beloved—and deadly—myths.

47. Malm, *op. cit.*, 8.

48. A complementary emphasis on *ecopessimism* emerges in the frankly exceptional dissertation of political theorist Witlacil, Mary E. 2023. "Pessimism and the Anthropocene." Order № 30568308. Colorado State University / ProQuest Dissertations Publishing. I have also learned a great deal from my friend Sean Parson's climate nihilism, the focus of his next book. It'll be a banger.

49. Malm, *op. cit.*, 9.

50. *Ibid.*, 146.

51. Interestingly, this is one of the primary drivers of political action on the climate crisis in Kim Stanley Robinson's widely hailed *Ministry for the Future* (New York: Orbit, 2020). Between targeted violence and national banks as superheroes, the novel's plot seems to register the end of Robinson's long commitment to imagining democracy. It is a little surprising, and deeply disquieting, that it was so positively received by so many political and business leaders.

52. Cf. Burke, Kenneth. 1945. "The Temporizing of Essence." *The Kenyon Review*, vol. 7, no. 4: 616-627.

53. I've addressed such questions in a limited way in Allen 2022, *op. cit.*.

54. For a more martial instance of community defense in the context of state breakdown, see Díaz, Antonio Fuentes, and Daniele Fini (trans. Victoria Furio). 2021. "Neoliberalism in the Grey Area: Community Defense, the State, and Organized Crime in Guerrero and Michoacán." *Latin American Perspectives*, vol. 48, no. 1: 84-102. Though "community self-defense" is a phrase especially associated with anarchist thought and practice, community defense has often been explicitly urged by states themselves. For a WWII-era example in the US, where the term is used synonymously with civil defense, see Jordan, Harry E. 1940. "Organizing for Community Defense." *Journal (American Water Works Association)*, vol. 32, no. 10: 1732-1736.

55. This section focuses on novel social forms that in one way or another resist

CaCaCo. I do not mean, though, to deny that thoughtful and useful sorts of social novelty emerge within even CaCaCo logics themselves. For a very fine instance of the latter, which will be amenable to the more business-minded reader, see Albareda, Laura, and Alejo Jose G. Sison. 2020. "Commons Organizing: Embedding Common Good and Institutions for Collective Action. Insights from Ethics and Economics." *Journal of Business Ethics*, vol. 166: 727-743.

56. For a carefully theorized discussion of Cooperation Jackson from my own discipline of rhetorical studies, see Bost, Matthew, and Joshua S. Hanan. 2023. "Capacitating the Deep Commons: Considering Capital and Commoning Practices from an Affective-Rhetorical Systems Perspective." *Rhetoric Society Quarterly*, vol. 53, no. 2: 186-201.

57. The project is detailed in the essays collected in Akuno, Kali / Cooperation Jackson, and Ajamu Nangwaya (eds.). 2017. *Jackson Rising: The Struggle for Economic Democracy and Black Self-Determination in Jackson, Mississippi*. Wakefield, Quebec: Daraja Press. See also the follow-up volume, Akuno, Kali / Cooperation Jackson, and Matt Meyer (eds.). 2023. *Jackson Rising Redux: Lessons on Building the Future in the Present*. Oakland: PM Press.

58. Akuno, Kali. 2017. "Build and Fight: The Program and Strategy of Cooperation Jackson," in Akuno / Cooperation Jackson and Nangwaya, *op. cit.*, 22.

59. For a very brief overview, see Dubb, Steve. 2023. "Advocates Gather to Advance Solidarity Economy Organizing." *Nonprofit Quarterly*, 24 May 2023. Web.

60. Akuno, *op. cit.*, 28.

61. Akuno, Kali. 2022. "Jackson, MS Water Crisis—Building Community Resiliency, Water Crisis Relief Phase 2." *Cooperation Jackson*, 22 September 2022. Web.

62. *Ibid.*

63. Disturbingly, Elizabeth Kolbert's *Under a White Sky: The Nature of the Future* (New York: Crown, 2021) details an awful lot of the worst, and likeliest, sort of geoengineering: "solar radiation management" (SRM), the deliberate blocking out of the sun by distributing particles in earth's atmosphere. In effect, such a scheme holds all of humanity hostage to whoever undertakes it. As GHG emissions continue, the base capacity of the earth system to retain heat when receiving the sun's rays—interrupted literally day-to-day by particles continuously distributed in the atmosphere via SRM—will continue to rise. So, any cessation of such geoengineering before vast quantities of carbon has been vacuumed out of the air (via not-yet-invented technologies) will result in ultrarapid, almost immediate, new heating. What's disturbing is that, while Kolbert presents the implementation of SRM as a virtually foregone conclusion, the book's received wildly enthusiastic praise from figures like Bill Gates and Barack Obama. It seems highly likely that one or more somebodies trying to maintain CaCaCo continuity will undertake SRM and other large-scale geoengineering projects before long. Never mind that dozens of millions of people already die from air pollution. Never mind that nobody knows how to grow food to feed eight billion people without an awful lot of direct sunlight. Never mind, never mind.

64. For the most fulsome future-anterior (what will have been) look at how stuck we are with producing a "hotter, darker future" I am aware of, see the monumental, two-volume work of Vollman, William T. 2019. *No Immediate Danger: Volume One* and *No Alternative: Volume Two*. New York: Penguin.

65. It's not outrageous to focus on making technological novelties, perhaps even to devote one's life to making them (in the time that remains). If I seem ambivalent

about CaCaCo innovation, it's because I am. We all should be. Material innovations of all sorts are absolutely necessary to pay enough of CaCaCo's deferred costs to avoid the most horrifying and worst possible futures. Listing some of them out would certainly brighten up this chapter. And yet, the old stories of abundance that such lists invoke are just not true. We're in for a future of widespread diminution of resource access. So, while I don't begrudge anyone working on grid electrification or left vanguardist politics (both of which are likely stillborn, but can leave positive legacies), this book takes another tack. More than anything, I'm urging forms of political localism (including in some domains we often don't think of as *political*) that extend to networks of immediate and near-immediate relations the excellent insights of Fyke, Jeremy, and Andrew Weaver. 2023. "Reducing Personal Climate Risk to Reduce Personal Climate Anxiety." *Nature Climate Change*, vol. 13: 209-210. Web.

66. For further instances of what this can look like, see Parson, Sean. 2019. *Cooking Up a Revolution: Food Not Bombs, Homes Not Jails, and Resistance to Gentrification*. Manchester: Manchester UP.

67. Anyone old enough to remember 9/11 may also recall the way CIA guy Chalmers Johnson's *Blowback: The Costs and Consequences of American Empire* (New York: Henry Holt, 2000) became an instant classic. I remember going to see Johnson speak in late 2001, as an undergrad at the University of Kansas, and thinking, "Of course! That makes so much sense!" Deferred costs look like externalities—discarded waste—until they fall due. At that point, they can only appear as consequences. But because they are still in fact costs, a systemic failure or inability to pay them results, as with American empire or CaCaCo broadly, in even the mightiest of enterprises going under.

68. Liboiron, Max, and Josh Lepawsky. 2022. *Discard Studies: Wasting, Systems, and Power*. Cambridge: MIT Press.

69. *Ibid.*, 127.

70. *Ibid.*, 3.

71. *Ibid.*

72. I should note that Liboiron and Lepawsky are critical of any universal "we," for reasons that (speaking as someone who came up as a scholar during the long moment of antifoundational thought) I'm basically sympathetic to. Chapter four of *Discard Studies* is devoted to the idea that "There's No Such Thing as We: A Theory of Difference" and is well worth reading. At the same time, as you know well, I'm committed here to "we" at a subatomic level. There's not room to make the (academic) argument for why in this book, but I trace it out to some extent in my last and also in the next one I'm working on, *Rhetoric, Witness, Loss, Truth*. The short of it is that I don't think anyone really escapes supra-identitarian or would-be transcendent "we"-talk. It's still worth criticizing, but critics should maybe take a little more into account the way they, too, will do it. Maybe not *universal*, but we're all more or less stuck with a *general* "we" as part of how language organizes experience. We are.

73. This latter is the organizing question, too, that motivates revolutionary communist journal *Salvage*. See, for instance, https://salvage.zone/salvage-perspectives-1-amid -this-stony-rubbish/.

74. Liboiron and Lepawsky, *op. cit.*, 128. It's noteworthy, too, that recycling turns out to be an utterly disastrous contributor to the global circulation of microplastics and nanoplastics. Plastic recycling, as a management system that licenses the ever-intensifying production of (fossil fuel-based) novel entities, has—in just the way Rachel

Carson warned of—ended up contributing its own unforeseen and horrific consequences to the novel chemical crisis. See especially Simon, Matt. 2023. "Yet Another Problem With Recycling: It Spews Microplastics." *Wired*, 5 May 2023. Web. The underlying study is Brown, Erina, *et al.* 2023. "The Potential for a Plastic Recycling Facility to Release Microplastic Pollution and Possible Filtration Remediation Effectiveness." *Journal of Hazardous Materials Advances*, vol. 10, art. no. 100309.

75. On forms of social critique and political work that might best support such novelty, and on the ways even our best efforts inevitably fall short and yet remain worth undertaking, see the brilliant Martel, James. 2022. *Anarchist Prophets: Disappointing Vision and the Power of Collective Sight*. Durham: Duke UP.

76. Bishop, Paul (Ed.). 2012. *The Archaic: The Past in the Present*. London: Routledge, 36-37.

77. *Ibid.*, 37.

78. Though not, as Jason Josephson-Storm shows in *The Myth of Disenchantment*, nearly as skeptical as we like to think. He notes that "roughly an amazing three-quarters of Americans hold at least one supernatural belief. Sure, we have plenty of skeptics, and one might hazard the guess that more of them are housed in the academy than elsewhere; still, evidence suggests that higher education merely opens one up to some paranormal beliefs rather than others. In most respects it would appear these skeptics are in the minority." Josephson-Storm, Jason Ā. 2017. *The Myth of Disenchantment: Magic, Modernity, and the Birth of the Human Sciences*. Chicago: U Chicago P, 34.

79. Exactly *how* concerning is debatable. A leaked FBI memo, for instance, registered one level of concern (as reported by the unhappy leaker, that tradcaths represent a terror threat). Seraphin, Kyle. 2023. "The FBI Doubles Down on Christians and White Supremacy." *UncoveredDC.com*, 8 February 2023. Web. Questioned about this concern by the Catholic News Agency, the FBI disavowed the memo the next day. Arnold, Tyler, and Joe Bukuras. 2023. "FBI Retracts Leaked Document Orchestrating Investigation of Catholics." *Catholic New Agency*, 9 February 2023. Web. That controversy aside, the non-initiate reader of a tradcath forum like reddit.com/r/TraditionalCatholics might be taken aback by the mixture of virulent anticommunism, anti-LGBTQ screeds, advice on confession, Elon Musk adulation, requests for prayer, thoughtful discussion of Traditionalist Catholic twentieth-century history, anti-abortion maximalism, covid denialism, and so on. It's all anchored in insistence, following French Archbishop Marcel Lefebvre (excommunicated 1988), that only the archaic Latin Mass can properly be thought of as Catholic.

80. Cf. Norris, Sian. 2023. "Frilly Dresses and White Supremacy: Welcome to the Weird, Frightening World of 'Trad Wives.'" *Guardian*, 23 May 2023. Web.

81. That distinction, between preference for a religious rite and exclusive insistence on this rite, is the difference between the (Vatican-affirmed) Priestly Fraternity of Saint Peter (FSSP) and the (Vatican-unsupported) Society of Saint Pius X (SSPX). The latter was Lefebvre's vehicle and remains a powerful outsider-movement within Catholicism broadly conceived. And the two may now be more closely affiliated than they for a time were, following on Pope Francis' 2021 quasi-suppression of the Latin Tridentine Mass that both value. But this all gets a little Catholic inside-baseball. What I'm interested in, and troubled by, is the exclusionary way of thinking or mindset sponsored by the SSPX-affiliated tradcath movement in its approach to archaism.

82. For a vision of what this move can look like when married to an emphasis on novel, egalitarian social forms (and also as evidence that this is in no way a "fundamen-

talist" impulse specific only to the Mosaic religions), see Miura, Takashi. 2019. *Agents of World Renewal: The Rise of the Yonaoshi Gods in Japan*. Honolulu: U Hawai'i P. On traditionalism as a force in modern history, see the fascinating and often bizarre Sedgwick, Mark J. 2004. *Against the Modern World: Traditionalism and the Secret Intellectual History of the Twentieth Century*. New York: Oxford UP.

83. Cultural theorist Svetlana Boym makes a powerful distinction between restorative and reflective nostalgias. For restorative nostalgia, the goal is to become one with the past, to make it whole again. This aim of recreating the lost world, Boym sees as proto-fascist. By contrast, reflective nostalgia is a basis for novel worldmaking. To rescue something of what's lost in service of something that's never yet existed opens social and political possibilities. Boym, Svetlana. 2001. *The Future of Nostalgia*. New York: Basic Books. Though I don't mean exactly the same thing by archaisms as Boym meant by nostalgia, there is a shared flavor and it is a (lovely) book that's shaped much of my thinking here.

84. For a partisan's view, see Chessman, Stuart. 2022. *Faith of Our Fathers: A Brief History of Catholic Traditionalism in the United States, From Triumph to Traditionis Custodes*. Brooklyn: Angelico Press. For a dated, but in outline still apt, critical view, see Dinges, William D. 1995. "'We Are What You Were': Roman Catholic Traditionalism in America." *Being Right: Conservative Catholics in America*. Eds. Mary Jo Weaver and R. Scott Appleby. Bloomington: Indiana UP. Lest this seem a sheerly or even primarily U.S. phenomenon, see on Austrian tradcaths in covid times Schmidinger, Thomas. 2022. "Profiting from Crisis? Catholic Traditionalism during the COVID-19 Pandemic." *Interdisciplinary Journal for Religion and Transformation in Contemporary Society*, vol. 8, no. 2: 466-486. On the role of Brazilians in making the tradcath movement itself (and on that movement's intensely inegalitarian hierarchical vision), see Cowan, Benjamin. 2019. "The 'Beauty of Inequality' and the Mythos of the Medieval: Brazil and the Forging of Global Catholic Traditionalism." *Luso-Brazilian Review*, vol. 56, no. 2: 105-129.

85. Voxxkowalski. 2023. "What's Happening to American Men?" *Tradcath.proboards. com*, 17 April 2023. Web. Partial ellipsis *sic*.

86. Voxxkowalski. 2016. "Trad Cath Rules." *Tradcath.proboards.com*, 24 April 2016.

87. For a popular take on both the fascizing implications of this view and its interweaving with restorative nostalgia for archaic variants of Christianity, see esp. chapter two of Sexton, Jared Yates. 2023. *The Midnight Kingdom: A History of Power, Paranoia, and the Coming Crisis*. New York: Dutton.

88. Holdsworth, Brian. 2021; 2023. "In Defense of the Crusades"; "Should Christians Be Friends with Non-Christians?" Youtube.com/@brianholdsworth. Web.

89. I thank Sean Parson for keeping me heedful of the danger in quests after authenticity, even if I remain dubious we ever quite escape them.

90. See, for instance, the discussion in Fox, Mira. 2023. "After Pope Benedict's Death, Who Will Claim His Legacy?" *Forward*, 5 January 2023. Web.

91. As a reminder for anyone who make have skipped chapter two, CaCaCo humanity's role in making Gaia uninhabitable for our species and others currently involves placing us on the wrong side of seven out of eight planetary boundaries. Rockström, Johan, *et al.* "Safe and Just Earth System Boundaries." *Nature*, forthcoming (advance web publication 31 May 2023).

92. Greenspoon, Lior, *et al.* 2023. "The Global Biomass of Wild Mammals." *PNAS*, vol. 120, no. 10, forthcoming (advance web publication 27 February 2023). See also

Bar-On, Yinon M., Rob Phillips, and Ron Milo. 2018. "The Biomass Distribution on Earth." *PNAS*, vol. 115, no. 25: 6506-6511. It's important to note, as the authors of both studies do, that biomass estimation is intrinsically tricky and fairly broad-strokes. Still, the general trend is desperately clear.

93. Jeremy Engels aptly observes, with Walt Whitman, that "the key to grief is how it is expressed. Does mourning lead us toward oneness and [more-than-]human interconnectedness, or away from it? Does grief encourage us to deny the reality of life, or affirm it?" Engels, *op. cit.*, 115.

94. My understanding of the purposes of scholarship has for many years been shaped by Silko, Leslie Marmon. 1986. *Ceremony*. New York: Penguin.

95. See, for instance, efforts to help biodiversity science learn from the governance principles of seventeen North American Pacific Coast First Nations in Salomon, Anne K., *et al.* 2023. "Disrupting and Diversifying the Values, Voices, and Governance Principles that Shape Biodiversity Science and Management." *Philosophical Transactions of the Royal Society B*, vol. 378, art. no. 20220196. Web.

96. Indeed, scientists and institutions at all levels, both laudably and, at times, more than a little ironically (*ahem*, World Economic Forum), have begun to treat indigenous knowledges as central to anything approximating climate and biodiversity solutions. On the one hand, that's great! On the other hand, there's a bit of "keep the colonialism, but add back in the indigeneity" going on here. The latter has led critics to call appropriation of indigenous knowledges not coupled with efforts to dismantle CaCaCo no more than a new form of colonialism. Anyone trying to do *not that* can benefit from Itchuaqiyaq, Cana Uluak. "Iñupiat Iḷitqusiat: An Indigenist Ethics Approach for Working with Marginalized Knowledges in Technical Communication." 2021. *Equipping Technical Communicators for Social Justice Work: Theories, Methodologies, and Pedagogies*. Eds. Rebecca Walton and Godwin Y. Agboka. Utah State UP.

97. And terrifically many other words. It is fitting that, as a term designating first principles or roots or origins, archē came to serve as the basis for most of our ways of thinking about organizing human societies. Monarchy is rule stemming from one (*mono*), oligarchy rule organized by the few (*oligos*), anarchy a state without a single first principle (*a-* or *an-* being a negating prefix). For a wonderful discussion of the dangers of archism, the insistence that social organization stem from some sole and superordinate "first principle," see Martel, *op. cit.* I leave open the question of what forms of rule or social organization might best serve the peoples of Gaia in a still-more-broken world to come, in part because I remain unsure my own self (though I have become increasingly persuaded that "anarchist prophets," as Martel puts it, see both possibilities and impossibilities the rest of us struggle to accept and so are an important source of inspiration). For one "prophet" whose thinking, especially of prefigurative politics and archaisms, is especially challenging and fruitful today, see Bookchin, Murray. 2004. *Post-Scarcity Anarchism*. Chico: AK Press. If this book had a motto, it'd read "Murray Bookchin: Wrong for 1974, Right for 2024."

98. As reported upon critically by Aristotle in *Metaph.* 983 b20-28. Aristotle. 1941. "Metaphysica." Trans. W.D. Ross. *The Basic Works of Aristotle*. Ed. Richard McKeon. New York: Random House, 694.

99. Estes, Nick. 2019. *Our History Is the Future: Standing Rock versus the Dakota Access Pipeline, and the Long Tradition of Indigenous Resistance*. London: Verso, 15.

100. *Ibid.*

101. *Ibid.*

102. For a good overview of the inclusion of rivers in CaCaCo legal systems, see Pecharroman, Lidia Cano. 2018. "Rights of Nature: Rivers that Can Stand in Court." *Resources*, vol. 7, no. 1, art. no. 13. Web; or O'Donnell, Erin L., and Julia Talbot-Jones. 2018. "Creating Legal Rights for Rivers: Lessons from Australia, New Zealand, and India." *Ecology & Society*, vol. 23, no. 1, art. no. 7. Web. For critical readings of and beyond this more restricted sense of the rights of nature, see the essays of Anker, Kirsten, *et al.* (eds.). 2020. *From Environmental to Ecological Law*. London: Routledge.

103. For a particularly compelling explanation of this fact, drawing on communication with Gerrard Albert (Whanganui Iwi lead negotiator for the Te Awa Tupua Agreement) and outlining a broad and emerging domain of indigenous law as global replacement for CaCaCo jurisprudential principles, see Rāwiri, Āneta Hinemihi. 2022. "Te Awa Tupua, Indigenous Law, and Decolonisation." *Victoria University Wellington Law Review*, vol. 53, no. 3: 431-462. Lest one mistake legal wins within CaCaCo for actual decolonization, however, Rāwiri observes, "For Whanganui Iwi, the Te Awa Tupua Agreement is a starting point towards decolonising New Zealand's legal and governance systems. The end point will be reached when Te Awa Tupua determines (instead of participating in) all decision-making that affects the River, and the natural world determines New Zealand's constitutional framework. In addition, Whanganui Iwi and New Zealand's respective nations and systems of law and governance will coexist interdependently" (432). I have benefited also from the brief overview of Hsiao, Elaine C. 2012. "Whanganui River Agreement: Indigenous Rights and Rights of Nature." *Environmental Law & Policy*, vol. 42, no. 6: 371-375.

104. As Rāwiri explains, to understand at all the scope of Te Awa Tupua, a person needs some sense of the underlying Whanganui Iwi legal philosophy, Te Kawa Ora. This is not merely abstract, but fully embodied; it rests on three core principles: "Te Kore = the world of the potential for life; Te Pō = the world of unseen life energy systems; and Te Ao Mārama = the seen physical" (Rāwiri, *op. cit.*, 434n10).

105. Estes, *op. cit.*, 256.

106. Estes' *Our History Is the Future* traces a lineage of indigenous resistance to carbon-burning, capitalism, and colonialism from long before the first massacre at Wounded Knee to and through the multination alliance of Water Protectors fighting the Dakota Access Pipeline at Standing Rock, a camp ten or twenty thousand strong. He notes that "Mni Wiconi, as much as it reaches into the past, is a future-oriented project. It forces some to confront their own unbelonging to the land and the river" and asks pointedly, "How can settler society, which possesses no fundamental ethical relationship to the land or its original people, imagine a future premised on justice?" While I'm—I hope obviously, given the underlying currents of this book—mostly amenable to Estes' claim that "whatever the answer may be, Indigenous peoples must lead the way" (*ibid.*), the same restorative nostalgia that makes tradcaths a dead end for humanizing haunts the edges of this view, too.

107. Boccaletti, Giulio. 2021. *Water: A Biography*. New York: Vintage, 293. This often illuminating book is premised on acceptance, even celebration, of CaCaCo at all levels; and it's framed by scaremongering about China. Great book about the deep political history of water, but wants salt.

108. Estes, *op. cit.*, 257.

109. Deloria, Jr., Vine. 1994. *God Is Red: A Native View of Religion, the Classic Work*

Updated. Golden: Fulcrum Publishing, 271. My thanks to Tom Hurley for lending me this book back in 2000 or so; I'll get it back to you sometime.

110. On the latter, see especially Yazzie, Melanie. 2018. "Decolonizing Development in Diné Bikeyah." *Environment & Society*, vol. 9: 25-39.

111. Kimmerer, Robin. 2013. *Braiding Sweetgrass: Indigenous Wisdom, Scientific Knowledge, and the Teachings of Plants*. Minneapolis: Milkweed Editions.

112. *Ibid.*, 4.

113. *Ibid.*, 33.

114. *Ibid.*

115. Tahawus, Kimmerer explains, "is the Algonquin name for Mount Marcy, the highest peak in the Adirondacks. . . . Tahawus, 'the Cloud Splitter,' is its true name, evoking its essential nature." *Ibid.*, 34.

116. *Ibid.*, 36.

117. *Ibid.*, 367.

118. *Ibid.*, 369.

119. *Ibid.*, 377.

120. *Ibid.*, 36.

121. Kimmerer asks, "What else can you offer the earth, which has everything? What else can you give but something of yourself? A homemade ceremony, a ceremony that makes a home" (38).

122. *Ibid.*, 37.

123. In the 1977 *Speed and Politics*, Paul Virilio foretells the likeliest outcome of this fact in terms that should feel chillingly prescient: "We will see the creation of a common feeling of insecurity that will lead to a new kind of consumption, the consumption of protection; this latter will progressively come to the fore and become *the target of the whole merchandising system*." Virilio, Paul. 2006 [1977]. *Speed and Politics: An Essay on Dromology*. Trans. Mark Polizzotti. Los Angeles: Semiotext(e).

124. For a wonderfully contrary view of that stale and deadly story, see Pennock, Caroline Dodds. 2023. *On Savage Shores: How Indigenous Americans Discovered Europe*. New York: Alfred A. Knopf.

125. Though there's a lot to be irritated by in the book, a good overview of the fluidity of "human species" designations appears in Harari, Yuval Noah. 2015. *Sapiens: A History of Humankind*. New York: HarperCollins.

126. Neely, Sol. 2016. "On Becoming Human in *Lingít Aaní*: Encountering Levinas through Indigenous Inspirations." *Environmental Philosophy*, vol. 13, no. 1: 83-104, 101.

127. Crystal Rogers, qtd. in *ibid*.

128. Rogers, qtd. in *ibid*.

129. Neely, *op. cit.*, 101.

130. *Ibid.*, 102.

131. Kant, Immanuel. 1983 [1795]. "To Perpetual Peace: A Philosophical Sketch." *Perpetual Peace and Other Essays*. Trans. Ted Humphreys. Indianapolis: Hackett.

132. *Ibid.*, 108.

133. *Ibid.*, 110.

134. *Ibid.*, 117.

135. On the Haitian revolution, see the dated but still essential James, C.L.R. 1989 [1963]. *The Black Jacobins: Toussaint L'Ouverture and the San Domingo Revolution, 2nd Ed.*

Rev. New York: Vintage. On Kant's uptake of the early American experiment, see Ypi, Lea. 2014. "On Revolution in Kant and Marx." *Political Theory*, vol. 42, no. 3: 262-287.

136. For the position that Kant's perpetual peace essay, and Kantianism generally, cannot be rescued from Kant's own deeply committed racism, see Lu-Adler, Huaping. "Kant and Slavery—Or Why He Never Became a Racial Egalitarian." 2022. *Critical Philosophy of Race*, vol. 10, no. 2: 263-294. For a still fuller version of the case, see Lu-Adler, Huaping. 2023. *Kant, Race, and Racism: Views from Somewhere*. New York: Oxford UP.

137. Wynter, Sylvia, and Katherine McKittrick. 2015. "Unparalleled Catastrophe for Our Species? Or, to Give Humanness a Different Future: Conversations." *Sylvia Wynter: On Being Human as Praxis*. Ed. Katherine McKittrick. Durham: Duke UP: 9-89, 25.

138. *Ibid.*, 72.

139. *Ibid.*, 73.

140. A comparable and similarly useful theory of change appears in Butler, Judith. 2005. *Giving an Account of Oneself*. New York: Fordham UP.

141. Wynter, *op. cit.*, 36.

142. *Ibid.*

143. *Ibid.*, 31.

Chapter 5

1. Graeber and Wengrow, *op. cit.*, 115.

2. *Ibid.*, 433.

3. *Ibid.*

4. The "planetary boundaries" framework has the disadvantage of not covering well CaCaCo's primarily intrahuman crises, such as the AI revolution and other annihilations of meaning, so I haven't structured *Panic Now?* by its terms. But, it has shaped my thinking quite a bit.

5. Steffen, Will, Katherine Richardson, Johann Rockström, *et al.* 2015 "Planetary Boundaries: Guiding Human Development on a Changing Planet." *Science*, vol. 347, issue 6223: 1259855.

6. Rockström, Johan, *et al.* 2009. "A Safe Operating Space for Humanity." *Nature*, vol. 461: 472-475. See also their own update, which tries to account for justitial considerations (in my view, a bit muddledly; it's a bigger question than the short format of a *Nature* article is ideal for tackling): Rockström, Johan, *et al.* 2023. "Safe and Just Earth System Boundaries." *Nature*, forthcoming (advance web publication 31 May 2023). Web. I anticipate a lot of the well-intentioned public discourse—which will still fail to avert climate genocide and CaCaCo collapse, since these outcomes are baked into CaCaCo's own logic—about climate justice in the next few years will (rightly) set out from this touchstone. For a good indication of how such conversations may unfold, see Humphreys, Stephen. 2023. "How to Define Unjust Planetary Change." *Nature: News and Views*, 31 May 2023. Web.

7. In their "Comment on 'Planetary Boundaries: Guiding Human Development on a Changing Planet'" (*Science*, vol. 348, issue 6240: 1217), Fernando Jaramillo and Georgia Destouni make a compelling case that the freshwater use boundary, too, has already been crossed.

8. I recently joined for dinner the president of a major U.S. labor union, in town to meet with a few billionaires who "believe in democracy." This person was doing what

they could with the tools available to them to safeguard democratic institutions. So, in their way, were the billionaires. So are you if you phonebank or put placards in your yard or go door-to-door to register voters. None of it will be enough. CaCaCo is failing. A drive toward fascism is the all but inevitable correlate of efforts to maintain business as usual while the whole system goes bankrupt, individual good intentions notwithstanding. As British communist Rajani Palme Dutt observed in 1935 (following on his 1934 book devoted to understanding the rise of fascism), "Fascism represents an extreme phenomenon of this process of capitalism in decay." Fascism, as the line is commonly misattributed to Lenin, is capitalism in decay. What is all of CaCaCo *in decay*, i.e., in its current and ongoing process of senescence? Dutt, Rajani Palme. 1935. "The Question of Fascism and Capitalist Decay." *The Communist International*, vol. 12, no. 14. Archived at Marxists Internet Archive. Web. On the rise of fascism in recent years, both globally and in the U.S. in particular, see Burley, Shane. 2017. *Fascism Today: What It Is and How to End It.* Chico: AK Press; and Ross, Alexander Reid. 2017. *Against the Fascist Creep.* Chico: AK Press.

9. In so saying, I find myself somewhat at odds with one indigenous story of growing popularity in the climate literature. For that story, the idea of "crisis" itself is part of the problem. Apprehending a fast-moving disaster and taking any measures necessary to hold it at bay is part and parcel of the colonial imaginary, is in Kyle Whyte's (Citizen Potawatomi) evocative phrasing a "crisis epistemology" that must be replaced by "epistemologies of coordination." Whyte, Kyle. 2021. "Against Crisis Epistemologies." *Routledge Handbook of Critical Indigenous Studies.* Eds. Brendan Hokowhitu *et al.* New York: Routledge: 52-64. As I hope has been clear, I do not believe CaCaCo can (or should) be saved and so do not affirm the versions of by-any-means-necessary that have been and will be mobilized to protect continuity with its core structures. And yet, by partial contrast with Whyte, I think it is *appropriate* to apprehend our polycrisis in terms of imminent threat and to act accordingly. That this should not be taken as justification for dissolving kinship relations—indeed, the very contrary—should be apparent especially from chapters three and four.

10. Graeber and Wengrow, *op. cit.*, 438.

11. A person really should read Graeber and Wengrow's *Dawn of Everything* in its totality. Besides being an eminently readable overview of the creative efflorescence of human social history, it's atypical in both celebrating non-CaCaCo ways of organizing societies *and* highlighting the many limitations of other and archaic lifeways.

12. Belgian rhetoricians Chaïm Perelman and Lucie Olbrechts-Tyteca describe this in terms of *presence*. As they put it, "one of the preoccupations of a speaker is to make present, by verbal magic alone, what is actually absent but what he considers important to his argument or, by making them more present, to enhance the value of some of the elements of which one has actually been made conscious . . . As far as possible, such an effort is directed to filling the whole field of consciousness with this presence so as to isolate it, as it were, from the hearer's overall mentality" (*The New Rhetoric: A Treatise on Argumentation.* Trans. John Wilkinson and Purcell Weaver. Notre Dame: U Notre Dame P, 1971, 117-118).

13. Incidentally, I didn't use any AIs, other than those involved in optimizing search engine algorithms and myriad other loci that dispose me, you, and everyone you know, to write this book. It is my strongly held view that any use of generative AI in symbol-production intended for human audiences should, at the very least, be flagged as such.

14. It's tempting to just assert this as axiomatic. To be frank, I think it has to be

taken that way. Beyond semantic tricks (ha!) and simple disavowals of the fact (double-ha!), I have been unable to find serious efforts to establish that humans are not, for human audiences, exemplarily symbolic animals. Two compelling efforts to tell this story may be found in Taylor, Charles, *op. cit.* and Ferber, Ilit. 2019. *Language Pangs: On Pain and the Origins of Language.* New York: Oxford UP.

15. Burke, Kenneth. 1969 [1950]. *A Rhetoric of Motives.* Berkeley: U California P; 1969 [1954]. *A Grammar of Motives.* Berkeley: U California P; 1966. *Language as Symbolic Action: Essays on Life, Literature, and Method.* Berkeley: U California P.

16. In *Language as Symbolic Action*: 3-24. As Jordynn Jack notes, Burke kept amending this definition up through the end of his life, gradually dispensing with the masculinist framing—in particular, through communication from Barbara Bate. Jack invites a wider sense of symbolicity, to include many gestural and non-linguistic forms of communication, to which I'm quite friendly. Jack, Jordynn. 2013. "On the Limits of Human: Haggling with Burke's 'Definition of Man.'" *Burke in the Archives: Using the Past to Transform the Future of Burkean Studies.* Eds. Dana Anderson and Jessica Enoch. Columbia: U South Carolina P.

17. Burke, *Language as Symbolic Action*, 16.

18. Chapter five of my *The Ethical Fantasy* reads Burke as characterizing humans in particular rather than uniquely. Even if he himself thought he was describing our unique traits, what he in fact was doing was characterizing traits that we exemplify, but do not have a corner on.

19. On primate symbolicity, see for instance Lyn, Heidi, and Jennie L. Christopher. "How Environment Can Reveal Semantic Capacities in Nonhuman Animals." *Animal Behavior and Cognition*, vol. 7, no. 2: 159-167. For a rhetorical take, see Parrish, Alex C. 2021. *The Sensory Modes of Animal Rhetorics: A Hoot in the Light.* London: Palgrave Macmillan.

20. I know no finer exposition of this point than that of Gadamer, Hans-Georg. 2004. *Truth and Method, 2nd Rev. Ed.* Trans. Joel Weinsheimer and Donald G. Marshall. London: Continuum, esp. chapter four.

21. Or, more excitingly, books like The Red Nation. 2021. *The Red Deal: Indigenous Action to Save Our Earth.* Brooklyn: Common Notions; or Gelderloos, Peter. 2022. *The Solutions Are Already Here: Strategies for Ecological Revolution from Below.* London: Pluto Press. Just because we cannot implement any of these strategies in time to avert CaCaCo's collapsing in devastating ways does not mean we are free to *not* pick one or another set and have a go at them.

22. Cf. McNutt, Charles H., and Ryan M. Parish (Eds.). 2020. *Cahokia in Context: Hegemony and Diaspora.* Gainesville: U Florida P.

23. See esp. Kelly, John E., and James A. Brown. 2020. "In the Beginning: Contextualizing Cahokia's Emergence." In McNutt and Parish, *op. cit.*

24. Graeber and Wengrow, *op. cit.*, 466.

25. *Ibid.*, 452.

26. *Ibid.*

27. *Ibid.*, 469.

28. On the centrality of Cahokia to what we now call Mississippian cultures, see Alt, Susan M. 2020. "The Implications of the Religious Foundations at Cahokia." In McNutt and Parish, *op. cit.*

29. Odell, *op. cit.*, 204.

30. Graeber and Wengrow, *op. cit.*, 502.

31. Jeffrey Winter's *Oligarchy* (Cambridge: Cambridge UP, 2012) is one of the most rigorous examinations of this. His dour conclusion, based on a historically wide-ranging assessment that leads up through the contemporary ubiquity of oligarchy, is one many people who too-readily believe themselves to live in "democracies" would do well to heed: "Expanded and meaningful participation has no necessary or deep impact on oligarchy. Oligarchs feared what the emergence of democracy and then universal suffrage would portend, but history proved the fears to be exaggerated. The reason is that participation by itself strikes at the heart of elitism, but poses only a *potential* threat to oligarchs and the distinct basis of their power. It is only when participation challenges material strati-fication specifically—when extreme wealth held by oligarchs is dispersed as a democratic outcome—that oligarchy and participatory democracy finally clash" (275). CaCaCo's age of polycrisis, as indicated in chapter one especially, is organized in fundamentally and intensifyingly oligarchic terms. It is safe to say this bodes ill for most of us.

32. The Westphalian order (the European system of more or less sovereign nation-states imagined as world-spanning in Kant's *Perpetual Peace* and eventually enshrined as the basis of international law in the United Nations and underlying quasi-formal mecha-nisms of global governance like the G7) was intrinsically a carry-forward of colonialism (see, for a defense of this system that only half-acknowledges and yet also lays bare its colonial organization, Spruyt, Hendrik. 2000. "The End of Empire and the Extension of the Westphalian System: The Normative Basis of the Modern State Order." *International Studies Review*, vol. 2, no. 2: 65-92). It is also, as Quinn Slobodian (*op. cit.*) has suggested, "cracking up." For an insiders' view of that crack-up's corollary, "deglobalization," see Keller, Christian, and Renate Marold. 2023. "Deglobalisation: What You Need to Know." *World Economic Forum*, 17 January 2023. Web.

33. There are a great many discussions of this. For two from entirely *inside* an ideo-logical position of which I am critical, so that you may be sure I am reporting not what I wish to see but what proponents of American hegemony themselves regard as occurring, see Nye, Jr., Joseph S. 2019. "The Rise and Fall of American Hegemony from Wilson to Trump." *International Affairs*, vol. 95, no. 1: 63-80; and Fukuyama, Francis. 2021. "Francis Fukuyama on the End of American Hegemony." *Economist*, 18 August 2021. Web.

34. As noted in chapter one, the USD's status as global reserve currency—a mid-20th-century "achievement" as the United States replaced the U.K. as planetary market-maker in the course and aftermath of World War II—has been one of CaCaCo's core sites of intertwining. Its unraveling has been hastened by the U.S. response to Russia's 2022 invasion of Ukraine, for which traditional economic sanctions were both central and largely ineffective. Roubini's (*op. cit.*) discussion of the end of dollar hegemony is useful. For up-to-the-minute developments, see literally any business press outlet. For an instance as I was finishing this book, see De Mott, Filip. 2023. "De-dollarization Is No Longer a Matter of If, But When—And Is a National Security Concern, Says Inter-national Crisis Group Cochair." *Business Insider: Markets*, 3 May 2023. Web. To say that de-dollarization, itself the necessary cost of maintaining CaCaCo business-as-usual in a world of escalating and mutually accelerating crises, will interrupt CaCaCo stability is extreme understatement. This, though very bad for many people in the global north and especially the United States, might be welcome news for those in global south countries whose debt is denominated in a rapidly inflating USD. That de-dollarization will shift global trade patterns and military relations, and so interfere with U.S. efforts to manage the consequences of the polycrisis, seems highly likely. Like any sufficiently complex oligarchic system's collapse, this is both bad and good.

35. On the 40% of America's road system that is in poor or mediocre condition, having languished there for years, see ASCE. 2021. "2021 Report Card for America's Infrastructure." American Society of Civil Engineers, Accessed 5 May 2023. Web. For a good overview of some energy delivery vulnerabilities—even before the polycrisis proceeds much further—see Brooks, Chuck. 2023. "3 Alarming Threats to the U.S. Energy Grid—Cyber, Physical, and Existential Events." *Forbes*, 15 February 2023. Web. What's important to note is that, as CaCaCo staggers deeper into collapse, long-deferred costs such as those of maintaining infrastructure become more and more difficult for states and most private entities to afford. Infrastructural breakdown is at once an effect and a resonator-cause of further collapse processes within the larger system (badly maintained roads, for instance, will make food transport increasingly expensive at the same time as fossil fuel prices rise due both to supply:demand ratio tightening and decarbonization efforts—that this pairing may well be necessary will not make the resulting hunger less painful and socially disruptive).

36. For a hyperbolic, but unhappily not ridiculous, assessment of this breakdown, see Marche, Stephen. 2022. "The Next US Civil War Is Here—We Just Refuse to See It." *Guardian*, 4 January 2022. Web.

37. The U.S. State Department-aligned Freedom House has been rating "democracy" around the world for five decades. Developed as an ideological tool in the anticommunist Cold War arsenal, it is anything but above reproach in methods and conclusions. So, it is striking that Freedom House records the United States as having dropped ten points in its scoring system (a full 10% less free!) over the last decade. Gorokhovskaia, Yana, Adrian Shahbaz, and Amy Slipowitz. 2023. "Freedom in the World 2023: Marking 50 Years in the Struggle for Democracy." *Freedom House*, March 2023. Web. For a duly dismal view of how matters stand in the U.K., see Boffey, Daniel, and Nicola Slawson. 2023. "Police Accused of 'Alarming' Attack on Protest Rights After Anti-Monarchist Leader Arrested." *Guardian*, 6 May 2023. Web. More scholarly perspectives on de-democratization in the global north may be found in the ever-larger array of worried tomes like Przeworski, *op. cit.*

38. Allen, Sarah. 2022. *Kairotic Inspiration: Imagining the Future in the Sixth Extinction.* Pittsburgh: U Pittsburgh P, 157.

39. Barnett, *op. cit.*, 153.

40. Allen, *Kairotic Inspiration*, 162

41. Gramsci, Antonio. 1971. *Selections from the Prison Notebooks of Antonio Gramsci.* Trans. and ed. Quinton Hoare and Geoffrey Nowell Smith. New York: International Publishers, 276.

42. *Ibid.*, 275.

43. *Ibid.*, 276.

44. Perhaps the visions of "we" that should drive us now lie somewhere between the fantasies of decentralized autonomous organization (DAO) beloved of left-libertarian tech bros, the at-once localist and superordinate vision of dual-power offered by groups like Black Socialists in America or Cooperation Jackson, the eco-romantic, re-enchanted future imagined in Le Guin, Ursula. 2019 [1985]. *Always Coming Home, Author's Expanded Edition.* New York: Library of America, and the big-city anarcho-communism detailed in the beautiful speculations of O'Brien, M.E., and Eman Abdelhadi. 2022. *Everything for Everyone: An Oral History of the New York Commune 2052–2072.* Brooklyn: Common Notions. For the sort of far longer horizon of "humanizing" that even a longtermist could love, try Newitz, Annalee. 2023. *The Terraformers.* New York: Tor / Tom Doherty Associates.